♦ The Two-Week Traveler Series ♦

THE BEST
OF
BRITAIN'S
COUNTRYSIDE

◆ The Two-Week Traveler Series ◆

THE BEST OF BRITAIN'S COUNTRYSIDE

THE HEART OF ENGLAND AND WALES
A Driving & Walking Itinerary

Bill and Gwen North

The Mountaineers/Seattle

Published by The Mountaineers
1011 SW Klickitat Way, Seattle, Washington 98134

Published simultaneously in Canada by Douglas & McIntyre, Ltd., 1615 Venables Street, Vancouver, B.C. V5L 2H1

Published simultaneously in Great Britain by Cordee, 3a DeMontfort Street, Leicester, England, LE1 7HD

Manufactured in the United States of America

Edited by Miriam Bulmer
Maps by Vikki Leib
All photographs by the authors, except page 107 (courtesy of the Wales Tourist Board) and page 109 (courtesy of Gladstone Pottery Museum).
Cover design by Watson Graphics
Book design by Barbara Bash, layout by Constance Bollen
Typography by Typeworks

Cover photograph: Carreg Cennen Castle, Wales
Frontispiece: Carreg Cennen Castle, Wales

Library of Congress Cataloging in Publication Data
North, Bill, 1947-
    The best of Britain's countryside : the heart of England and Wales:
a driving & walking itinerary / Bill and Gwen North.
        p.   cm.—(The Two-week traveler series)
    Includes bibliographical references and index.
    ISBN 0-89886-341-4
    1. Automobile travel—England—Guidebooks. 2. Automobile travel—
Wales—Guidebooks. 3. Landscape—England—Guidebooks. 4. Walking—
England—Guidebooks. 5. Landscape—Wales—Guidebooks. 6. Walking—
Wales—Guidebooks.   I. North, Gwen. II. Title. III. Series.
DA650.N595   1992
914.2'04859—dc20   92-41891
                                                                    CIP

For Harlan,
Warm, resolute, yet possessed of the creativity
and curiosity of a child
. . . the soul of a Welshman

Contents

PART ONE

Introduction

A Note About Safety

Safety is an important concern in all outdoor activities. No guidebook can alert you to every hazard or anticipate the limitations of every reader. Therefore, the descriptions of roads, trails, routes, and natural features in this book are not representations that a particular place or excursion will be safe for your party. When you follow any of the routes described in this book, you assume responsibility for your own safety. Under normal conditions, such excursions require the usual attention to traffic, road and trail conditions, weather, terrain, the capabilities of your party, and other factors. Keeping informed on current conditions and exercising common sense are the keys to a safe, enjoyable outing.

Political conditions may add to the risks of travel in Europe in ways that this book cannot predict. When you travel, you assume this risk, and should keep informed of political developments that may make safe travel difficult or impossible.

The Mountaineers

About This Guidebook

We see nothing until we truly understand it.
— John Constable
English landscape painter

John Constable understood the secret of traveling; notice that he doesn't say "We understand nothing until we see it." He was not a "sight-seer." Most guidebooks tell you a lot about *what* and *where* things are, but seldom *why*—why a castle was built on this particular site and not another, why a village looks so perfectly charming, why a great cathedral arose in a remote place, or simply why the scenery looks the way it does. It's impossible to capture the feeling of a country like Britain by "taking in the sights," because so much meaning is to be found in the places in between. This book, like the first two volumes in the *Best of Britain's Countryside* series, is designed to help you truly "see" Britain—to make sense of the shape and form of the landscape and the imprints of man upon it by illuminating both the stories behind the sights and, even more important, the countryside in between.

In addition, this third volume, *The Heart of England and Wales*, is a kind of quest for the Britain of our imaginations, for the heart and soul of this ancient isle. Is it in East Anglia, the peaceful countryside seized by wave upon wave of invaders over the centuries, including the Angles who gave England ("Angle-land") its name? Is it in the Midlands, where the Industrial Revolution and the Age of Empire were born? Is it in the wild mountains of Wales, to which the last true Britons were driven by the Saxons and their successors? Or is it in the Cotswolds, whose patchwork hills, cozy villages, and flower-bedecked cottages are so beloved by visitors and by the English themselves?

The answer, of course, is that the real Britain is in all of these places and more. To get the most from a visit to this "green and pleasant land," you need to get off the beaten track and deep into the countryside. In the sixteen-day itinerary presented in these pages, you'll explore:

◆ Four designated **Areas of Outstanding Natural Beauty**;
◆ Four **National Parks**;
◆ Four official **Long Distance Footpaths**;
◆ Nearly a dozen **prehistoric sites**;

- Three great **castles**;
- Five sumptuous **stately homes** and **gardens**;
- Five soaring **cathedrals** and **abbeys**, both ruined and intact;
- One of Europe's oldest **universities**;
- Four delightful **open-air historical museums**;
- And many of the most charming **villages** in England and Wales.

Each chapter of this book covers a different day in the itinerary (for a longer trip, just link up the itineraries in the other two books in this series). You'll spend much of your time tooling along through the countryside by car, but roughly every other day we encourage you to experience Britain at a more relaxed pace—with delightful day and half-day walks, canal boat trips, steam-driven mountain train rides, and cycling outings, among other choices. You can follow the itinerary closely, or simply use it as a working outline. Be adventurous; plunge down a narrow country lane and get lost!

In the end, what you will remember most fondly isn't this great castle or that famous cathedral, but the simple grace of a parish church, the luxuriant chaos of a cottage garden in a small village, the heart-stopping drama of a narrow mountain road, a friendship struck up in an ancient country pub. These things, and more, are *The Best of Britain's Countryside*.

Bill and Gwen North

How This Book is Organized

Each chapter covers a different day in the itinerary and includes:

1. ORIENTATION. A brief description of the character and history of the landscape through which you'll be traveling—just enough to give you a taste of what's to come.

2. THE ROUTE. Detailed directions to guide you through the day's drive or walk, with a running commentary to illuminate the passing scene.

🚗 This symbol indicates driving portions of a day's trip.

🚶 This symbol indicates walking portions of a day's trip.

3. DIVERSIONS. Alternatives to the main route (or additions to it) so that whatever the weather or your mood you have more than one way to spend the day.

4. CREATURE COMFORTS. Guidance on where to spend the night ("Daily Bed") and where to find a good dinner ("Daily Bread").

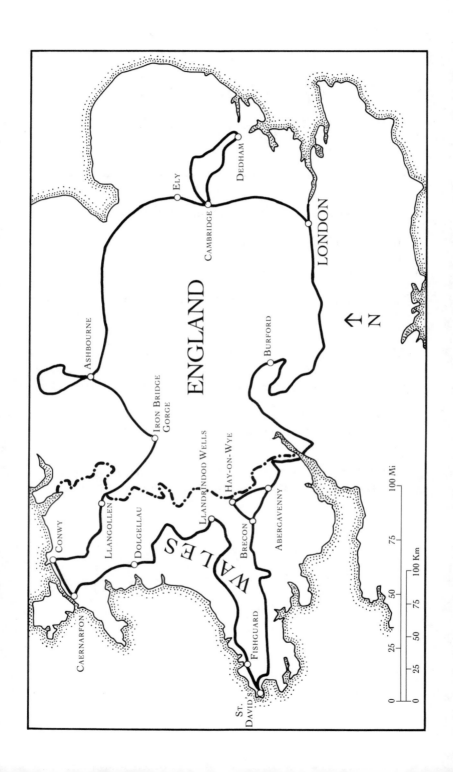

The Itinerary at a Glance

DAY 1: Arrive in London and head north to **East Anglia** for a walking tour of **Cambridge University** and a visit to **Wicken Fen**, one of England's first nature reserves.

DAY 2: Tour the **medieval villages** of **Suffolk**, take a riverside walk in **"Constable Country,"** and visit the birthplace of the **Magna Carta**.

DAY 3: Explore **Ely Cathedral** and drive across the **Great Levels** to the hills of the **Peak District National Park**.

DAY 4: Hike to the summit of **Kinder Scout**, take a car tour of the Peak District that includes two **stately homes** and a **prehistoric stone circle**, or try **cycling** and **walking** trips around scenic **Dovedale**.

DAY 5: Step back into the Industrial Revolution at **Iron Bridge Gorge**, or **"the Potteries"** of Stoke-on-Trent, then slip across the border to the mountains of **Wales**.

DAY 6: Drive across North Wales and visit the great **castles** of **Conwy** and **Caernarfon**, with an optional visit to **Bodnant Gardens**.

DAY 7: Plunge deep into the spectacular mountains of **Snowdonia National Park**, climb or take the steam train to the summit of **Snowdon**, the highest peak in England or Wales, then head south to handsome **Dolgellau**, near the coast.

DAY 8: Climb to the breathtaking summit of **Cadair Idris**, take a car tour that includes a **steam train** ride and the **Centre for Alternative Technologies**, or take the easy but rewarding **Precipice Walk**.

DAY 9: Drive through the **Cambrian Hills** to the Victorian spa town of **Llandrindod Wells**, then take an ancient **drovers' road** through the "desert of Wales" to the coastal **Pembrokeshire National Park.**

DAY 10: Visit **St. David's Cathedral**, then walk around the windswept cliffs of **St. David's Head**, or tour **prehistoric sites** scattered among the **Preseli Hills.**

DAY 11: Drive across South Wales to the **Brecon Beacons National Park**, visit clifftop **Carreg Cennen Castle** on the way, and detour either to poet **Dylan Thomas's home** or the **Museum of the Welsh Woolen Industry.**

DAY 12: Hike to the highest of the **Brecon Beacons**, or drive through the **Black Mountains**, visiting lonely **Llanthony Abbey** in the secluded **Vale of Ewyas** and **Hay-on-Wye**, the "town of books," with a short hike high above the English border on the **Offa's Dike Path**. Optional visit to the **Big Pit** coal mine museum.

DAY 13: Head south to the **Wye River Gorge** and **Tintern Abbey**, cross back into England, visit Stone Age **Belas Knap** and the **Cotswold** villages of **Upper and Lower Slaughter** and the handsome market town of **Burford**. Optional side trip to the **Welsh Folk Museum** near **Cardiff**.

DAY 14: Drive through the scenic **Coln River valley** with stops at **Filkins Mill, Bibury**, and the ruins of **Chedworth Roman Villa**, then head east to **London** and **Greenwich**. Optional **bicycle tour** or **walk** in the Cotswold Hills.

DAY 15: A day along the **Thames** between central London and Greenwich, with a **walking tour** of Greenwich, a **boat trip** on the river, and a **light rail** ride through the newly rejuvenated **London Docklands.**

DAY 16: Home.

Preparations

Of the world's romantic travel destinations, none is more accessible or affordable than Britain. It's easy to get to, easy to get around once you've arrived, and (with a little imagination) easier on the pocketbook than almost anywhere else in Europe. What's more, no nation has a more competent tourism agency than the British Tourist Authority (see Useful Addresses for the branch nearest you). Here's what you need to know to get started.

WHEN TO GO

The best times for visiting Britain are late spring (after April 1) and fall (before November 1). The weather tends to be more stable then, virtually all attractions are open, and crowds are mercifully absent. On the other hand, if your taste runs to melancholy landscapes and evenings around a fire (with daylight savings time, it gets dark very early), winter can be a romantic time to visit. But most vacationers visit Britain in the summer. The great advantage of doing so is that the country fairly blazes with flowers and the days are long and (if the sun cooperates) have a golden glow possible only in England. The disadvantage is that everyone and his brother will be there as well. If you have a choice, avoid July and especially August. But even if you can't, this itinerary has the advantage of taking you "far from the madding crowd." Moreover, with a little prior planning you can reduce your worries even in peak season.

RENTING A CAR

Traveling off the beaten track means, almost by definition, traveling to places trains and buses don't go. Here's what you need to know about renting a car.

THE BEST PRICES. You have three options for getting a good deal on car rental in Britain: check your airline for fly/drive promotions (but be sure the discounted car rental doesn't require a premium airfare); reserve (and sometimes prepay) from a multinational—Hertz, Avis, Budget, Thrifty, Alamo, Eurodollar, National/Europcar—*before* you leave (renting once you get to Britain is much more expensive than doing it in advance); or rent through "wholesalers" which negotiate discounted rates from either the multinationals or major British firms. With multinationals or wholesalers, your travel agent can make the arrangements for you, or you can contact them directly. Wholesalers with toll-free numbers include Connex, Kemwel, and Auto Europe, among others. Some discounted rentals require prepayment, most require a minimum seven-day rental, and some will add a hefty "drop fee" if you pick up the car in one place and leave it in another. (**Note:** Unless you rent with a credit card, be prepared to post a sizable deposit before you drive away.)

INSURANCE AND VAT. When you compare rental rates, be sure you know whether they include accident insurance and taxes. Your rental car will come with free roadside breakdown coverage from either the British Automobile Association (AA) or Royal Automobile Club, but you also will be expected to purchase collision damage waiver (CDW) coverage for accidents. As at home, beware: the insurance can increase the cost of the rental significantly. You can avoid the CDW by charging the rental on a MasterCard Gold, Visa Gold, Diners Club, or American Express card. All provide free collision coverage, but check the fine print beforehand; terms vary and some limit coverage to fifteen days. If you don't charge the rental, pay for the insurance. Without it, you will be liable for any damage, often up to the full value of the car. In addition, there is a 17.5 percent nonrefundable value added tax (VAT) on car rentals. As with the CDW, be sure you know whether the VAT is included in the quote. "Inclusive" rates from a wholesaler, including both the CDW and the VAT and unlimited mileage, start at about $275 per week for a Ford Fiesta or similar car. (Sign up *all* potential drivers, despite the extra cost; if an unregistered driver has an accident, your insurance may not cover it.)

CAR SIZE. British rental cars range from tiny subcompacts to station wagons ("estate wagons"). Unless you specify otherwise, expect a manual transmission. A small automatic will cost as much as a large standard-transmission car, but if you've never driven with a manual shift this is not the time to learn.

WHAT TO TAKE WITH YOU

OFFICIAL DOCUMENTS. You need a valid passport, but not a visa, if you're a citizen of the United States, the European Community, or most Commonwealth nations. Others should check with the nearest British consulate. To rent a car, all you need is a valid driver's license

from home. If you're interested in staying in a youth hostel, join Hostelling International/American Youth Hostel (P.O. Box 37613, Washington, D.C. 20013, telephone 202-783-6161). When joining, order the *YHA Accommodation Guide for England and Wales.*

MONEY. Buy VISA/Barclay's Bank traveler's checks in *pounds*, not dollars before you leave home. (These are available at most large banks.) Because they are already in the local currency, they can be used as cash in most restaurants, shops, and hotels (though not bed and breakfasts). And when you need cash, Barclays Bank has branches in virtually every town of any size in England. Keep the serial numbers separate from the checks and know how to report lost or stolen checks for a refund. Avoid cashing checks in a Bureau de Change or at Chequepoint branches; their exchange rates are poor and they charge hefty cashing commissions. (**Note:** Prudent guidebooks recommend a money belt. We've never felt the need in England, but you may.)

Credit cards are accepted in virtually all shops, hotels, restaurants, and petrol stations (but, again, not in B&Bs). In addition, they come in handy if you suddenly need a cash advance.

CLOTHES. Most guidebooks recommend you travel light. We don't. English weather is notoriously fickle; even in midsummer it's just as likely to be chilly and damp as sunny and hot. Since your bags will spend most of the time in the trunk ("boot") of your car, pack enough to be prepared. Coordinate around a single color scheme, layer light clothes as needed, and plan to spend an hour doing a wash at a coin-operated laundry halfway through the trip. Also, remember the British are a bit formal; in restaurants (but not pubs), men typically wear jacket and tie, women a skirt or dress.

WALKING GEAR. Several of the walks in this book are over rugged terrain. You'll be happier—and safer—in boots or any of the new generation of walking shoes. Also, remember this is Britain; even if it doesn't rain while you're walking, the chances are good the ground will be wet. Really waterproof shoes, lined with a breathable fabric like Gore-Tex, will make a big difference. The same goes for rainwear; make sure it's truly waterproof and breathable or your chances of being wet and miserable at some point are pretty high. As for walking socks, the best combination is a wool or polypropylene outer sock and a thin polypropylene inner sock to wick moisture away. Year-round, plan on layers of light clothes: a cotton T-shirt (and/or a turtleneck if it's cold), cotton (or flannel) overshirt, light sweater, wind- and waterproof rainwear, and light to midweight cotton or wool slacks (shorts in summer). A hat and gloves can make a big difference in the fall. A few other items, packed in a small knapsack, can make your walks and picnics more pleasant: a Swiss army knife, a small tablecloth, collapsible cups (or just save some of the plastic cups from the flight over), and moleskin and adhesive bandages for blisters.

BOOKING ACCOMMODATIONS IN ADVANCE

If you're willing to be adventurous, you don't really need to reserve accommodations in advance, especially if you stay at B&Bs. Most of the areas covered by this itinerary are well supplied with B&Bs that advertise themselves along the roadside (see Understanding Britain for tips). In addition, the British Tourist Authority's Tourist Information Centre (TIC) network is poised to help daily travelers; TICs are located in every town of any importance in England and Wales. In this book, the address of the local TIC is included in the Creature Comforts section of each day's itinerary. You can write or call a few months in advance, ask for their accommodations brochures, and then contact the establishments that interest you. If you prefer to play it by ear, local TICs are prepared to find you a room for the night. You can also use their "Book-A-Bed-Ahead" (BABA) service to arrange accommodations a day or two in advance as you are traveling. We recommend advance reservations for the B&Bs featured in this book, and for your first and last nights in Britain, when looking for a room is the last thing you'll want to be doing. (**Note:** Beware public holidays, when the English take to the country: Good Friday and Easter Monday, the first and last Monday in May, and the last Monday in August.)

OTHER BOOKS TO READ

For detailed listings of accommodations, restaurants, and pubs, along with a selection of the best background books, consult the Further Reading section at the back of the book.

Understanding Britain

A recent poll of world travelers found that men and women alike feel safer, by far, traveling in Britain than anywhere else on the globe. (The United States wasn't even close.) There is simply something inherently cozy and comforting about the place. Maybe we remember all those bedtime stories we were read as children—*The Wind in the Willows*, *A Child's Garden of Verses*, *Winnie the Pooh*. Whatever the reason, it feels like home . . . or what we *wish* home were like.

The temporary terrors of driving on the wrong side notwithstanding, travel in Britain is remarkably hassle-free. It is, nonetheless, a foreign land. Understanding something of the customs of the natives will not only smooth but enrich your visit.

THE LANGUAGE

Yes, it's English. But it's *British* English. George Bernard Shaw described America and Britain as "two nations separated by a common language." Never assume that just because you understand what they're saying, you also understand what they *mean*. Lots of words are either completely or subtly different. Moreover, when you get to Wales you'll be faced with a wonderfully impenetrable language that neither looks nor sounds like anything you've ever seen or heard before. (Don't worry, they're bilingual.) Here's a short glossary of British English; the Day Six chapter includes a guide to Welsh.

A Practical Guide to British English

BRITISH	U.S. EQUIVALENT
At Hotels/B&Bs:	
twin	= two single beds
double	= one double bed
bathroom	= little room with a bathtub in it
loo, toilet, W.C. (water closet)	= bathroom
flannel	= washcloth
torch	= flashlight
fortnight	= two weeks
porridge	= hot oatmeal
fully cooked breakfast	= fried egg, bacon, sausage, etc.
At Restaurants:	
cream tea	= tea with scones, jam, clotted cream
clotted cream	= a bit like whipped cream
jam	= jelly, preserves
jelly	= Jell-O
chips	= french fries
crisps	= chips (potato)
sweet, pudding	= any dessert
bill	= check

BRITISH	U.S. EQUIVALENT
Shopping:	
chemist	= drugstore
plaster	= bandage
jumper	= sweater
pinafore	= jumper (dress)
tights	= pantyhose
braces	= suspenders
suspenders	= garters
waistcoat	= vest
vest	= undershirt
pants	= underpants
trousers	= pants
plimsolls	= sneakers
trainers	= running shoes
first floor	= second floor
ground floor	= first floor
off-licence	= retail liquor store
Transportation:	
queue ("cue")	= line
return	= round-trip ticket
single	= one-way ticket
Underground	= subway
subway	= underground walkway
Miscellaneous:	
football	= soccer
American football	= football
redundant	= laid off, idled
cheers	= thanks/good-bye
"a nice cuppa"	= tea, solution to all ills

DRIVING IN BRITAIN

It's a bit unnerving at the outset, but you'll be surprised at how quickly you get used to driving on the left. The most important first step—no matter how busy the rental agency is—is to ask for a complete run-through of your car's features. Be sure there's a good spare tire ("tyre"), a jack in the trunk ("boot"), and an owner's manual. Also, get instructions from the rental agency about what to do in case of a mechanical breakdown or an accident. Then, drive around the lot a bit to get used to things. Finally, relax. While you may never quite get the hang of gauging how close things are on the passenger side, the rest will come with practice.

Near Trapp, South Wales

Diwedd y gwaharddiadau

End of prohibitions

Wild fowl

DRIVING ETIQUETTE. The British drive accurately and fast, will pass ("overtake") on curves and blind hills, but never use their horns (they blink their lights instead). On the other hand, they unfailingly come to a full stop as lights turn red, stop for pedestrians at crossings with blinking yellow lights or white "zebra" stripes on the road, yield at traffic circles ("roundabouts") to cars already in the circle, use directional indicators religiously (especially when exiting a roundabout), and on one-lane roads will politely back up to the last passing place when confronted by an oncoming car. (You're expected to show similar courtesy; blink your lights to signal you're yielding.)
Note: Use of front seat belts is mandatory. Also, police check for drunk drivers and use breath analyzers. Punishment in both cases is swift and stern.

BRITISH ROADS. There are four classes of roads in Britain. **"M"** roads are motorways (freeways). **"A"** roads are the major "arterials"; the fewer the digits following the *A* (e.g., A4, A40, A404), the more important the road. **"B"** roads connect smaller villages with nearby market towns and are generally two lanes wide. **Unclassified** roads, with no letter or number, run through rural areas, are by far the loveliest, and may be only one lane wide with passing places. *All* roads, no matter how minor, will be well paved. Unless otherwise noted, the speed limit on motorways and divided highways ("dual carriageways") is 70 mph (112 km/h), on other open roads 60 mph (96 km/h), and in built-up areas 30 mph (48 km/h).

Two other tips: (1) road signs tell you not just what road you are on, but what other roads (indicated in parentheses) that road will take you to; (2) when you come to an unmarked fork in a very rural area, the *less* important branching road will have a dotted white line painted across its entry; if you are *on* the lane with the dotted line across the entry you must yield to the traffic on the more important road.

PARKING. On-street parking limitations are indicated by curbside lines on the pavement and corresponding signs. A dotted yellow line indicates parking is permitted, except as posted on the sign. A single solid line generally means no parking during working hours, also indicated on signs. A double yellow line or a white zigzag line means no parking, period. In most towns, follow blue-and-white P signs to parking lots. Most have "pay and display" machines from which you buy a stick-on parking stamp.

GASOLINE. Gasoline (petrol) is expensive (two to three times the U.S. average), but British cars get great gas mileage and the imperial gallon equals 1.2 U.S. gallons (about 4.5 liters). Most rental cars take 4-star (97 octane) unleaded fuel.

A Driver's Glossary

bonnet	= hood
boot	= trunk
cark park	= parking area
cul-de-sac	= dead end
diversion	= detour
dual carriageway	= divided highway
estate car	= station wagon
flyover	= overpass
give way	= yield
lay-by	= pull-over place
lorry	= truck
petrol	= gasoline
roundabout	= traffic circle
silencer	= muffler
tailback	= traffic jam
windscreen	= windshield
zebra	= crosswalk

BRITISH HOTELS, B&Bs, AND RESTAURANTS

The best accommodations in Britain are at the extremes of the cost spectrum: lavish and expensive country house hotels, and charming and relatively inexpensive bed and breakfast accommodations in private homes and, even better, farms. In between is a wide range of hotels and guest houses that often offer no more than a B&B and cost much more. In a special category are historic old inns, which will cost a bit more than a B&B, may have terrific atmosphere, but may also have a noisy pub downstairs. Choose inns with care (write for the British Tourist Authority's booklet *Stay at an Inn*; see Useful Addresses).

FINDING THE BEST B&Bs. If chic country-house hotels are your preference, consult the guidebooks specializing in them in Further Reading. To spot the best B&Bs (in addition to the ones described in each chapter of this book), adhere to this rule: *If the place looks well cared for, you'll be well cared for.* Because they're in private homes, B&Bs are as different as people. The B&B idea started out as a way for hospitable grannies to let out rooms no longer needed by their grown children.

Beechenhill Farm, a B&B in the Peak District

But today—and this is the case with the B&Bs described in the Creature Comfort sections of this book—offering B&B accommodations may be a key source of income for a couple restoring a historically important country house or a family managing a remote hill farm. You might share a bathroom with the family, but, overall, standards are high.

The English and Welsh tourist boards have a "crown scheme" to classify the level of facilities offered by B&Bs and hotels. The more crowns on the plaque displayed outside the door, the better the facilities. But crowns tell you nothing about charm, cuisine, or hospitality. For that, the Welsh have established a rigorous quality-commendation system culminating in the Welsh Dragon Award for truly superior friendliness and comfort; look for it in B&B listings. Expect to pay $20 to $30 per person for most B&B accommodations, more in cities and in fancier "country house" B&Bs.

Unless you've reserved ahead (be sure to guarantee your time of arrival and phone ahead if delayed), begin looking for B&B vacancies between 4:00 P.M. and 5:00 P.M. (earlier in the fall and winter, when it gets dark earlier). Most B&Bs, whether in cities or out in the country-side, identify themselves with a small sign hung out at the roadside or in a front window (though an increasing number rely on guidebook listings). The choice is greater near famous sites, national parks, and beaches, but demand is also higher. If you get stuck, the local Tourist Information Centre can always help.

THE SECOND "B" IN B&B. For decades, no matter where you were in Britain, a B&B breakfast had an immutable menu: juice and/or corn flakes, fried eggs, bacon, grilled sausage, possibly grilled tomatoes and mushrooms, toast (well cooled in little holding racks), marmalade, and tea (with an extra pot of hot water) or coffee. Massive and sustaining, it's still a terrific bargain and may last you all day. Recently, however, the increasingly health-conscious English have begun to offer more choices, including fruit, yogurt, and whole-grain cereals.

B&B EVENING MEALS. Perhaps the best value (and some of the best food) in Britain is the evening meal sometimes offered by farms in remote areas and "upscale" B&Bs. You usually need to let your hosts know in advance, so phone ahead, ask what's on the menu, and choose accordingly. If you wish, you can purchase wine to accompany dinner at an "off-licence" (liquor store), wine merchant, or supermarket in town.

RESTAURANTS. It is still possible to eat badly in Britain, but you have to work at it. During the last decade, superb little restaurants and country inns have sprung up even in the remotest corners of Britain (see Further Reading for listings). Using fresh local ingredients, these restaurants have created a "new British cuisine" that is imaginative without being fussy (in Wales, look for TASTE OF WALES signs on restaurant doors for traditional dishes). At last, eating is one of the joys of Britain's countryside. (Be forewarned: dinner for two, with wine, at a very good restaurant will run from $50 up.)

PUBS

Hundreds of years ago, ale making was a cottage industry and some people were licensed to sell pitchers of it from a "public room" in their house. Soon these public houses—*pubs* for short—became freestanding businesses. Today, some 80 percent of all pubs are *tied houses* (owned by breweries); only 20 percent are *free houses* (where the proprietor, not the beer, is free).

There is nothing comparable to the pub outside of Britain. An English pub is a neighborhood's or village's communal living room, where folks go to spend the evening together. During World War I, pubs

The George, in Alstonefield in the Peak District—the place for good, affordable lunches and dinners

were closed in the afternoon to improve quality control in munitions plants. Recently, afternoon closing was abolished and pubs are permitted to remain open from 11:00 A.M. to 11:00 P.M. Monday through Saturday, and noon to 3:00 P.M. Sunday. But the English are traditionalists, and many country pubs still close between 2:30 P.M. and 5:30 P.M. Even those that remain open generally stop serving lunch after 2:00 P.M. (**Note:** You go to the bar to order drinks and food and usually pay after each order. Also, children under fourteen can be barred from pubs, except those with a "family room." It's up to the publican, so ask.)

THE MYSTERIES BEHIND THE BAR. In any pub, but especially in free houses, the number of beers on tap—not to mention the bottled beers arrayed behind the bar—can be bewildering. In general, British ales (technically, they're not beer) fall into four categories: *bitter*, the traditional cool, mildly carbonated, light brown ale (which tastes nutty, not bitter); *best bitter* or *special*, with a slightly higher alcohol content and a slightly higher price; *strong*, which, as its name suggests, is a bit stronger still and tends to have a sweet aftertaste; and *mild*, a dark brown, malty, creamy ale less alcoholic than the others (called *brown ale* when bottled). In a well-run pub, they're neither warm (they're kept at 55 degrees) nor flat (all have varying degrees of natural or artificial carbonation).

Thanks to the Campaign for Real Ale, most pubs now carry a range of the real thing, fresh and unpasteurized. Look for taps with long white handles; unpressurized real ale is drawn up from cellar casks by the vacuum created when the handle is pulled down. The taps with little flip levers deliver "keg beer"—pasteurized, artificially carbonated, and less distinctive ales kept in pressurized aluminum kegs. Stick to the real ale.

Also available in most pubs are bottled *pale* or *light ale* (fizzier versions of draft ale), *stout* (the black, malty drink favored in Ireland), and *lagers* (thin and uninteresting). Alcoholic cider, dry and quite refreshing, may also be on tap.

Of course, hard liquors are also sold. When ordering Scotch, ask simply for "whisky," specify a brand, and indicate whether you want it "neat" (plain), with ice, or with water (there are no other respectable options). A "martini" in Britain is a glass of Martini-brand vermouth, so if you want a "gin martini," specify. A gin and tonic will come with lemon, not lime. For some reason, ice cubes are distributed grudgingly, as if they were being rationed.

PUB GRUB. There may be no better lunch or dinner bargain than eating at a pub. Sandwiches, "Ploughman's lunches" (fresh cheese, bread, salad), hearty soups, fish, game, and meat pies of various types can often be had for less than a "fast food" lunch in the States. True, dreadful pub food hasn't been banished entirely, and it's sometimes high in starch and fat, but the good pub food campaign has spread almost as fast as the real ale campaign and many pubs serve fresh, homemade meals. Some inns now have separate dining rooms, but approach these with skepticism; while an inspired chef may be toiling in the kitchen, it's possible that the menu is little different from the one in the pub, just more expensive (and the mood much less convivial).

THE CURRENCY

The coin of the realm in England is the pound sterling, worth between $1.50 and $2.00 U.S. in recent years. Bank notes come in denominations of £5, £10, £20, and £50. There are 100p (pronounced *pee* and short for "pence") in a pound. Coins come in denominations of 1p, 2p, 5p, 10p, 20p, 50p, and £1. The 1p and 2p coins are copper, the 5p and 10p are silver, the 20p and 50p are silver and six-sided, and the

£1 coin is thick and brassy. You may still come across 1 shilling and 2 shilling coins, equal to 5p and 10p respectively, left over from the days before the decimal system was introduced.

THE PHONE SYSTEM

Public phones come in two types: those that take coins (keep a handful of 10p coins at all times) and those that take Phone Cards (which you buy at post offices for between £2 and £20). At coin-operated phones, you put money in first (10p is the minimum), then dial. When your party answers, a digital readout on the phone tells you how much money you're using up as you talk. When it reaches zero you either add another coin, hang up, or get cut off. If the readout shows you still have credit and you want to make another call, *don't hang up*; press the "follow-on call" button and dial the next number. The subtraction process continues when you are connected.

Most British phone numbers are composed of a regional dialing code of several numbers, usually printed in parentheses, and the individual's phone number (which may be from three to seven digits). If all you have is a town name and the individual's number (e.g., Anytowne 123), dial the operator (100; no coin needed) and ask for the regional dialing code for that town. If you don't know a number, dial Directory Enquiries (also a free call); the number is 142 in London and 192 elsewhere. The International Operator is 155. Emergency (police, fire, ambulance) is 999—a free call and one that sometimes can be made even from nonworking phones. (**Note:** Some public phones cannot receive incoming calls, but they're not marked as such.)

The British are a bit wary of letting strangers use their phones, but if you must use a residential phone, dial the operator and ask to place an *ADC* ("advise duration and charge") call. After the call is completed, the operator will call you back with the charge. An ADC call, because it is operator-assisted, will be *much* more expensive than a call from a phone box. To call overseas cheaply, dial the operator and ask for the Home Country Direct dialing code for the country you want.

WALKING IN BRITAIN

No nation on earth has more public footpaths than Britain (120,000 miles/193,000 kilometers) or protects them more zealously. Whether you're a hiker at home or not (we're not), the plain fact is that there is no better—or more delightful—way to experience the best of Britain's countryside than at walking speed. Ten of the sixteen days of this itinerary feature a walk (sometimes more than one). They range from an hour to all day and were chosen with an eye not just for sce-

Ascending the lower slopes of Cadair Idris, North Wales

nery, but for variety too—of landscapes, history, archaeology, architecture, and more.

DIFFICULTY. Though three of the walks included involve physically challenging summits, all can be done by reasonably fit folks. Long walks—four or five hours—typically have shortcuts, and most chapters offer shorter alternative walks as well. Walks described as *easy* involve level or gently undulating ground along well-maintained paths. Walks described as *moderate* involve some steady climbs or cover generally hilly terrain with occasional steep slopes, again on well-marked paths. While there are no *difficult* summit climbs, three of the walks have difficult or strenuous stretches, sometimes over loose or rough terrain.

TRAILS AND MAPS. The descriptions and accompanying maps are really all you'll need to negotiate these walks. For those who prefer a bit more detail, however, recommended Ordnance Survey maps (available in local bookstores and newsagents en route) and locally produced walking guides are also listed. Virtually all paths are marked with signposts and *waymarkers*—posts painted with yellow arrows for public footpaths, blue arrows for public "bridleways," and acorn symbols for official Long Distance Paths. Signposts inscribed with the baffling legend LLWYBR CYHOEDUS simply say "public footpath" in Welsh.

SAFETY. None of these walks is dangerous, provided you take reasonable care (especially on steep downhill descents). As a general rule, tell the people with whom you're staying what your plans are (they may have useful suggestions). Remember that even in midsummer, bone-chilling high winds and rain are common on summits and ridge tops; layered clothing and thoroughly waterproof outerwear can make the difference between a miserable or memorable walk. As an extra precaution, you may want to carry a flashlight or whistle (six flashes or whistle blasts is the International Distress Signal; three is the answering response).

THE COUNTRY CODE. Most public footpaths predate the advent of roads and virtually all are on private land. The system works because people cooperate to make it work: landowners agree to let walkers pass; walkers agree to stay on the footpaths and follow the Country Code.

The Country Code

- ◆ Enjoy the countryside and respect its life and work.
- ◆ Guard against all risk of fire.
- ◆ Fasten all gates.
- ◆ Keep dogs under close control.
- ◆ Keep to public paths across farmland.
- ◆ Use gates and stiles to cross fences, hedges, and walls.
- ◆ Leave livestock, crops, and machinery alone.
- ◆ Take your litter home.
- ◆ Help keep all water clean.
- ◆ Take special care on country roads.
- ◆ Make no unnecessary noise.

PART TWO

The Itinerary

MILES
LONDON.
220
DOLGELLEY.
18
CAERNARVON.
23
BALA.
22
CERNIOGE.
20
BEDDGELERT.
10
HARLECH.
10
BABMOUTH.
20

Cambridge and the East Anglian Fens

LONDON ♦ CAMBRIDGE ♦ WICKEN FEN

- ♦ **Arriving at Heathrow or Gatwick**
- ♦ **Renting your car (or detouring to London)**
- ♦ **The short drive north to Cambridge**
- ♦ **A walking tour of the colleges**
- ♦ **A night in the fens**

*They have a beauty of their own, these great fens . . . a
beauty as of the sea, of boundless expanse and freedom.*
——Charles Kingsley, 1866

As evening comes to Wicken Fen, the dying sun turns the dark waters of Adventurers' Mere to molten gold and burnishes the wispy plumes of the reeds that drift in gentle green swells to the marshy horizon. Then, abruptly, the light fades and color drains from the sky. Ground fog steals through the sedges and curls around the twisted trunks of buckthorn that haunt the featureless landscape in the deepening darkness. The wind rises, tearing holes in the mist and setting the reeds to whispering. The fen, so tranquil at twilight, turns sinister, primeval—a sodden, timeless, impenetrable wilderness.

In the morning, when the sun melts away the mist, the mood here in Britain's first nature reserve lightens and visitors return. A reedy remnant of the vast marshland that once covered thousands of square miles of eastern England, Wicken Fen is a naturalist's paradise. And yet it is anything *but* natural; perhaps nowhere in Britain has the landscape been more thoroughly manipulated by man than in the East Anglian fens. Long before the Middle Ages, men managed the marshes, harvesting reeds for thatch, cutting and drying peat for fuel, stalking wildfowl, and fishing for the eels that gave the nearby cathedral town of Ely ("eel isle") its name. The Romans tried to drain the fens; so did the medieval monasteries that controlled vast estates here. Both failed. It was not until the seventeenth century that Dutch engineers and English entrepreneurs (called "adventurers") finally succeeded, building a complex drainage system to shunt the flood waters of the meandering rivers Nene and Great Ouse to the sea.

The result is some of the finest farmland in Europe—rich, black, and as flat as a snooker table. To the north, across the shallow bay known as the Wash, brilliant blankets of tulips, daffodils, and lilies stretch away into Lincolnshire. To the west and south, long straight rows of vegetables—giant crinkled purple-green heads of savoy cabbage, feathery fennel, blanched-white cauliflower, sharp onion stalks, and bulbous brussels sprouts run to the horizon, punctuated here and there by brilliant yellow patches of rapeseed and jubilant fields of cutting flowers.

But East Anglia is much more than horizons and skyscapes. Settled by successive waves of invaders from across the North Sea, including the Angles who gave England ("Angle-land") its name, the counties of the original Kingdom of East Anglia—Norfolk (for the "North Folk") and Suffolk ("South Folk")—along with Essex (a corruption of "East Saxons") farther south, have absorbed them all and prospered quietly. Then, bypassed almost entirely by the Industrial Revolution, the region languished. Today, the result is an unspoiled countryside of gently folded valleys, narrow winding lanes, and charming old villages with some of the finest medieval architecture in Britain. But this morning our destination is a group of ancient colleges gathered around a bridge over the River Cam: Cambridge, on the region's western border. The good news is that the East Anglian countryside is just an hour from London.

ARRIVING IN BRITAIN

You will arrive, typically early in the morning, at either **Heathrow**, just west of the city, or **Gatwick**, south of the city on the Surrey/West Sussex border. After you "deplane," as they say in airline English, you'll go for a brisk (and long) morning walk through endless (but well-marked) corridors, eventually arriving, along with hundreds of other fellow travelers, at the immigration hall. Here, immigration agents will engage you in small talk while attempting to determine if you are an international terrorist or drug courier and (assuming you are not) stamp your passport and wave you through to the baggage retrieval area. As Britain is a civilized country, baggage carts here are free. Unless you are bringing in large quantities of cash or valuables, head for the green NOTHING TO DECLARE signs, where, in most instances, you'll simply be waved through to the chaos of the arrivals hall.

GETTING YOUR RENTAL CAR

At **Heathrow**, most international flights arrive at Terminal 3. In the arrivals hall there is an airport information desk, a Bureau de

Change (get some cash if you don't have some already), and check-in desks for several of the major international car-rental companies. To call companies located outside the airport, head for the phones under the MEETING POINT sign (dial 192 for Directory Enquiries if you don't know the number). Then go through the doors in the **left** front corner of the hall to a well-marked rental car pickup area and await the company's minivan.

At **Gatwick** the process is the same but the directions are different. Hertz, Avis, Budget, and National/Europcar have their check-in desks and car lots just outside the arrivals building; call any other rental firms from the pay phones in the hall. Then head for the **right** front corner of the arrivals hall and follow car hire signs down the spiral ramp to the ground level. The major companies are just along the sidewalk to your **right**; the pickup area for others is to your **left**.

DETOURING TO LONDON

If you choose to spend a few days in London before heading north into the country, you have two good transportation options from Heathrow, but only one practical option from Gatwick. From Heathrow, a **taxi** makes sense if you are traveling with a lot of luggage or in a group of three or four people. The ride into town will set you back more than £20, plus tip, but the cabs are roomy and clean, and the drivers are uniformly polite, knowledgeable, and often entertaining as well. If you're on a budget, take "the Tube," as the **Underground**, London's subway, is known. It's cheap, clean, safe, and almost as fast as a cab, especially at rush hour. Push your baggage cart down the ramp marked for the Underground and, after a short walk, you will find yourself in the airport Tube station. An added bonus is the Tourist Information Centre located in the station; be sure to buy an official British Tourist Authority London Map (75p at this writing). When you're ready to buy your Tube ticket, think about how you plan to use the rest of the day. If it's a weekday and after 9:30 A.M., or any time on a weekend, buy a One Day Travelcard good for unlimited rides on the Tube, the London Docklands Light Railway, most buses, and even parts of the BritRail Network Southeast rail system. At a cost of only a few pence more than a one-way ride into the city, it's one of the best bargains in London. While you're at it, pick up a free Tube map; the system is simple but the map's a must. Actually, there is a third transport option from Heathrow, the **Airbus**. It's cheaper than a cab, more expensive than the Tube, has the advantage of operating above-ground so you see more of the city, but has the disadvantage of having only two routes and a limited number of stops. If your hotel is at one of the stops, it's a good deal; if not, it's not.

From Gatwick the decision is simple: take the **Gatwick Express**,

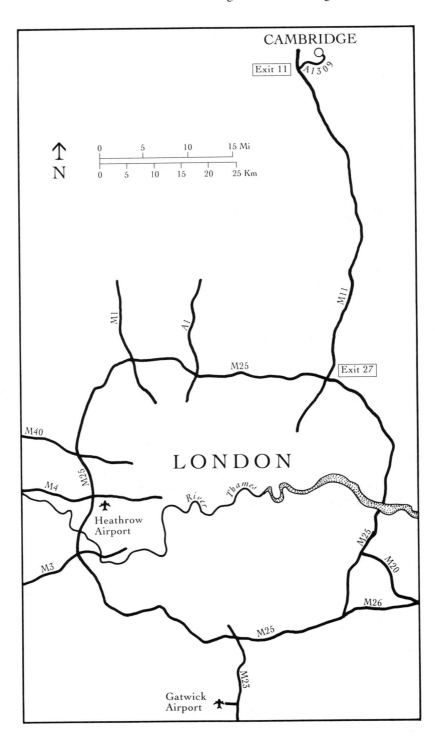

BritRail's nonstop train to Victoria Station. It runs every 15 minutes from the arrivals building (follow the BritRail signs), and takes about 30 minutes. When you reach Victoria, stop in at the excellent Tourist Information Centre and Book Store. If you don't already have your accommodations booked, the tourist authority runs an excellent booking service, next door to the TIC, that will find you a room in your price range for a modest fee. Then walk outside to the taxi queue and head for your hotel.

But this is a book about Britain's countryside, not London. While we offer a city sampler at the end of this itinerary (see Day Fifteen), East Anglia is our destination today.

🚗 NORTH TO CAMBRIDGE

Distance: About 90 miles/145 kilometers (from Gatwick)
Roads: Motorways and major arterials
Driving Time: 1.75 hours, depending on airport and traffic
Map: Michelin Map #404

From **Heathrow**, pick up the **M4** motorway heading west and, almost immediately, turn onto the **M25**, London's outer ring road, heading north. The M25, obsolete even before it was completed, can be a bit frantic any time of the day, so stay to the **left** until you've grown accustomed to the traffic flow. If the M25 were a clock face, with London in the center, you would have joined it at "9:00"; you will be driving clockwise past eleven exits until you reach, at "1:00," the **M11** at **Exit 27**. Take the ramp marked for **Cambridge**, and settle in for a pleasant 45-minute ride through the country.

From **Gatwick**, the ride around London is a bit longer. From the car-hire agency lot, follow the blue-and-white motorway signs for the **M23** north toward London. In a little more that 10 miles (16 kilometers), watch for signs for the **M25**. Exit **left** off the M23, but then stay to the **right**, following signs for **Dartford**. There is little evidence here that London sprawls just to the north beyond the chalk ridge on your left; neat hedgerows divide small fields of grain and meadows dotted with black-and-white cows, obviously prosperous farmsteads are scattered here and there, and the horizon is punctuated by graceful church spires.

After crossing into Kent, the motorway divides; stay on the M25 toward Dartford, where the highway tunnels beneath the **River Thames** (a new bridge will open soon), and continue around London.

At **Exit 27**, a little more than 50 miles (80.5 kilometers) from Gatwick, turn north onto the **M11** toward **Cambridge**. Near Bishop's Stortford the ground rumples gently as the road traverses a range of low chalk hills, then evens out again, carpeted by barley and wheat that

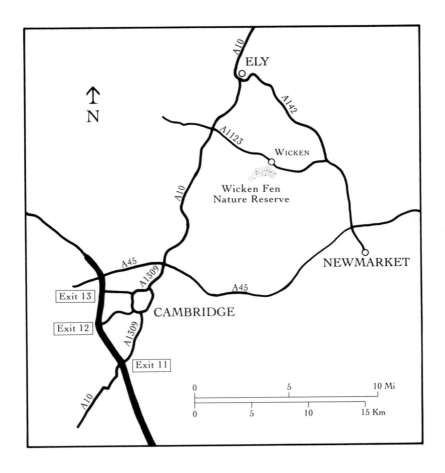

ripples across fields unrelieved by the hedgerows common elsewhere.

Leave the M11 at **Exit 11**, less than 1 hour and 45 minutes after leaving Gatwick, and take the **A1309** (which becomes Trumpington Road) into Cambridge. Follow signs for the City Centre and in minutes you'll be driving through "the Backs"—the leafy parkland bordering the River Cam just in *back* of several of Cambridge's oldest and most beautiful colleges.

Parking in Cambridge—legal parking, that is—is in short supply. There is a public parking area in Lion's Yard (there are signs as you enter town), but the entry queues can be long. A more attractive option is to look for **Sidgwick Avenue**, a block or so south of the famous view of King's College Chapel across the Backs (you may have to turn around if you've gone too far; the colleges and the river will be on your **left** when you travel south). Turn into Sidgwick Avenue, drive past Newnham

College (Cambridge's first women's college, founded 1871), and turn **left** onto **Grange Road**. In this area you'll find space to park that's both legal and free. Then it's time to stretch your legs and shake off the jet lag. **Note:** If you have not made prior arrangements for accommodations tonight (see Creature Comforts below), park in Lion's Yard; the Tourist Information Centre, which has a booking service, is next door.

𝝲 STROLLING AMONG "THE MANSIONS OF THE MUSES"

Distance: Negligible, but allow at least 2 hours
Difficulty: A pleasant afternoon stroll
Total Elevation Gain: None
Gear: Comfortable shoes/sneakers, loads of film
Map: Any town map from the Tourist Information Centre, or take the guided walking tour

Younger than Oxford, Cambridge *seems* older and more perfect. There is something about its layout, embraced by a gentle curve in the River Cam and adorned by the broad lawns and leafy walks of the Backs, that gives Cambridge a physical integrity and beauty that Oxford cannot match.

Technically, Cambridge University began in 1209, when a disaffected group of scholars left Oxford to establish their own academic community. The first true college, Peterhouse, was not founded until 1284. Ancient as this seems, the town was by then already more than twelve centuries old. Archaeologists have found evidence that Cambridge may have been the site of a Neolithic settlement, but the city's recorded history begins with the establishment of a Roman fort on the north bank of the river (which they called the Granta) in A.D. 70. The settlement, called Grantacaester (later Grantabric, then Cantabridge), was strategically sited at the head of navigation on the river. But fenlanders, like the fens themselves, are not easily conquered. Queen Boadicea, by all accounts a formidable lady, led a local Celtic tribe called the Iceni in a furious but ultimately fruitless resistance against the Romans. When the Romans withdrew, Cambridge and the inviting East Anglian coast proved irresistible to new invaders. Vikings, Danes, and Saxons each found their way upriver, struggled with the locals, then settled in. Even after the Normans had managed to subjugate the rest of Britain, William the Conqueror had to build a castle at Cambridge from which to wage a three-year battle against the Saxon rebel Hereward the Wake, who resisted the Normans from Ely, then an island deep in the fenland swamps. And as recently as the seventeenth century, defenders of traditional uses of fenland resources waged so stubborn a guerilla war against engineers who drained the fens for farming that they earned the name "Fen Tigers."

From Cambridge's present tranquil vantage point, however, these struggles seem almost impossible. Despite the traffic and the swarms of bicycling students, Cambridge manages to seem unhurried—as if the languor of an afternoon upon the River Cam had seeped into the city's lifeblood.

There are three ways to appreciate Cambridge: take the official guided tour; wander off on your own, map in hand, to whichever colleges capture your fancy; or take a self-styled course in architectural appreciation while drifting lazily in a punt on the placid river, enjoying a bit of cheese, a bottle of wine, and perhaps a slim volume of poetry (to keep up appearances). It's a difficult choice.

If the weather is fine, the river may be hard to resist. But the Tourist Information Centre's two-hour guided walking tours are probably your best bet. Tickets cost about £3 per person. The "Blue Badge" guides are knowledgeable and entertaining and have one advantage over you: in addition to knowing all the best nooks and crannies, they know which colleges are open to the public on any given day. Each of Cambridge's thirty-one colleges is private and can close its grounds at any time to individuals or groups as it sees fit. From the second week in October, when students come up (one doesn't arrive at Cambridge, one "comes up"), through April, access can be iffy, and the colleges are completely closed to visitors during exams in May. In the summer, the colleges are open and access is gained through the main gates or through each college's "Porter's Office." The guides know the schedules and vary the walking tours accordingly. Tours leave daily all year at 11:15 A.M. and 2:00 P.M. from April through October; tours at 1:00 P.M. and 3:00 P.M. are added in July, August, and September; and noon tours are also offered in July and August only (try to get there early during the summer). The Tourist Information Centre is on the ground floor of the Guildhall Building just across the street from the Lion Yard Shopping Centre and is open (with slight seasonal variations) from 9:00 A.M. to 5:00 P.M. Monday through Saturday year-round, and Sunday from 10:30 A.M. to 3:30 P.M. Easter through September.

If the guided tour schedule isn't convenient or you prefer to appreciate the university at your own pace, structure your own walk (but remember that even the self-guided walking tour described below is subject to the opening and closing whims of the individual colleges). Leave your car in the **Grange Road** area, walk back up **Sidgwick Avenue**, and cross **Queen's Road**, at which point Sidgwick becomes **Silver Street**. Continue straight ahead, past a crescent of gable-ended attached houses on your left, and cross over **Silver Street Bridge**. Pause for a moment on the left side of the bridge to look at **Mathematical Bridge**, a vaguely Oriental wooden bridge built in 1749 with such mathematical precision that it required no nails. It has been rebuilt twice since . . . with bolts.

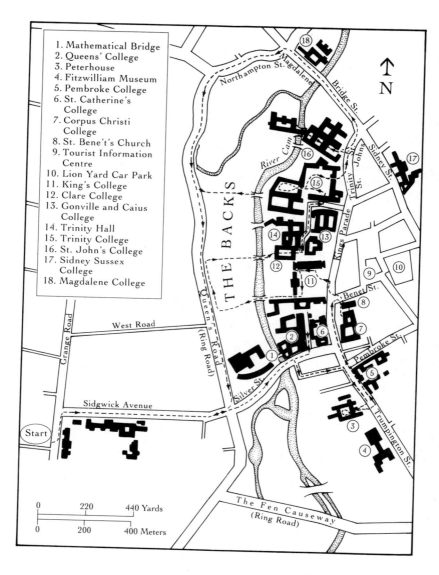

1. Mathematical Bridge
2. Queens' College
3. Peterhouse
4. Fitzwilliam Museum
5. Pembroke College
6. St. Catherine's College
7. Corpus Christi College
8. St. Bene't's Church
9. Tourist Information Centre
10. Lion Yard Car Park
11. King's College
12. Clare College
13. Gonville and Caius College
14. Trinity Hall
15. Trinity College
16. St. John's College
17. Sidney Sussex College
18. Magdalene College

Walking in Cambridge is like a game of hide-and-seek. The true character of many colleges is disguised by a modest public face. The soot-covered brick building on your left as you continue up Silver Street is a perfect example: dull, unprepossessing. But turn **left** into **Queens' Lane** and **left** again through the massive gatehouse and you'll discover why **Queens' College** (founded by two queens, Henry VI's wife Margaret of Anjou in 1448 and Edward IV's wife Elizabeth in

1465) is felt by many to be the prettiest in Cambridge. Its Front Court, built in the mid-1400s, is the oldest complete courtyard in the university and the half-timber Cloister Court beyond is even lovelier. In many of the oldest colleges, the passage from archway to courtyard, from dark to light, yields a continuing string of visual surprises and a wide range of architectural styles, from Norman to Elizabethan, Georgian to Victorian—most of it original.

Now backtrack, out through the gatehouse, **right** into Queens' Lane, and **right** again into Silver Street. Cross over and then turn **left** down narrow **Laundress Lane**, named for the laundrywomen who once dried their laundry on the riverbanks nearby. If you landed in London early in the morning, as most transatlantic travelers do, it should be lunchtime about now and two riverside pubs, **The Mill** and **The Anchor**, sit facing the river at the end of this lane. There is a weir on the river here, so you may well have the spectacle of kayakers working the rapids as you sip a pint of local ale.

Next, walk up **Mill Lane**, away from the river, and turn **right** into busy **Trumpington Street**, staying on the right side. **Peterhouse** (not "college") lies ahead. Little of the original thirteenth-century buildings remains today, but the symmetry of the Georgian-style buildings around the school's courtyard is pleasing and the formality is eased by bicycles piled up near the gates and exuberant flower baskets hanging beneath the arcade arches.

The imposing building just ahead on the right is the **Fitzwilliam Museum**, a treasure house of Egyptian, Roman, and Greek antiquities and painting by Europe's masters, but one that should probably be left for another day. Instead, cross Trumpington Street and head back toward the center of town, passing the medieval gateway of **Pembroke College** (1347) on the next corner.

Cross over **Pembroke Street** and continue straight ahead along Trumpington. On your left, with its simple streetside courtyard, is **St. Catherine's College** (1473). **Corpus Christi College** (1352) is on your right. The view through Corpus Christi's gatehouse to its chapel is essentially Victorian; the buildings in this part of the school, called the New Court, date from the mid-1800s. Walk past the main gatehouse and turn **right** into **Benet Street**. On your right, so old that the ground on which it is built is below grade today, is **St. Bene't's Church** (short for St. Benedict); its Saxon tower, built in 1025, is the oldest building in Cambridge. Duck through the alley behind the church, and you'll find yourself in Corpus Christi's Old Court, the oldest and most complete medieval courtyard in either Cambridge or Oxford. Church and court are linked because St. Bene't's served as the college's chapel. (The Tourist Information Centre is just a block farther up Benet Street, in the Guildhall Building facing the small square.)

Now walk back out to the main street, which here changes its name

from Trumpington to **King's Parade**, cross the street, and pass under the elaborately carved cupola of **King's College's** gate. Founded in 1441, all that remains of the original school is **King's College Chapel**, across the courtyard to the right, arguably the finest example of English Perpendicular architecture in the land. An eloquent expression of Renaissance advances in engineering and art, the chapel's delicate fan-vaulted ceiling, slim columns, and soaring stained glass windows contrast sharply with the squat bulk of St. Bene't's. Flemish craftsmen spent twenty-six years creating the magnificent windows, twelve pairs of which march down the nave from the altar (crowned by Rubens's *Adoration of the Magi*) to the great west window. On a sunny day, the long, narrow interior is suffused with light and color, as if hundreds of rainbows arched through the airy aisle.

Time now, perhaps, for a respite from buildings. Walk from the chapel to the opposite side of Front Court and turn **right** after passing the somewhat austere **Fellows Building**. Continue along this walk, over the River Cam via **King's Bridge**, and then turn **right** at **Queen's Road**. Across the meadow, usually grazed by perhaps the most photographed cows in Britain, is the most famous view of Cambridge, with King's College Chapel and Clare College dominating a remarkably pastoral scene.

Continue through the Backs along Queen's Road 100 yards or so and take the first footpath to the **right**, down a leafy *allee* to **Clare Bridge**, arching gracefully over the Cam. Then duck under the massive copper beech at the other end, past Fellow's Garden, and enter **Clare College** (1326). Fire has twice destroyed Clare and the present buildings were built in the seventeenth and eighteenth centuries with the precise classical proportions of the period. At the other side of the compact courtyard go through the gatehouse and turn **left** into narrow **Trinity Lane**.

You are dwarfed here by the back of **Gonville and Caius** (pronounced *Keys*) **College** (founded 1346 and 1557, respectively) on the right and **Trinity Hall** (1350) on the left. Go to the end and, a few steps after the bend, turn **left** through a gatehouse to enter the vast Great Court of **Trinity College**. Created by Henry VIII in 1546 to outshine Oxford's Christ Church College, built by his nemesis Cardinal Wolsey, Trinity today is the largest college in the university. Detour **left** first to see the **Wren Library**, by the river in Neville's Court, then come back through the Great Court and go out by the main gatehouse, turning **left** into **Trinity Street**.

In that charming, if confusing, way that English street names keep changing, Trinity Street becomes **St. John's Street** as it passes the tur-

Peterhouse, the oldest college at Cambridge

reted Tudor gatehouse of **St. John's College**. St. John's was founded in 1511 by Lady Margaret Beaufort, mother of Henry VII (that's her coat of arms over the door). St. John's has four courtyards. First Court, built in the early sixteenth century, contains the school's Victorian chapel. Second Court was built in 1598, and Third Court during the mid-seventeenth century. One makes this pilgrimage principally to reach the river and the "Bridge of Sighs," an exquisite, enclosed stone confection built in 1831 in the style of the sixteenth century original in Venice. On the other side of the bridge is the Gothic New Court ("new," that is, when it was built in the mid-nineteenth century).

Next, go back out through the main gate, turn **left** into St. John's Street, and walk out to **Bridge Street**, with the round **Church of the Holy Sepulchre** (1130) dead ahead. Then turn **left** and walk along Bridge Street to Magdalene (pronounced, for some reason, *Maudlin*) Bridge. The punt rental yard here, while atmospheric, is really just a pale shadow of the earlier life of this section of the River Cam, which served as the city's port from Roman times well into recent history.

Across the bridge, Bridge Street becomes **Magdalene Street**, with **Magdalene College** (1542) on the right above the river. Here you have a decision to make. If the countless bookstores and shopfronts of the old part of town have caught your eye, you can turn around and follow Bridge Street, which becomes **Sidney Street** in front of **Sidney Sussex College** (1596), to plunge into the thick of it. (Take the same route to return to Lion's Yard if you parked there.) If your car is in the Grange Road area, however, continue straight ahead and turn **left** at the corner just beyond Magdalene College and return to your car by way of Queen's Road and the Backs.

🚗 LATE AFTERNOON IN WICKEN FEN

Distance: 14 miles/22.5 kilometers
Roads: Fast, uncrowded primary roads
Driving Time: Less than 30 minutes
Map: Michelin Map #404

Most people who visit Cambridge stay in the city. Don't. Once you've "done" the colleges, Cambridge is just another city: busy, crowded, and noisy. Be adventurous. A few minutes to the north lies a unique corner of England, alternately breathtaking and eerie—like Holland with a bit of mystery thrown in for spice. Head for Wicken. There are comfortable farmhouse bed-and-breakfast accommodations scattered across the countryside (at least one of them haunted—see Creature Comforts below) and there is the added attraction of Wicken Fen, one of Britain's first nature reserves.

The reedy expanse of the Anglian Fens rolls to the horizon like a gentle green tide.

From the Backs, head north on Queen's Road and follow signs for the **A1309** (Milton Road) and **A10** north toward **Ely**. As Cambridge falls behind you, the landscape flattens and farmland stretches in green abundance to the horizon. At the **Stretham** roundabout, about 9 miles (14.5 kilometers) outside of Cambridge, turn **right** onto the **A1123**. The village of Wicken is about 5 miles (8 kilometers) to the east. Just before reaching the village, turn **right** into the entrance to the Wicken Fen Nature Reserve.

You bump along a short rutted lane and then reach a sort of gap in the time-space continuum: behind you, a twentieth-century English village; ahead, a squat late-nineteenth-century thatch-roofed fenland cottage, an ancient wooden windmill, and, beyond, the timeless fen itself, a lush green morass of reeds and sedges stretching off to the edge of the sky. To be fair, this is not a place for everyone. But it has a lonely beauty, a deep affecting quiet. You have to wait a bit for the fen to reach you. For the birdsong to penetrate. For the low hum of bumblebees and dragonflies and hundreds of other insects to reach that primitive part of the ear that senses nearly inaudible frequencies. For the wind-rustled reed music to uncurl your urban fingers. It is a place of tiny illuminations—like the amazing range of flowers that can occupy a small patch of marshy ground: yellow flag iris, purple loosestrife, spiky yellow ragwort, pink marsh pea, feathery meadow rue, frothy cow parsley.

Wicken Fen is the last accessible, undrained remnant of the 2,500-square-mile (6,475-square-kilometer) marsh called the Great Level. As recently as the last century, some 700 windmills were employed to drain the Levels for farming; today, the windmill at Wicken Fen, which became a nature reserve in 1899, pumps water *into* the fen to maintain its unique habitat. But the fen is no wilderness; it is managed to demonstrate how traditional uses of the fens (reed-cutting for thatch, peat-cutting for fuel, and so on) maintained and enhanced the natural diversity of the habitat. There is a good nature center near the entrance where you pay a small admission fee and pick up a guide to the trails in the reserve. Wicken Fen is managed by the National Trust, a private nonprofit body that is Britain's leading conservation organization. It is open year-round.

CREATURE COMFORTS
Daily Bed

On a foggy evening, the featureless fens of Cambridgeshire are the kind of mysterious place in which you can imagine almost anything happening. At **Spinney Abbey**, an imposing stone farmhouse on the edge of Wicken Fen, things have been "going bump in the night" for centuries. The house is built on the foundations of the Priory of St. Mary and the Holy Cross, an isolated monastic community founded in the thirteenth century. According to local records, the prior, one William of Lode, was murdered by three of his canons in 1403. They were convicted, but the Bishop of Ely claimed clerical privilege and took the murderers back to the priory, imprisoning them in the basement. They were never heard of again. The priory cellar still exists, beneath the current house, and the chains that once held the prisoners still dangle from the dank stone walls. Over the years, the Fuller family, which has farmed the surrounding land for generations, has had more than its share of unexplainable happenings and "sightings"—an invisible choir singing in the midst of Easter dinner, hooded figures appearing and disappearing in the garden, and more.

Today though, Valerie Fuller runs a delightful farmhouse bed and breakfast to help restore and maintain Spinney Abbey while her husband, Robert, manages the farm. The house, built in 1775 and formally listed as historically important, is quite grand as farmhouses go, with spacious rooms, an elegant central stairway, and doors that belonged to the original abbey. The hospitality, ghosts notwithstanding, is warm and informal. As you approach Wicken on the A1123, Spinney Abbey is the large double gable-roofed stone farmhouse off to the right; there is a small sign by the road. But book ahead: write Valerie Fuller, Spinney Abbey, Wicken, Ely, Cambridgeshire CB7 5XQ, or phone (0353) 720971.

The Fullers are part of a program called "Cambridge Farm Tourism." In addition to promoting the pleasures of staying in the countryside, the program makes it easier for travelers to *find* B&Bs, which for some reason are not as well developed in East Anglia as elsewhere in Britain. For a brochure providing pictures, a description of the facilities at participating farms, addresses, and phone numbers, write for the *Cambridge Farm Tourism* brochure at the Tourist Information Centre, Wheeler Street, Cambridge, or phone (0773) 317336. Some of the same farms are listed in *Stay on a Farm: The Official Guide of the Farm Holiday Bureau*, listed in Further Reading in the back of this book. Others are listed in the *Bed and Breakfast Touring Map for the East of England*, published by the East Anglia Tourist Board, Toppesfield Hall, Hadleigh, Suffolk IP7 5DN, phone (0473) 822922. There are youth hostels at Cambridge and Ely; consult the YHA guide in Further Reading for addresses. Wherever you decide to stay, book in for two nights.

Daily Bread

There are, of course, plenty of places to eat in Cambridge; if you stay in the city tonight you can either ask your host or hostess for recommendations or simply forage on your own. But if you're out in the countryside, head for the local pub with the best menu. Your B&B hostess will be a reliable guide. Jet lag by now having nearly overcome you, you won't want to venture too far afield. If you stay at Spinney Abbey, there is a good pub with a better-than-average menu right on the green at the center of Wicken.

In Constable Country

NEWMARKET ♦ LONG MELFORD
DEDHAM VALE ♦ KERSEY ♦ LAVENHAM

- ♦ **A driving tour through Suffolk's medieval wool towns**
- ♦ **A riverside walk through Dedham Vale**
- ♦ **An optional visit to the birthplace of the Magna Carta**

I associate my careless boyhood with all that lies on the banks of the River Stour; these scenes made me a painter. . . . I had often thought of pictures of them before I ever touched a pencil.

——John Constable, 1821

*I*t is a luminous autumn afternoon in 1832 as the London–Ipswich stagecoach clatters through peaceful Dedham Vale on the Essex–Suffolk border. One of the two gentleman sharing the carriage comments on the beauty of the passing scene—the cerulean blue East Anglian sky, the intense viridian green of the watermeadows along the meandering River Stour. The stranger opposite him puffs up his chest and exclaims: "Yes, sir. This is Constable's country!" The other gentleman smiles. His name is John Constable.

His smile that afternoon would no doubt have been pained. Today, Constable's pastoral landscapes are what England thinks of when it thinks of itself. But in the early 1800s he was a Romantic visionary, his sweeping six-foot canvases savaged by the Royal Academy as "nasty green things" even as he was being celebrated in France. He was elected, finally and just barely, to the Academy at age fifty-three. Eight years later he was dead.

Constable's best paintings depict a world he knew intimately: a short stretch of the little River Stour above and below Flatford Mill, one of two mills his father owned in Dedham Vale. It is a peaceful, domesticated landscape of lush meadows, rippling fields of silvery green barley, crooked country lanes lined with hedgerows of hawthorn and blackberry bramble, sleepy thatch-roofed Tudor villages and, through it all, the willow-lined river itself, drifting in lazy loops across the valley floor. So unchanged is Dedham Vale that scenes like *The Haywain*, *Boat Building at Flatford*, *Willy Lott's Cottage*, and *Mill Stream* survive today much as he painted them a century and a half ago. The main objective of today's itinerary is to slip quietly into the foreground of a Constable painting by means of an easy amble beside the banks of the River Stour. Along the way, however, there is much to see of this underrated corner of England.

🚗 THROUGH SUFFOLK TO THE STOUR RIVER VALLEY

Distance: About 55 miles/89 kilometers
Roads: Mostly secondary roads and narrow country lanes
Driving Time: 2–3 hours, depending on stops
Map: Michelin Map #404

We begin today's sojourn into south Suffolk by heading east from Wicken village on the **A1123** toward **Soham**. When you reach the intersection with the **A142**, turn **right** and drive south toward **Fordham**. There, turn **left** onto the **B1102** and, after perhaps a mile, bear **right** onto the **B1085** toward **Chippenham** (if you stayed elsewhere in Cambridgeshire last night, drive to Newmarket and pick up the itinerary there).

Here along the Cambridgeshire–Suffolk border you'll see none of the quaint stone cottages that are characteristic of so much of the rest of Britain. There simply is no stone to be had. The earth beneath these rolling fields is young, sedimentary, and soft, a mix of chalk and clay. In place of stone, builders resorted to an eclectic mix of locally available materials. Many newer buildings are made of brick and roofed in terracotta tile; others are faced with mortar studded with flint nodules (the compressed remains of prehistoric sponges) that have been chipped, or "knapped," to expose a decorative glassy surface. The oldest surviving buildings, dating to medieval times and earlier, are timber-framed and have walls made of interwoven "wattles" (split hazel or willow branches) and "daub" (a mix of mud, cow dung, and horsehair) surfaced with a skim coat of plaster. In the old days the plaster walls were painted with a mix of whitewash and pig's blood; even today, you know immediately that you've entered East Anglia by its pink cottage walls. They don't use pig's blood anymore, but the palette is the same, ranging from palest pink to deep rose, bright magenta, or even claret red. For roofing, the East Anglians harvested reeds and bound bundles ("fathoms") of them together to form thick thatching. Flimsy as these materials may sound, they actually put more modern materials to shame; thick wattle-and-daub walls are excellent insulators and a roof

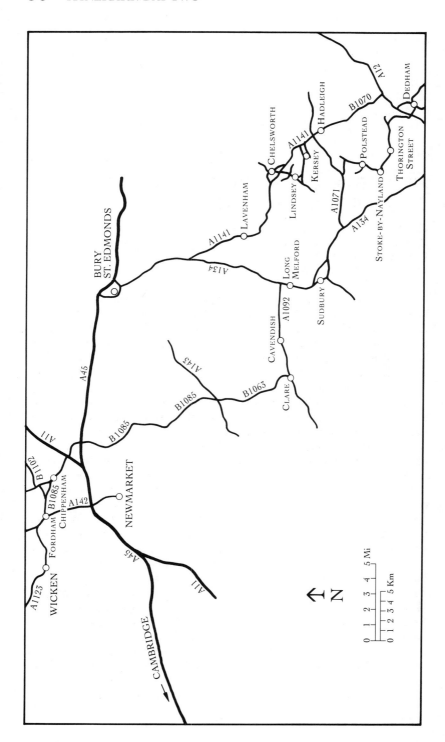

made from Norfolk reed can last as long as eighty years.

The chalk and clay soils also determined how the land was used and, as a result, how the scenery looks today. As you drive south along the B1085 east of **Newmarket**, for example, huge horse farms carpeted in rich green turf and edged with neat boundary fences stretch off beyond the hedgerows in all directions. To an extent, Newmarket's importance as an equestrian center is a fine example of making a virtue out of necessity; the surrounding heath sits upon a fast-draining belt of chalk that produces calcium-rich grass in abundance. Like the bluegrass country of Kentucky, it was tailor-made for raising horses, but little else.

When you encounter the A11 a few miles beyond Chippenham, stay on the B1085, which jogs **right**, then **left**, and continues south into the pleasant valley of the River Kennett. (Take care driving along the B1085 and some of the other country lanes you'll travel this morning; they were laid out long after the farms were established, and often turn sharply around field corners without a great deal of warning.) At the intersection with the **A143**, you once again jog **right**, then **left**, and continue south following signs for the B1057 and **Clare**.

Only 30 miles (48 kilometers) separate Wicken from Clare, but the landscape changes you experience in the 50 minutes or so it will take you to cover this distance are remarkable. First, the tabletop flatness of the peaty brown fens yields to the high chalk heathland of Newmarket's horse farms. Then the grassy heath yields to a rumpled tapestry of softly undulating fields of wheat and barley, clumps of forest, and tightly clustered villages with pretty whitewashed thatched cottages. Then, at Clare, you enter the gentle world of Constable's beloved Stour Valley.

Clare is worth a stop. The town gets its name from the clarity of the river at this point. Situated near the head of the river, the town has had strategic importance since the Iron Age, when the Iceni tribe had a fort here. Castle Mound, from which there are sweeping views of the surrounding countryside, is all that remains of a castle built by the Normans in 1090. The fifteenth-century flint-faced church in the center of town is airy and austere, partly due to the fact that its original stained glass windows were destroyed by William Dowsing, Oliver Cromwell's "Parliamentary Visitor from Suffolk," whose job it was to destroy "Popish" churches. He seems to have relished the task; he is said to have destroyed or damaged more than 1,000 East Anglian churches, 200 of them personally.

From the market center of Clare, turn **left** onto the **A1092** to **Cavendish**, just downriver. Here, in addition to the conventional pastels, cottages are washed in mustard yellows and oxblood reds, as if darkened with age. As it enters the center of the village, the road squeezes around the corner of an ivy-covered shop and then curves around the edge of a rather grand village green, with Cavendish's handsome church towering above a beautifully restored group of thatched

The Art of Pargeting

The problem with buildings made of split logs and willow branches is that, after a century or two, the wood warps and the building settles, fracturing the mud walls. To keep out drafts, East Anglians slathered thick layers of plaster over their exterior walls, often embellishing the plaster by combing it in abstract patterns or sculpting it into ornate decorative forms—a process called *pargeting*. Beginning as early as the fifteenth century and peaking in the seventeenth, when half-timber construction went out of fashion, pargeting became more and more elaborate, sometimes depicting family crests, guild signs, representations of the business of the owner, or intricate floral patterns. One of the finest examples of pargeting in Suffolk is Clare's "Ancient House," a fifteenth-century priest's house whose elaborately carved and brilliantly whitewashed walls face the church's tiny cemetery in the center of town.

cottages. Continue east on the A1092 and, after 4 miles (6.4 kilometers), turn **right** at the T-junction onto the **A134** and enter **Long Melford**.

Long Melford's 3-mile-long main street—broad, tree-lined, and trimmed with elegant Georgian and Victorian shopfronts—is like a necklace encrusted with architectural gems. It has not one but two great houses, both built in the fifteenth century: **Kentwell Hall**, a perfectly proportioned Tudor masterpiece complete with moat (open afternoons Thursday and Sunday from April to mid-June, Wednesday through Sunday from mid-June through September), and **Melford Hall**, a fabulous confection of turrets and topiary off to your left as you enter the village (open afternoons Wednesday, Thursday, Saturday, and Sunday from April through September). Melford's Church of Holy Trinity has so many soaring windows (ninety-seven in all) and so little apparent structure that the roof seems almost to float in midair. The town itself is a bit self-consciously precious, as if it had been "done" by one of the many interior decorators whose shops line its main street. Still, it is a sumptuous creation.

From Long Melford, continue south on the A134 in the direction of **Colchester**, bypassing the town of **Sudbury**, and then turn **left** onto the **A1071** toward **Hadleigh**. Just beyond the turning for **Boxford** (on the left), turn **right** toward **Whitestreet Green** and **Polstead** and plunge into the world of the seventeenth century: a maze of narrow hedge-lined country lanes dotted with tiny hamlets of color-washed cottages that Constable knew well. Turn **right** again at the sign for Kelly Street, Whitestreet Green, and Polstead, a charming clutch of cottages gathered around a pond (*Polstead* means "place by a pool") and surrounded by an old cherry orchard. At the next T-junction, turn **right** in the direction of **Stoke-by-Nayland**, past deeply thatched half-timber cottages. Then, at the next T-junction, bear **left** entering Stoke. Turn **right** at the top of the hill, then **right** again as the splendid Church of St. Mary the Virgin comes into view. Pause here briefly to admire the intricately carved south doors and vaulting hammer-beamed ceiling of the church and the ancient half-timber Guildhall and Maltings buildings nearby, with their overhanging second stories and tiny leaded windows. Then, at the Angel Inn, head in the direction of **Higham**. Drive through the village of **Thorington Street**, past Thorington Hall, with the pretty River Stour off on your right, and at Higham turn **right** for **Stratford St. Mary**, another tiny village of crooked timbered houses close by the river. As you climb the hill, bear **left** toward **Dedham**. Then, at the T-junction for the **B1029**, turn **left** down into Dedham village. At the center of the village, turn **left** and park in the well-marked car park on the way to the river.

Dedham, where Constable went to school and the site of one of his father's mills, is warm and welcoming, a happy little jumble of medi-

The artistry of Suffolk's medieval carpenters

eval, Georgian, and Victorian shops and buildings. Despite the central role it plays in so many of Constable's paintings, Dedham somehow manages to avoid being deluged by the crowds that flock to nearby Flatford Mill on midsummer weekends. For that reason alone, but also because it has an excellent Tourist Information Centre, down a narrow lane beside the Royal Grammar School, Dedham makes an excellent base for exploring the Stour valley. It's also a good place to have lunch before you head off downriver, perhaps at the venerable Marlborough Head inn, between the town center and the car park.

大 A WALK THROUGH CONSTABLE'S ENGLAND

Distance: About 4 miles/6.4 kilometers; allow 2 hours
Difficulty: An easy riverside stroll with one short hill
Total Elevation Gain: Negligible
Gear: Sneakers (but waterproof shoes preferable), long trousers (to protect against stinging nettles), camera
Map: *Walking in Constable Country*, a brochure available from the Tourist Information Centre; Ordnance Survey Pathfinder #1053; this book

The little River Stour (more a dilettante stream than a purposeful river) is the official boundary between the counties of Essex and Suffolk, but the river unifies, rather than divides, the scene, creating a broad, enchantingly pastoral vale—a patchwork of vivid green watermeadows, irregular fields of barley and wheat, forested ridge tops, and wildflower-dappled grasslands grazed by unperturbable black-and-white cows. So unspoiled is the scene that Dedham Vale was desig-

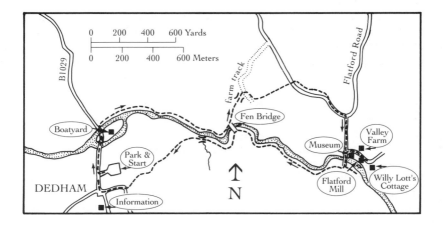

nated an Area of Outstanding Natural Beauty in 1970.

From the car park entrance, turn **right** and walk toward the river. After crossing the first bridge, just beyond Dedham Mill (now renovated for residences), you are faced with a pleasant choice. If your mood is romantic, stop right here. Just to your right is Dedham Boatyard; for a modest £4 per hour, you can hire a graceful Victorian rowboat, complete with lapstrake wooden hull and delicate wrought-iron railings, and row lazily downriver to Flatford Mill; the trip takes roughly 45 minutes each way and the current is almost imperceptible. (The little boatyard ought to rent straw "boater" hats for gentlemen and lace parasols for ladies, just to complete the picture, but, alas, does not.)

If, on the other hand, you prefer the freedom of the footpaths, continue over the second bridge, turn **right** at the footpath sign, and head downriver along the north bank. The river, glassy and silent, is overhung here and there by gnarled old willow trees, and the whispery rustle of their silver-green leaves complements the birdsong that fills the air. It's remarkable how quickly you can leave the twentieth century behind. From the broad valley floor, virtually the only signs of human beings are a splendidly situated Georgian country house away on a far ridge and the ever-present spire of Dedham's church in the distance to your right. At the river's edge are reeds and bullrushes, yellow flag iris, and magenta foxglove. Along the footpath, blush red campion and creamy clouds of cow parsley bloom in profusion.

The scene is so enchanting that it is difficult to imagine the Stour as the hard-working river it was well into the twentieth century, lined with mills and busy with barges hauling grain, coal, lime, and bricks. Indeed, it was that more muscular landscape—of boatbuilding at Flatford, of wagons hauling hay to riverside wharves, of millraces and corn grinding—that Constable committed to canvas, not the placid scene that is the river today.

After clambering over several stiles, you reach Fen Bridge. Turn **left** away from the river up the gravel path through a hawthorn thicket, cross another small bridge, then cross a farm track and go over the stile opposite, continuing up the well-marked footpath along the right side of a field, paralleling the river. Partway along the field, the footpath turns away from the river and **climbs** to the crest of the hill. From this spot there are sweeping 180-degree views of Dedham Vale and the great blue arc of clear East Anglian sky—a scene Constable once described as "the calm sunshine of the heart."

At the narrow country lane at the top of the hill, turn **right**, first following a footpath and then the road itself. Then bear **right** at **Flatford Road** and walk downhill between the ivy-clad banks to **Flatford Mill**. The mill itself, its brickwork fading to deep rose, Willy Lott's white-washed cottage with its massive chimneys, and the half-timber masterpiece of Valley Farm (all owned by the National Trust and managed as the Flatford Mill Field Studies Centre) compose a scene instantly recognizable from Constable's work. The trees are a bit higher, the mill pond a bit more overgrown and reedy, but the feeling of the place is just as he evoked it a century and a half ago. Bridge Cottage, a few steps from the mill, houses a small Constable museum.

Afterwards, **cross** over the bridge beside the museum. Turn **left** for a few yards for the best view of the mill, then turn and walk past the bridge, taking the footpath along the **left** side of the river, back toward Dedham. At Fen Bridge, stay on the left bank. A short distance ahead, just beyond a small cement bridge over a tributary ditch (and very near the site depicted in Constable's painting *The Leaping Horse*), a signpost guides you **left** away from the river and diagonally across a field toward Dedham. Just outside the village, the path passes behind a farm that features rare domestic animal breeds, enters another farmyard, cuts **left** to a stile with a yellow marker arrow, then crosses yet another field. On

Victorian-style rowboats for hire at Dedham Boatyard

Willie Lott's cottage at Flatford Mill, much as it was when Constable painted it

the other side you go over one last stile and meet the road into town by a pretty cream-colored, gambrel-roofed cottage. At the village center, turn **right** to return to the car park.

🚗 TOWNS THAT SHEEP BUILT

Distance: 50 miles/80 kilometers
Roads: Both secondary and primary roads, well signed
Driving Time: The balance of the afternoon
Map: Michelin Map #404

From Dedham, turn **right** out of the car park, drive over the river, and a mile or so later, turn **left** toward the **A12** to **Ipswich**. You duck underneath the highway, then swing onto its entrance ramp. In less than a mile, turn off the A12 onto the **B1070** and at the first intersection turn **right** in the direction of **Hadleigh**.

Coming up the hill out of Hadleigh turn **left** at the T-junction with the **A1071**, but then turn **right** immediately onto the **A1141** sign-posted for **Lavenham**. Then, after perhaps a mile, look for a signpost for **Kersey** and turn **left** down a narrow lane. The lane brings you to **Kersey Street**, where you turn **right** and slip down the hill.

From the little churchyard overlooking the village you can read the history of Suffolk in a single horizon-sweeping glance, if you recognize the clues. There is the hammer-beamed church itself, which, like so many in this county, seems much grander than this sleepy village should command. There is the small but centrally placed stream, through which the town's narrow main street splashes on its way up the opposite hill. There are the stout medieval houses arrayed cheek-by-jowl along the pavement, leaning against one another like proud but aging soldiers on review, their cocked hats tilting at all angles. Some are bright pink with color-washed plaster, their thick oak doors nearly obscured by riots of purple clematis and ivory-pink "New Dawn" roses. Others are framed with intricately joined and ornately carved half-timbers, such as the commanding Bell Inn, halfway up the hill on the left. Beyond the Bell are the billowing Suffolk hills, here cloaked in barley that ripples in the soft breeze, there dotted with the creamy flecks of grazing sheep.

Kersey—or Lavenham, or Long Melford, or Chelsworth, or any of a dozen similar villages—may be humble rural backwaters today, but "good bones" show through the neat but modest fabric of their somewhat reduced present circumstances. There was money here once, a lot of it; the evidence is everywhere. But it was a long time ago: Suffolk had its "industrial revolution" in the fourteenth and fifteenth centuries, when Edward III banned the import of foreign cloth. Unable to move their goods into England, Flemish and Dutch weavers moved themselves instead, combining forces with English sheep farmers to create one of the premier textile centers of Europe. Little Kersey became famous for its blue serge. Its neighbor over the hill, Lindsey, may have given its name to the linen-and-wool fabric called linsey-woolsey. Lavenham and Long Melford flourished as centers for the wool and cloth trades. The merchant families displayed their wealth by building elaborate half-timber homes (framed with oak logs split in half) and parish churches so grand they would have been cathedrals elsewhere.

But when the first power loom appeared a few centuries later, the economy of the entire region collapsed. In a landscape of chalk and clay like Suffolk's, there are few fast-flowing streams to drive looms. Consequently, by the mid-eighteenth century, the entire industry had moved on to the rainy Peak District, where there was plenty of water (and later coal) to power the vast mills of the real Industrial Revolution. Ever since, Suffolk has slept, like a pretty princess under a spell.

After you've explored Kersey, drive to the top of the hill beyond the Bell Inn and turn sharply **left** at the T-junction in the direction of **Lindsey**. At the next signposted intersection, turn **right** up a single-track lane toward **Chelsworth**. Turn **left** at the Y-junction ahead, then

Kersey, one of Suffolk's medieval gems

right at the next intersection, and drive through a tiny hamlet of cottages with thatch so deep and smooth it looks like golden meringue. At the intersection with the **A1141** (careful, visibility is poor here), **cross** over and continue **straight** toward Chelsworth, a mile ahead. At the next intersection, bear **left**. You plunge downhill through a dark green tunnel of trees, bump over a two-hump eighteenth-century stone bridge, and are deposited in Chelsworth, a little candy box of a village, full of plump bonbon-like cottages in cream, orange, and pink icing. After a quick look around, press on to **Lavenham**, Suffolk's medieval treasure.

Lavenham boasts perhaps the finest array of medieval buildings in Britain, and it's hard to keep your eye on the road given the multiple distractions. Before reaching the center of town, turn **right** up **Lady Lane**. At the top of the hill, a handful of shops with bright awnings edge the pavement along one side of a broad market square. The town's crown jewel is the sixteenth-century Guildhall on the opposite side, its ancient timbers weathered silver-gray by centuries of English rain and East Anglian sun. Over the years the Guildhall has been the town hall, a prison, a workhouse, an almshouse, and a wool store. Today, under the management of the National Trust, it houses an exhibition on the medieval wool industry (open daily April through October, 11:00 A.M. to 5:00 P.M.) and the town's Tourist Information Centre.

Lavenham's "sights" are the Guildhall, the Swan Inn, and the impressive Church of St. Peter and St. Paul on the edge of town, each in its own way a monument to the early wool trade. But take some time this afternoon to wander through Lavenham's back alleys, where the craftsmanship of the medieval builders can be best appreciated. Watch for details: intricate carvings on cornerposts, tiny leaded windows of wavy old glass, weathered grotesques carved on the ends of overhanging joists, massive (though short!) oak doors held together by hand-wrought nails hammered in decorative patterns, and more. The state of preservation, thanks to the town's having gone broke and never having recovered, is astonishing. Lavenham is at its best late in the afternoon, when the vivid orange rays of the setting sun bring the color back out of the ancient timbers and set the rosy plaster walls aglow; when the only company on the street may be a stray cat and your own long shadow; when the only sound is the evening birdsong and the distant bark of a dog; when the pungent fragrance of a coal fire evokes scenes from Dickens novels. Then, at this magical hour, you can know Lavenham as it once was.

From Lavenham it's a quick ride home. Take the **A1141** (High Street), which joins the **A134** to **Bury St. Edmunds**. Then take the **A45** west to Newmarket and, if you stayed in Wicken, take the **A142** north nearly to Soham, then the **A1123** to home. If you stayed in the Cambridge area, stay on the A45 straight into Cambridge.

DIVERSIONS
The Abbots and Barons of Bury St. Edmunds

If you skipped this afternoon's walk or simply have the luxury of one of England's endless summer afternoons, a short detour into **Bury**

St. Edmunds will take you to the birthplace of the Magna Carta and the ruins of one of the grandest abbeys in Europe. Bury St. Edmunds is, as you might guess, where St. Edmund is buried. King Edmund, the last ruler of the Kingdom of East Anglia, was killed by invading Danes in A.D. 869. But the martyred king had a peripatetic sort of death; devoted monks hauled his remains around the countryside for three decades before finally laying him to rest here in A.D. 903, in what then was called Beodricksworth. In A.D. 945, Danish King Canute gave the monks permission to establish a shrine for Edmund in a monastery that had been at this site since A.D. 633. A place of pilgrimage, both the town (by then called St. Edmondsbury) and the monastery grew. After the Norman Conquest the abbey, which was one of the five richest in the country, expanded almost continuously, its church attaining a length of more than 500 feet (152 meters). It was at the altar of this church, on November 20, 1214, that twenty-five barons of England swore an oath before the Archbishop of Canterbury that if King John did not sign their Charter of Liberties, they would oust him at Runnymede. He did, of course, accede to their demands and the Magna Carta became a cornerstone of representative governance from that day forward.

Meanwhile, the autocratic rule of the rich and dissolute abbots of St. Edmundsbury became unendurable for the townspeople. They sacked the abbey in 1327, beheaded the prior in 1381, and burned the church again in 1465. The abbey survived these attacks, but the end was near anyway; St. Edmundsbury was one of the many abbeys dissolved by Henry VIII in 1539. After the Dissolution, the abbey was treated as a quarry for precut building stone. What the townspeople couldn't cart away, they colonized; there are several Tudor and Georgian homes built right into the ruined west wall of the church.

CREATURE COMFORTS

The same as yesterday.

Flat Fens and White Peaks

ELY ◆ THE LINCOLNSHIRE FENS
THE DERBYSHIRE PEAKS

◆ **A morning in the ancient precincts of Ely
Cathedral**
◆ **An afternoon drive across the Lincolnshire Fens
to the Peak District National Park**

*Mile after mile the flat road reeled away behind them.
Here a windmill, there a solitary farmhouse, there a row of
poplars strung along the edge of a reed-grown
dike. . . . And as they went, the land flattened more and
more, if a flatter flatness were possible.*
——Dorothy Sayers, *The Nine Tailors*

On a fine day in 1851, a small group of men walked out into
the limitless expanse of Holme Fen and drove a long iron post
straight down into the soft, rich earth until its top was level with the
ground. A hundred years or so later, more than 13 feet (4 meters) of the
post were *above* the ground. It had not been raised by some mysterious
force. It had not moved at all. Instead, the ground around it—for as far
as the eye could see—had dropped, leaving much of the post high and
dry. The same thing was happening throughout the fenland. After centuries of trying, man had finally "won" the battle to drain the fens, but
the peaty soil was shrinking and blowing away. It still is.

The East Anglian fens began forming thousands of years ago, when
the combined effects of a rising sea level and a gentle down-tilting of
eastern Britain raised the water table and caused streams and rivers to
drift aimlessly across the eastern lowlands. The more sluggish the rivers
became, the more waterlogged the landscape grew, creating a vast
swamp. Vegetation grew and died in the increasingly acidic water,
gradually building beds of peat up to 20 feet (6 meters) thick. In time,
prehistoric settlements grew where hummocks of dry land rose above
the water, their inhabitants fishing and hunting in the marshes. (To this

day, the location of these island settlements can be pinpointed on a map by a town's name alone; the suffixes *ea* and *ey* are Old English for "isle.")

But in the early 1600s, the fourth Earl of Bedford, whose family had been given the monastic estates of Thorney and Whittlesey after the Dissolution, set about turning the "useless" marsh into productive farmland. He called in Dutch engineer Cornelius Vermuyden, whose plan was simple—hurry the Great Ouse to the sea by digging a straight channel 21 miles (34 kilometers) long, 70 feet (21 meters) wide. Traditional users of the fens fought back, rioting in Soham and other places and sabotaging engineering works, but the project continued, nonetheless. So successful was this "Bedford River" that Vermuyden was commissioned to build another (the New Bedford River) less than a kilometer away. Soon the fens were crisscrossed with channels, the rivers Great Ouse, Nene, and Welland were disciplined, and the wild Great Level was tamed.

Or so it seemed. But Mother Nature fought back stubbornly. First the river mouths silted up, reflooding the newly drained land and forcing the engineers to deepen the channels. Then seasonal and storm-driven high tides in the shallow bay called the Wash backed salt water into the canals, and sluice gates had to be built near the coast to keep out the tides. In addition, the rivers continued to flood each winter.

Steam engines, like the one in this building in Stretham, gradually replaced windmills as the drainage of the Fens continued in the 1800s.

Fenland Windmills

When the east wind howls across the North Sea, which is almost always, it blows unimpeded all the way from Siberia. The only things in its way are East Anglia's windmills. Once there were thousands of them, some draining the fens, the rest grinding the grain produced from the drained soil. Many still stand; the oldest, in the village of Bourn west of Cambridge, dates from 1636. Though each windmill is different, there are three general types: the *post* mill, which has a timber "body" that revolves around a fixed post so the sails can point into the wind; the *tower* mill, a fixed stone or brick body with a "cap" that rotates to face the wind; and the *smock* mill, a wooden version of the tower mill, usually with eight tapered sides creating a shape resembling a miller's smock. The smock mill in the center of Wicken village is one of only two in the country to have twelve sides. In the early 1800s, wind-powered mills were gradually replaced by steam engines. Stretham's steam engine, built in 1831 and still operable, is capable of lifting 124 tons of water to a height of 12 feet (3.7 meters) each minute.

But these were minor inconveniences compared to the main problem: like a great sponge working in reverse, the peaty soil of the fens shrank as water was drained, and the ground level dropped. To keep their fields from reflooding, farmers installed windmills—hundreds of them—to lift water up into the drainage channels, which by now were well above the level of the surrounding fields. And, of course, the more water the windmills lifted, the faster the ground dropped.

Over time, an entire vocabulary evolved to describe the new landscape: a *drain* is a canal dug to drain the fens; a *mere* is a lake that has been drained for farming; a *load* is a navigable canal cut through a marsh; a *drove* is also a canal, but with a footpath alongside; and a *hythe* is a wharf. Road maps are strewn with remote hamlets with dampish-sounding names—Landwade, Waterbeach, Horningsea, and Walsoken—and hopeful ones—Highfields, Dry Drayton, Landbeach, and Lakesend. Curious words for an even curiouser landscape, a topsy-turvy topography where roads climb *up and over* rivers and canals that flow far above the level of the surrounding fields.

🚗 THE SHIP OF THE FENS

Distance: 10 miles/16 kilometers
Roads: Primary roads, well signed
Driving Time: 20 minutes from Wicken
Map: Michelin Map #404

This morning head for Ely, a charming little market town clustered around perhaps the finest Norman cathedral in all of England. From Wicken, drive west to Stretham, then north on the **A10** (from Cambridge, simply take the A10 north).

Almost from the moment you clear the Stretham roundabout, Ely's cathedral is visible on the northern horizon. It sails serene as an ocean liner above the shimmering green sea of the surrounding fields, the buildings around it like tiny tugboats and tenders skittering about in its wake.

As you enter the center of Ely, watch for the house in which Oliver Cromwell lived (well marked on your right) and turn **right** into the next lane. Even on market day Ely seldom is thronged with tourists, so parking is usually available directly opposite the cathedral green, and elsewhere nearby as well.

Ely's first church was founded in A.D. 673 by Etheldreda, daughter of the Saxon King of East Anglia, who fled her husband after twelve years of marriage and established a community of nuns on a large island in the midst of the fenland swamps. The invading Danes sacked the church in A.D. 869, but it was refounded in A.D. 979 by the Benedictines. In 1081, the Normans began the present cathedral, completing

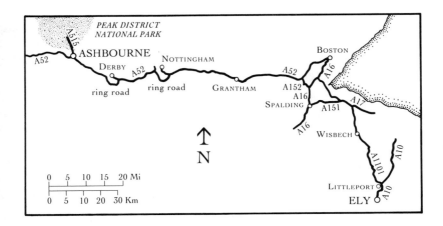

what is arguably the finest example of Romanesque ecclesiastical architecture in England in about 1200. Most great cathedrals have a kind of
assertive masculinity, but Ely is feminine: its corners are softly curved;
its pinnacles and towers are rounded and composed of gently arching,
rather than peaked, leaded windows; its 215-foot (66-meter) west
tower looks like an ornate wedding cake. Entering through the twin
arches of the great west door, you are struck immediately by the vast-
ness of the interior, a grand, uninterrupted space that sweeps 517 feet
(158 meters) from the west tower, through the nave, past the transept,
to the choir and presbytery beyond. Far above the floor is a jubilantly
painted wooden ceiling. But the ceiling is not Ely's pride. For that you
must walk to the east end of the nave, where the ceiling explodes upward to a magnificent and completely unique octagonal dome, arching
high above the transept and capped by the cathedral's famous lantern
tower.

On the night of February 12, 1322, the people of Ely were awak-
ened by a fearful din that shook the earth like an earthquake. The reality
was, if anything, worse. The central tower of the cathedral had collapsed into the transept. Instead of rebuilding the original square
tower, Alan of Walsingham, an architect and the cathedral sacrist, designed an octagon topped by a dome. Aside from its great beauty, the
lantern tower is also a remarkable piece of engineering; some 400 tons
of lead and wood are suspended above the cathedral floor with no apparent means of support. The great weight is transferred through the
delicate fan vaulting to the elegantly carved trunks of eight prodigious
oak trees cut in Bedfordshire (one of the eight was hollowed to permit
workers to reach the lantern).

The cathedral holds many more surprises. There is Bishop West's
Chapel in the southeast corner of the cathedral, delicately carved but in-

Ely Cathedral from its gardens, with the graceful Lady Chapel on the right

complete. Begun in the 1530s, it was still under construction when Henry VIII dissolved the monasteries; the statues in niches near the ceiling were only roughed in when all work stopped. Bishop Alcock's Chapel in the northwest corner is even more ornate than Bishop West's, a fantasia of intricate carving made possible in part by the fact that it is made of easily carved local chalk, not imported limestone. (Alcock seems to have been proud of his name; there are representations of cockerels at every turn.)

Many cathedrals have quirky interiors: the odd pulpit here, a little chapel there, tombs scattered about the aisles, as if each new bishop called in his own decorator. Not so Ely. From the rear of the church, at the shrine of Etheldreda, the view backwards to the west door is almost perfectly harmonious. The whole panorama of the church is framed by the carved wooden choir stalls, drawing the eye first to the soaring columns and fan arches of the octagon and then to the long nave, stretching out into the distance, each pair of massive Romanesque support columns framing the next pair all the way to the west door.

Turn now to the Lady Chapel, through a door in the north transept. Designed by Walsingham and begun in 1321, the Lady Chapel is a dramatic example of how ecclesiastical architecture changed in 300 years. Flooded with light and delicate to the point of fragility, it is a superb example of the high Gothic period and contrasts sharply with the heaviness of the Romanesque cathedral. Of course it is even lighter today than it was meant to be; virtually all of the stained glass (along with all but one of the statues, hidden behind an arch) was destroyed during the Dissolution and later replaced by clear glass.

Before you leave Ely, spend some time exploring the cathedral grounds. South of the cathedral (**left** out the west door) is perhaps the largest collection of medieval monastic buildings still in use in England, many with lovely gardens. The buildings are not open to the public, but browsing among them begins to give you a sense of the day-to-day life of the larger monastic community, of which the cathedral was just a part.

🚗 WEST TO THE WHITE PEAKS OF DERBYSHIRE

Distance: 145 miles/233 kilometers
Roads: Primary roads, well signed
Driving Time: About 3 hours
Map: Michelin Map #404

Time now for a dramatic change of scene, the kind of change possible only in Britain, where, in the span of an hour or so in any direction, the landscape can change so completely that you feel as if you've entered another country. The destination: the Peak District National Park, smack in the middle of the Midlands.

From Ely, take the **A10** north in the direction of **Littleport** and **King's Lynn**. Just outside Littleport, turn **left** onto the **A1101** toward **Wisbech**. About 4 miles (6.4 kilometers) from this intersection, the A1101 turns sharply **right** and runs along the foot of a high embankment. After a few hundred yards the road climbs up the side of the embankment and reveals, first, Vermuyden's New Bedford Level and, a little farther on at the edge of the village of **Welney**, his original Old Bedford Level. In between are the **Ouse Washes**, originally land "sacrificed" to winter flooding to keep water from inundating the reclaimed farmland but today so valued as habitat for migrating wildfowl that the area is formally protected as a Site of Special Scientific Interest.

Out on the Great Levels, under a huge sky curving like a bell jar from horizon to horizon, villages and farmsteads don't cluster as they do elsewhere in Britain. Instead, they are strung out along lonely, ruler-straight roads like laundry hung out on a line to dry. Beyond Welney, the abundance of the drained fens reaches away from the raised highway in regimented rows: in the fall there are rippling seas of ripe grain, great purple-black swaths of cabbages, entire miniature forests of brussels sprout plants, glossy-leafed sugar beets, pole beans as far as the eye can see, feathery carrot tops, and enough broccoli to give children nightmares for life. As you approach Wisbech, lush orchards and fields of raspberries replace the vegetable crops. Beyond Wisbech (still on the A1101) flowers replace the fruit; there are acres of bright asters and huge fields radiant with roses and soft pink dianthus.

At **Long Sutton,** turn **left** onto the **A17** and, after just a few miles, bear **left** onto the **A151** toward **Spalding,** a historic fenland town straddling the banks of the **River Welland.** This is Britain's own Holland; in the springtime, the rich black fields around Spalding are ablaze with mile upon mile of blooming tulips, daffodils, narcissus, and hyacinths (the town holds a flower festival in May). From Spalding, take the **A16** north in the direction of **Boston,** but branch **left** onto the **A152** at **Gosberton** in the direction of **Grantham.** At **Donington,** turn **left** again onto the **A52,** still following signs to Grantham. Incredibly, after all this driving, you are *still* in the fens—here the **Lincolnshire Fens,** much of it reclaimed not from swamp but from the sea, which once extended much deeper into the county than the shallow bay called **The Wash** does today.

The landscape finally begins to rise and rumple gently as you approach Grantham. The wide open fenland fields, with their tall poplar windbreaks, fall behind, replaced by pastures broken into neat patches by mile after mile of dense hedgerows.

About 8 miles (13 kilometers) beyond Grantham the A52 dashes across a remote corner of **Leicestershire,** then plunges deep into **Nottinghamshire.** The pace quickens, the A52 widens, alternating between four and six lanes, and industrialization and urbanization begin to close in. You know you've reached the twentieth century again when you begin to see signs for the Tales of Robin Hood Fun Park. Ignore them. Stick to the A52, which eventually becomes a ring road around the southern edge of Nottingham, and follow signs for **Derby** (pronounced *DAR-bee*). After passing through a series of roundabouts, you clear Nottingham and the road heads cross-country again to Derby. Once again you want the ring road that carries through-traffic around the southern edge of the city through another series of roundabouts. Follow signs for the **(A52)**—here in parentheses because the ring road is actually the **A5111**—in the direction of **Ashbourne.** (There is one roundabout that, uncharacteristically, is not well marked; in this case follow signs for **Alton Towers,** a park in the same direction as Ashbourne.)

Outside of Derby, the landscape steepens, the valley folds deepen, and the fortunes generated in the industrial Midlands are evident in the

The World's Longest Wildlife Refuge

There is something deeply satisfying about the pattern of hedgerows and small fields that carpets central England, something quintessentially "English," yet it is actually a relatively new development. Before about 1750, most of the countryside was open "common" farmland. But in the mid-eighteenth century it was discovered that smaller parcels of land made for more efficient grazing and farming and within only 100 years much of this open land was subdivided by Parliamentary "Acts of Enclosure." Because wood was too scarce for fences and the availability of stone varied, most of the new fields were bounded by hedges, chiefly of hawthorn. Four-year-old saplings were planted at 4-inch intervals and permitted to grow to a height of about 7 feet (2 meters). Then the strongest stems were split lengthwise to just above ground level and one of the halves (called a *plasher*) was bent horizontal and woven in and out of the nearest upright stems. Still nourished by their roots, the lattice of plashers and uprights quickly produced an impenetrable barrier of thorny branches.

Though designed only to contain wandering livestock, the hedgerows soon were "colonized" by a wide variety of plants that provided shelter and food for a complex web of small animals, birds, and insects. (Naturalists say you can estimate the age of a hedgerow by counting the species of woody shrubs established in a 30-yard (27.5-meter) section and allowing 100 years for each.) From the road, hedgerows have a pleasing effect on the landscape, breaking it into understandable pieces. Wildflowers thrive along their edges. Their greatest value, however, may be that, with an estimated total length of 600,000 miles (966,000 kilometers), English hedgerows constitute, in effect, the longest wildlife preserve in the world.

number of estates you pass on the A52 between Derby and Ashbourne.

Despite encroaching urbanization, Ashbourne is still a charming small town with a delightful collection of shops and a busy little market square. Take **St. John Street** through the center of town, underneath the unique sign for the combined Green Man Inn and Black's Head Royal Hotel that spans the road, and turn up the steep hill heading out of town to the north, following signs for **Dovedale** and the **A515**.

The moment you crest the hill above Ashbourne you enter another world: ahead the Derbyshire dales undulate to the horizon, a counter-pane of greens and browns sewn together with an intricate network of dry stone walls. At the bottom of the hill, bear **left** onto a minor road signposted for **Thorpe**, **Dovedale**, and **Ilam**. Cross the valley floor, crest another hill, and, in the blink of an eye, you enter one of England's small miracles: the ruggedly pastoral **Peak District National Park**, a region of peaceful valleys, lonely moors, and charming villages hud-dling in the deep folds of the southern terminus of the Pennines, the mountain range that forms England's backbone. Less than an hour from most of the gritty cities of the Midlands and a day trip for more than half of the population of England, the Peak District is industrial England's "backdoor wilderness."

It is also home for the next two nights.

CREATURE COMFORTS
Daily Bed

The view from the kitchen window of Sue and Terry Prince's **Beechenhill Farm**, high on a ridge above Ilam, hasn't changed in cen-turies. Beyond the flower and vegetable garden, daisy- and buttercup-strewn meadows shimmer in the summer sun as they slope south to the confluence of the rivers Dove and Manifold. Off to the left, Bunster Hill—once a coral reef in a prehistoric sea—climbs to the sky, high above the cliffs and crags of Dovedale. Ancient walls of gleaming white limestone race across meadows and over hills that rise and fall like great green ocean swells rolling away into the distant haze. The house, barn, and outbuildings are long and low, with thick stone walls that seem, in the right light, to grow directly out of the rocky soil. It is a scene that radiates stability, continuity, timelessness.

Yet hill farming in Britain is a precarious business. Limited to graz-ing by soils too shallow for crops (Terry and Sue are dairy farmers), hill farms are less versatile than the flatland farms of the fens. And yet, were it not for hill farms like the Princes' there would be no one to care for the fragile upland environment or to restore and maintain the an-cient stone buildings that are so much a part of Britain's architectural heritage.

Like other farm families, the Princes have diversified into providing bed-and-breakfast accommodations, but few have done it as creatively. In addition to their two redecorated B&B rooms (one double, one fam-ily), they have converted one attached outbuilding into a one-bedroom "self-catering" flat and another set of buildings into an award-winning three-bedroom suite with kitchen, bathrooms, and other facilities spe-

The limestone walls and deep vales of the White Peak region create pastoral landscapes that beg to be explored.

cifically designed to accommodate wheelchair-bound travelers. Both buildings (rented by the week) are decorated with witty *trompe l'oeil* murals by Sue, who is an illustrator. The Princes are part of the Peak District Farm Holiday Group, an association of farm families providing B&B accommodations that, along with some seventy other local associations, form the Farm Holiday Bureau. To contact the Princes directly, write Beechenhill Farm, Ilam, Ashbourne, Derbyshire DE6 2BD, or phone (033527) 274. For a brochure describing all the farms in the group write Mrs. Angela Whatley, The Hall, Great Hucklow, Tideswell, Buxton, Derbyshire SK17 8RG, or consult the Farm Bureau's national guidebook (see Further Reading).

If you prefer to live dangerously (remember, the Peak District is a popular destination), you can take potluck: there are lovely B&Bs in Thorpe, Ilam, Alstonefield, Wetton, and many other villages in the area, as well as in Ashbourne. In addition, there is a youth hostel at Ilam Hall. For reservations, write Ilam Hall, Ashbourne, Derbyshire DE6 2AZ, or phone (033529) 212. For other possibilities, including hotels, see Further Reading.

Daily Bread

This is good pub country, and there are several tucked away here in the dales (try the villages of Alstonefield or Hopedale).

If you prefer something a bit more formal than a pub, you might consider the restaurants at the Izaak Walton or Peveril of the Peak hotels near Thorpe, or any of several small restaurants in Ashbourne, just a few minutes away. As always, ask your hosts for suggestions; restaurants change hands and local recommendations will often be superior to guidebooks.

Britain's "Backdoor Wilderness"

BUXTON ◆ KINDER SCOUT
BAKEWELL ◆ DOVEDALE

◆ **A day walk to the Dark Peak summit of Kinder Scout**
◆ **An alternative drive in the Peak District National Park, including two stately homes**
◆ **Cycling in the White Peak**
◆ **An alternative walk in Dovedale**

From the mountains on every side, rivulets descended that filled all the valley with verdure and fertility.
—Samuel Johnson, *Rasselas*

A howling wilderness . . . the most desolate, wild, and abandoned country in all England.
—Daniel Defoe, 1725

*T*he soul of the Peak District is sorely divided—one part pastoral, the other primeval—and the conflict runs deep. Even its name is a contradiction; there are no peaks in the Peak District. The name comes from the Old English *peac*, or "hill," and the early tribes that lived here were known as the Pecsaetan, or "people of the hills." It is a Dr. Jekyll and Mr. Hyde sort of place. There are two Ordnance Survey Outdoor Leisure maps for the Peak District, one for the "White Peak," the other for the "Dark Peak," and the two regions they chart have sharply contrasting personalities.

The White Peak region of the park, beginning at Thorpe and spreading northward in an gradually widening V, is the one with the sunny disposition. It sits upon a giant limestone plateau formed some 300 million years ago by the gentle accumulation of tiny marine skeletons in a shallow desert sea. When temperatures moderated after the last Ice Age, torrents of meltwater were released that not only eroded the limestone but reacted chemically with it, dissolving the porous stone along fissures and fault lines. The result is a dramatic landscape called *karst*, riven with ravines, punctuated by steep crags, and honeycombed with caves and underground watercourses.

The countryside of the White Peak is irrepressibly cheerful. The lime-rich soil produces verdant grazing meadows and supports an incredible array of wildflowers. The carefully crafted limestone walls and well-kept farmsteads scattered across the landscape gleam dazzlingly white in the sunshine. And the compact hamlets tucked away in the deep folds of the hillsides, with their flower-bedecked cottages and tiny parish churches, seem to radiate goodwill, even on a rainy English day.

But the Dark Peak is something else again. The hulking sandstone mass of the Dark Peak plateau reaches around the western, northern, and eastern edges of the White Peak like the arms of some great sinister beast. The people in the villages of the Dark Peak are just as warm and welcoming as their neighbors to the south, but the towns are dark, almost dreary, as if unable to wash off the accumulated soot of the centuries. The somber mood of the Dark Peak plateau is created by the dirty-brown sandstone from which it is made. Called "millstone grit," the stone was once silt deposited millions of years ago in the broad delta of a prehistoric river. Compressed over the eons into rock, it is hard enough to be used for millstones (the symbol for the Peak District National Park), yet soft enough to be carved by wind and water into some of the most eerily dramatic climbing and and walking country in Britain.

Today, you have several options, depending upon weather and whim. You can spend the day driving from village to village through both the White Peak and Dark Peak regions and take in one or two of Britain's grandest stately homes. You can also take a leisurely walk through the narrow and beautiful valley of the little River Dove, about which countless romantic poets have rhapsodized. You can spend the day tooling around by rented bicycle, following old railroad rights-of-way that have been converted to bike paths. Or, if the weather is good and you're ready for something a bit more adventurous, you can spend the day exploring the Dark Peak summit of Kinder Scout. Of the four, the last is the most exciting.

🏃 A WALK ATOP KINDER SCOUT

Distance: About 8 miles/12.9 kilometers; allow 4–5 hours
Difficulty: A moderately strenuous first 1.5 hours to gain the ridge top, but easy thereafter
Total Elevation Gain: About 1,345 feet/410 meters
Gear: Sturdy, preferably waterproof walking shoes, raingear (just in case), scarf (for wind), camera
Map: Ordnance Survey Outdoor Leisure Map #1

From wherever you decided to stay while in the Peak District, this morning head for **Buxton**, about 30 minutes north of Ashbourne on the **A515** (parts of which follow the route of a Roman road). Buxton is a handsome market town that the fifth Duke of Devonshire had hoped to turn into a spa as fashionable as Bath. It had great prospects: warm mineral waters, magnificent Georgian architecture (thanks to the duke's deep pockets), and a choice location near many of the country's fastest-growing cities. Unfortunately, Buxton is also the highest market town in England, so windy, cold, and rainy that the spa never quite fulfilled the duke's dreams (locals still call the town's upper market area "Little Siberia"). On the other hand, Buxton has a wonderful delicatessen, on Terrace Street, that's a great place to buy the makings for a picnic lunch (see Daily Bread below).

From the center of Buxton, follow signs for the **A6** toward **Stockport** and **Manchester**. Roughly 5 miles (8 kilometers) north of Buxton, bear **left** off the A6 into **Chapel-en-le-Frith** ("chapel in the forest") and take the second **right**, joining the **A624** to **Glossop** and **Hayfield**. About 3 miles (4.8 kilometers) later, turn into the village of Hayfield, go past the general store, drive over the small bridge, and, a few yards beyond, turn sharply **right** onto **Kinder Road** (marked UN-SUITABLE FOR MOTORS). Roughly a mile up the valley, turn into the Bowden Bridge car park on the left (there are public toilets on the right).

To begin the walk, turn **left** out of the car park and up a one-lane road that parallels the little **River Kinder**. At the entrance to the reservoir property, cross the bridge over the river and continue gently uphill on the single-track lane. Where the track begins to tilt uphill towards a house, the footpath, clearly marked, continues along the right bank of the river, through a gate, and beneath the dark green canopy of a wood. When the path appears to dead-end, cross **left** over a steel bridge and then turn **right** up the stone-paved footpath that begins just to the **left** of the pillared entrance to the waterworks.

Quite suddenly, you pass from leafy lowland scenery to the wide open spaces of the upland moors. Rich green bracken fern covers the hillside on your left and ancient rhododendrons line the slopes along the shore of **Kinder Reservoir** on the right. Ahead in the distance, beyond the reservoir, the steep heather-clad flanks and dark gritstone cliffs of Kinder Scout rise into the sky. The path soon curves left around a narrow finger of the reservoir that points roughly north. When you reach the tip of this finger a National Trust sign marks the entrance to the **High Peak Estate**. Here, ignore a small wooden bridge and a path that continues around the reservoir and turn **left** instead, up **William Clough** ("valley").

Unlike those in the United States or Canada, Britain's national parks are neither "parks" in the sense of being pristine nature reserves, nor "national" in the sense of being owned by the nation. Virtually all of the land within the Peak District National Park (and all other national parks) is privately owned and under some form of economic use: arable farming, upland grazing, villages, reservoirs, and so forth. Rather than "roping off" a single-purpose nature reserve, the park boundaries simply mark a special region in which a multiagency planning board ensures that recreational uses of the land, as well as other uses, are managed to protect and enhance the area's unique resources.

In a very real sense, it is a system that was born on the very path along which you now are walking. Back at the beginning of the century and especially following World War I, workers in the grim industrial cities that ring the Peak District—Manchester, Sheffield, Stoke-on-Trent, Derby, Leeds—began to turn to the wild moorlands of the Peak District as an escape from the drudgery of city life. However, the moors were privately owned and managed principally for grouse hunting by gamekeepers little interested in the recreational needs of the working classes. While some landowners issued permits to walkers, most posted their land, and conflicts between walkers and gamekeepers grew. On April 24, 1932, the simmering resentment came to a boil: some 400

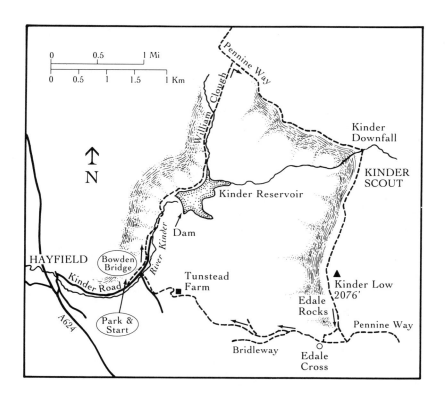

walkers organized a "mass trespass" on Kinder Scout, setting out from Hayfield and climbing up William Clough to the plateau summit. There they met an equally organized group of gamekeepers. Fights erupted, some walkers were arrested, and five ultimately received prison sentences. It took another two decades before the Peak District National Park, the nation's first, was created. And it all began here, on the trail to Kinder Scout.

For about half of the climb up the clough you have the pleasant company of a stream that clatters merrily over huge slabs of exposed gritstone. Above the stream, both right and left, acres of heather cloak the slopes, blooming in brilliant magenta in late summer. Then, roughly an hour into the walk, the stream wanders off and the footpath veers **right** up a gravel ravine. Here the large slabs of gritstone give way to crumbly shale and the path is deeply eroded. The going is slow, but the drudgery is relieved by occasional bright flashes of red grouse and the spectacle of small groups of glassy-eyed, dim-witted sheep exploding into terrified flight as you approach, typically careening into each other as they scatter.

Eventually, a little over 1 mile (1.6 kilometers) from the reservoir, you emerge from the ravine to the broad saddle of **Leygatehead Moor**, with the Dark Peak plateau very close now on the right and the low summit of **The Knot** off to the left. At this point you cut **right** along an obvious path to the ridge top, well marked by a cairn. When you reach the top of the ridge, turn **right** onto the well-worn path—the **Pennine Way**, Britain's oldest and longest Long Distance Path.

The scene atop Kinder Scout is alien, primordial. Weird stacks of dark gritstone carved into eerie shapes by the relentless wind grow out of the barren ground. For as far as the eye can see, mounds of black peat smother the surface like soot-stained snowdrifts. Boggy low spots suck greedily at your boots. There is no vegetation; nothing lives. Deep, narrow drainage channels, called *goughs*, zigzag through the thick peat like blind alleys in a maze. Wander away from the cliff edge a few hundred yards and the desolation of the lifeless landscape engulfs you. Each quadrant of this wasteland begins to look like every other and disorientation seizes you like a fever. Snatches of T. S. Eliot swim up from deep within your subconscious: "This is the way the world ends . . ."

And indeed this *is* what the world looks like when it has been used up. Eons ago, after the last Ice Age, dense forests flourished on the Dark Peak, but by the time the Romans arrived they had all been cleared—stripped away and burned off by prehistoric farmers to create grazing land. The earth never recovered. Altitude, an unforgiving climate, and the limitations of the underlying geology dictated steady deterioration, not regeneration. Because it is high, the Dark Peak's growing season is short. Because it stands in the way of prevailing weather patterns, it rains a lot. And because the ground is underlain

Atop Kinder Scout, in the Dark Peak region

with impervious gritstone, rain does not drain away easily. Under such conditions, plants do not fully decompose in the sour, sodden soil when they die. Peat bogs form and spread, and fewer and fewer living things are able to survive in the increasingly acidic environment.

The edge of the Dark Peak plateau is far more inviting than the interior; the towering cliff face, which runs for miles, is composed of huge blocks of brown gritstone, sliced horizontally by frost fractures like a multilayered chocolate torte. Wind and rain have combined forces artfully, carving the edges of the stone outcroppings into such massive and fantastic shapes that you might easily imagine you were strolling amid one of Henry Moore's monumental sculpture gardens. Off to your right are sweeping views out across the western Midlands, and on a clear day you can see far across the Cheshire Plain to the Irish Sea beyond.

Kinder Scout gets its odd name from the old Saxon *Kyndwr Scut,* which means "water over the edge," and the derivation lies straight ahead, about 1.5 miles (2.4 kilometers) southeast of the point where you joined the Pennine Way. It is **Kinder Downfall**, the point at which much of the water that falls on the plateau comes together and plummets over the cliff edge into a ravine far below. The Downfall is, in fact, infamous for not falling "down" at all; when the wind howls from the west (which is often) the river is caught in mid-fall and flung back up and over the cliff as a furious swirl of mist.

From Kinder Downfall, continue southward along the edge of the escarpment, picking your way among the massive boulders and around the ravine cut by Red Brook, heading toward the rocky tor called **Kinder Low**—yet another contradiction since, at 2,077 feet (633 meters), this is the highest point along this route (*low* is ancient English for a burial site). At Kinder Low, the Pennine Way bears **left** somewhat, away from the cliff edge, taking a shortcut across the base of a finger ridge that juts west, and heading instead across a spongy desert of peat "dunes" in the direction of the next high point, **Edale Rocks**. Near this point, the Park Authority has improved the footpath by paving it with flat stones to halt further erosion. The effect is actually quite pleasing, not so much as if civilization were intruding as that Mother Nature has suddenly been seized by a fit of neatness.

Beyond Edale Rocks, the Pennine Way curves partway around a hillside called **Swine's Back**, then veers left straight down the hill. At this point a narrower footpath branches **right**, staying on the upper flank of the hill. Take this path around the hillside, following a fenceline, until it appears to dead-end at a stone wall. Here, turn **left** past an old stone sheepfold and head downhill with the wall on your right. After only a few yards, this path ends at a bridleway. Turn **right** through a stone gate, continuing downhill along the bridleway. Just around the edge of this gate, carefully sheltered, is the **Edale Cross**, a

Along the Pennine Way, far above Kinder Reservoir

beautifully carved medieval stone cross protected as a "monument of national interest."

At this point, some 3.5 hours into the walk, it will be mid- to late afternoon, depending upon how early you began. As you walk westward, downhill into the sun, the Peak District ridges roll away before you in range upon range of hazy blue-green swells, becoming misty gray and merging with the sky in the far distance. The bridleway parallels a magnificent stone wall—completely mortar-free, artfully constructed of carefully split stone, curving sinuously with the contours of the slope. After about 5 minutes of walking along the bridleway, go over a stile in the wall and follow the path downhill signposted HAYFIELD VIA TUNSTEAD CLOUGH. After another 10 or 15 minutes the path branches; bear **left** around the side of the hill and down to a ladder stile where a small stream comes down from the right. On the other side of the stile, the clear path peters out into a gloriously green, flower-dappled meadow. You simply continue in roughly the same downhill direction, passing through one field after another, over a series of stiles, into an increasingly pastoral vale that contrasts dramatically with the wild, wind-blasted moorlands up on the plateau. This is what walking in Britain is all about: a sensory overload of landscape scenery, distributed over remarkably short distances. It is very hard to be bored here.

As the sun dips lower in the western sky, the serpentine stone walls stand out in sharp relief on the velvety green slopes of the valley above Hayfield. Trees cast long purple shadows and the dark eastern slopes of the surrounding moors contrast sharply with the burnished west-facing hillsides. Here and there, thin blue plumes of coal smoke curl up from stone chimneys into a still yellow sky.

When you reach a National Trust sign marking the boundary of the Kinder Estate, go through the "kissing gate" and walk down a stone-wall-lined farm lane. Just beyond Tunstead farmhouse, turn sharply **right** down a cobblestone lane, cross a small stone bridge, and follow the stream downhill until you reach a paved road. Here, turn **right**, still following the stream, until you reach **Kinder Road**, where you turn **left** and return to the car park, just a few yards downhill. To return to your home base, just go back to Chapel-en-le-Frith and retrace the route south into the White Peak region.

🚗 BY CAR THROUGH THE WHITE AND DARK PEAK

Distance: About 80 miles/129 kilometers
Roads: Primary, secondary, and unclassified roads, well signed
Driving Time: Allow all day
Map: Michelin Map #403

A leisurely driving tour of the Peak District takes in a remarkably varied menu of sights: charming little villages; enormous stately homes; pastoral limestone valleys cut by clear rivers teeming with trout; craggy moorlands pocked with mysterious underground caverns, prehistoric stone circles, and contemporary stone quarries and mines.

To begin, assuming you stayed in the White Peak area near Ashbourne, head for **Ilam** (a few miles northeast of Ashbourne on minor roads) and visit the National Trust Information Centre at Ilam Hall, a nineteenth-century country house now turned into a youth hostel. In addition to excellent displays about the Peak District, the center has a large three-dimensional map of much of the region that will help you get your bearings.

Then drive out through the gates again, turn **left** up the hill, and bear **right** at the fork signposted for **Wetton** and **Alstonefield** (pronounced *All-stun-feld*). The tree-lined narrow road climbs up and up high above the lovely valley of the **River Manifold**, eventually running along a high ridge. Bear **left** at **Stanshope Hall** and, a short distance

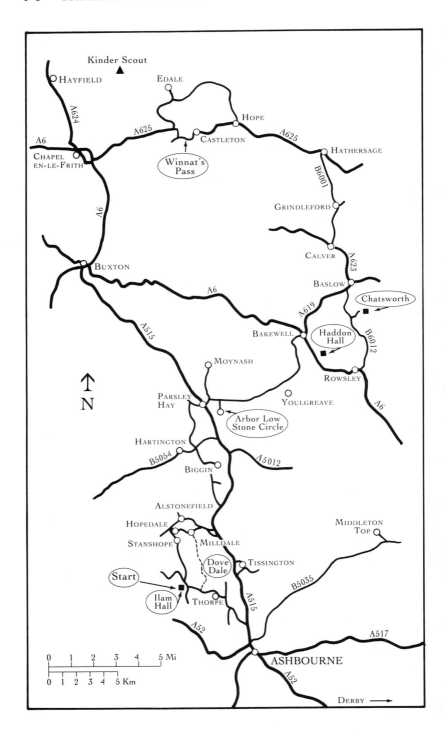

later, turn **right** at a T-junction in the direction of Alstonefield. Almost immediately, turn **right** into the hamlet of **Hopedale**—little more than a few buildings surrounding a pub called the Watts-Russell Arms. Then plunge down a gradually narrowing valley to another tiny hamlet, **Milldale**, beautifully situated by an ancient packhorse bridge over the crystal-clear River Dove. The road now runs upriver through a narrow section of Dovedale. At the next junction, turn **right**, over a narrow stone bridge, and climb up out of the valley. At a V-junction bear **right** and, when you reach the **A515**, turn **right** in the direction of **Ashbourne**. A couple of miles ahead, take the second **left** into **Tissington**, through a stone gate and down a lane lined with massive old beech trees.

Tissington, claimed by many to be the prettiest village in the Peak District, is a good example of a manor village; the town and the surrounding land have been owned by the Fitzherbert family since the days of Elizabeth I. While it includes a Jacobean manor house, a fine collection of stone cottages and larger dwellings, a parish church, and a duck-filled pond, it also seems a bit sterile. There is none of the hustle and bustle of a lively village and—a bad sign—no pub. What Tissington *does* have is the distinction of being the birthplace of the colorful tradition of "well-dressing." In any limestone karst region watercourses are, at best, fickle. At Tissington, the reliability and purity of the town's well was believed to have saved it from both drought and the Plague and, in the early 1600s, the town gave thanks by draping its well with flowers. The practice caught on and today many Peak District villages hang elaborate floral murals—composed of petals, seeds, mosses and other natural materials pressed onto a clay "canvass"—on their respective "well-dressing day."

Now, drive out the northern end of Tissington and, when you reach the A515 again, turn **right** in the direction of **Buxton**. Turn **left** off the A515 by a quarry onto a minor road signposted for **Biggin**, through an upland region crosshatched with gleaming white limestone walls. Go past Biggin and then bear **left** in the direction of Hartington; at each successive intersection, keep following signs for Hartington. When the road drops down into a limestone valley turn **left** onto the **B5054** and drive into Hartington, a handsome market town that is one of the few places that still produces true Stilton cheese (see Daily Bread below).

Next, backtrack out of town on the B5054 again and take the first **left**, turning north into lovely **Long Dale** (signposted for **Crowdicote**), a lonely, emerald green, dry river valley bounded by beetling limestone crags. When the valley shallows out, after about 2 miles (3.2 kilometers), turn **right** in the direction of the delightfully named hamlet of **Parsley Hay**. Pass the car park marking the junction of the Tissington and High Peak trails (there is a cycle-hire concession here), then turn **left** onto the A515 and, immediately, bear **right** onto a minor road in the direction of **Moynash**. After just a few yards, turn **right** onto a minor road signposted for **Arbor Low** and watch for another sign pointing **right** up a gravel track toward a farm, with what is obviously an earthworks in the distance off to the left.

Arbor Low is a sort of slumbering Stonehenge. Created some 4,000 years ago, it is composed of a circle of some forty prone stones, each weighing in excess of 8 tons, within a ditch and rampart perimeter roughly 250 feet (76 meters) across. Like so many stone circles, its purpose is unknown, but evidence of nearby burial chambers built over the succeeding 1,000 years suggests the people who lived here held it in great reverence. You approach Arbor Low, which is on private land, through a farmyard (depositing a small admission in a simple brass bowl by the farmhouse door), cross over a stone stile, and then turn **left** along the wall and walk to the top of the hill. It is a theatrically dramatic site, high and windy, with sweeping views across the swelling Peak District hills to the north. The fallen stones themselves, crude and weather-pocked but somehow more moving than the almost too perfect slabs at

Chatsworth House, a neoclassical jewel set in a carefully crafted "natural" landscape

Stonehenge, clearly did not fall willy-nilly. Whenever they were pulled down (assuming they were indeed erected in the first place) it was done with a plan in mind; they look to have been blown down from some powerful force at the center of the circle, each megalith pointing to a different quadrant of the compass. Arbor Low is a baffling and somehow disturbing place.

From Arbor Low, drive back down the gravel track and turn **right**, heading east. The unclassified road here runs along high ground for about 2 miles (3.2 kilometers). At the first intersection, bear **left** toward **Youlgreave**, but at the next intersection ignore the route to Youlgreave (though it is a pretty village) and bear **left** again instead, soon thereafter tipping steeply over the edge and down into **Lathkill Dale**, a classic limestone valley perhaps second only to Dovedale in natural beauty. At the bottom of the ravine, you cross a narrow medieval stone bridge over the lovely little **River Lathkill** and then continue to **Bakewell**. As you enter town, turn **right** at the T-junction and follow signs to the town center. Bakewell, an ancient market town by a ford of the **River Wye**, was already centuries old when the Domesday Book— William the Conqueror's booty list—was drawn up in the eleventh century. It is worth a stop for at least two reasons. First, as the headquarters of the Park Planning Board, it has an excellent National Park Information Centre. Second, it has at least two bakeries claiming to be the home of the original "Bakewell pudding" (see Daily Bread below) and you will no doubt wish to decide for yourself which is superior. Possibly several times.

Having done so, head southeast on the **A6** in the direction of **Matlock**. Just outside of Bakewell, to the left on a bluff above the River Wye, is **Haddon Hall**, one of the best-restored medieval manor houses in Britain, the ancestral home of the Dukes of Rutland (open 11:00 A.M. to 6:00 P.M. daily from April through September, but closed Sunday and Monday during July and August).

Continue southeast on the A6, through the broad Wye River valley, and at **Rowsley** turn **left** onto the **B6012** in the direction of **Baslow**. A short distance later, after crossing a one-lane bridge over the **River Derwent**, it becomes increasingly obvious that you have strayed into someone's *very* extensive estate, complete with acres of neatly trimmed lawn, magnificent specimen trees, and decorative cows and sheep. About 1 mile (1.6 kilometers) farther on, the suspicion is confirmed. Ahead on the right, beyond an artfully situated lake, is **Chatsworth House**—with 175 rooms, 24 baths, 21 kitchens, 17 staircases, 7,873 panes of glass, and 1.3 acres of roof, one of the stateliest of Britain's stately homes. Home of the Duke and Duchess of Devonshire (the British nobility never seem to live where their titles suggest), it is a stunning neoclassical pile, begun in 1686 and fussed with almost continuously until the mid-1800s. Its interiors, while a wee bit formal, display extraordinary craftsmanship—ornate plaster ceilings, deeply carved woodwork, lush tapestries and furnishings, and one of the finest art collections in the world (a self-guided tour takes about an hour). But in many respects, Chatsworth House is best appreciated from the outside, as the jewel in a carefully crafted setting of stone, water, and greenery. The house sits amid a 100-acre (40-hectare) garden of perennials, roses, and specimen plants neatly defined by stone and hedge borders and punctuated by pools and fountains. The garden is itself set amid a 1,000-acre (405-hectare) park designed by the indefatigable "Capability" Brown (who never saw a piece of nature that didn't have the "capability" to be improved upon). Chatsworth is open March 24 to November 3 from 11:00 A.M. to 4:30 P.M. (garden till 5:00 P.M.).

Next, continue north on the B6012 to Baslow. There, after crossing the river, turn **left** onto the **A623**. Continue up the valley through the handsome mill town of **Calver** and turn **right** onto the **B6001** toward **Hathersage**, with the massive gritstone cliffs looming above the village of **Froggat** across the valley ahead. You're in the Dark Peak region now and the mood of the landscape has been getting more solemn by the mile. The sharp-edged cliffs here owe their existence to the thick layer of gritstone that caps them. As the softer shales beneath this cap erode, the harder rock above remains intact, often overhanging the valley until weathering causes even the gritstone to yield to gravity.

Keep following signs for Hathersage, turning **left** at **Grindleford** before you reach the bridge and continuing north with the river off to the right. In Hathersage, cross the river and then turn **left** onto the **A625** at the George Hotel in the direction of **Hope** and **Castleton**. Drive through Castleton (guarded by the ruins of Peveril Castle) and, after about 0.5 mile (0.8 kilometer), bear **left** at a sign for **Speedwell Cavern** (one of several caves in the honeycombed limestone hills here open to the public). The A625 here was closed because the roadbed was found to be unsafe, so the only "safe" route to the west is up the minor road through spectacular **Winnat's Pass**. The mountain to your right, which looks like a giant took a bite out of it, is **Mam Tor**, also known as "Shivering Mountain" because its shale slopes are constantly crumbling. At the top of the pass, turn **right** and shortly thereafter turn **left** to regain the A625 across the moors to **Chapel-en-le-Frith**. Just outside of the town watch for the **A6** and take it south to **Buxton**. There, pick up the **A515** and return home to the White Peak area.

DIVERSIONS
Cycling the Dales

Railroad lines pushed into the Derbyshire dales in the southern Peak District at the turn of the century, chiefly to haul out milk and limestone, but they never quite proved profitable and had all been closed down by the 1960s. The Park Planning Board converted this liability to an asset by turning the old rights-of-way into well-maintained (and mercifully level) cycle paths. The longest segments are the **High Peak Trail**, which begins in **Middleton Top**, just off the **B5036** between **Cromford** and **Wirksworth**, and the **Tissington Trail**, which begins in **Ashbourne**. The two trails meet at **Parsley Hay**, and a triangular trip of about 35 miles (56 kilometers) can be created by following the **B5035** between Ashbourne and Middleton Top. Cycle-hire centers are located at the picnic sites at Ashbourne (Mapleton Lane), Middleton Top, and Parsley Hay (just off the A515). There is a £5.00 deposit and hire rate is £5.00 per day for adults, £3.50 for children fifteen and under. Children's bikes and tandems are also available. For details and reservations, write the Parsley Hay Cycle Hire Centre, Parsley Hay, Buxton SK17 0DG, or phone (0433) 51261. The centers at Parsley Hay and Ashbourne are open from 9:30 A.M. to 6:00 P.M. every day from April through October and most weekends thereafter, the Middleton Top center somewhat less frequently. For brochures on the trails and hiring cycles, write the Peak District National Park, Aldern House, Baslow Road, Bakewell, Derbyshire DE4 1AE, or phone (062981) 4321.

Walking Dovedale

The prettiest and most visually varied walk in the White Peak region is the walk along the **River Dove** in Dovedale, just northwest of Ashbourne, near **Ilam**. Drive to Ilam Hall, pick up their color *Dovedale Guide*, then drive back to the turnoff for the Izaak Walton Hotel, turn left, and drive a few yards to the car park. Don't be dismayed by the crowds; few visitors go beyond the stepping stones. After the first bend, as you walk upstream, you'll have the valley, the limestone crags and pinnacles, and the pretty river nearly to yourself. At Milldale (3 miles/4.8 kilometers), you can either return by the opposite bank or follow a longer walk detailed in the second volume of this series, *The Best of Britain's Countryside: Northern England & Scotland*.

CREATURE COMFORTS
Daily Bed

The same as yesterday.

Daily Bread

The Peak District is a great place to work up an appetite and to satisfy it once developed; a remarkable range of sweet and savory specialty foods is produced in the region. Perhaps the best known local product

One of two bakeries claiming to have the original recipe; you may have to sample them—repeatedly—to decide which is best.

is the **Bakewell pudding**, more a tart than a pudding, really, but folks here are sensitive about what they call it and what they call it is "pudding." It seems that sometime around 1860 the cook at Bakewell's White Horse Inn botched a recipe for a strawberry tart. It turned out to be a delicious disaster: a custard with a faint almond aftertaste, and a strawberry jam surprise on the inside). At least three bakeries produce the puddings (which come in both dinner-plate size and handy "bite" size), and two claim to own the original recipe.

The savory side of things, however, has the edge in the Peak District. The J. M. Nuttall Creamery in Hartington produces more than 250,000 **Stilton cheeses** each year, a quarter of the national total. (Officially, true veiny Stilton can be made only in the counties of Leicestershire, Nottinghamshire, and Derbyshire; Nuttall's, a bare quarter mile from the Staffordshire border, just qualifies.) The Hartington creamery, which began in 1870 and has a "factory shop" in the village, also produces milder **Buxton Blue Wensleydale cheese**. Both are award-winners.

As might be expected in the valleys that inspired Izaak Walton's *The Compleat Angler*, **smoked trout** is another local specialty, produced in Mayfield, near Ashbourne. These and others—more cheeses, local hams and sausages, breads, and more—are available at Pugson's of Buxton, a delicatessen that acts as both the larder and spokesman for the Peak District's food entrepreneurs. Wash it all down with **Buxton Spring Mineral Water**, in continuous production since roughly the dawn of time and recently judged Europe's finest in a blind taste test.

A Trip Through the Industrial Revolution

IRONBRIDGE GORGE ◆ STOKE-ON-TRENT LLANGOLLEN

- ◆ **Take a walk through the birthplace of the Industrial Revolution**
- ◆ **"Do China in a Day" in the Potteries**
- ◆ **Cross into Wales**

It was a squalid ugliness on a scale so vast and overpowering that it became sublime. Great furnaces gleamed red in the twilight, their fires were reflected in horrible black canals; processions of heavy vapour drifted in all directions across the sky.

——Arnold Bennett, 1907

Not far from the border of England and Wales, among the rolling Shropshire hills, the River Severn slips swiftly through a deep, thickly wooded valley. Here and there, tightly clustered brick buildings cling to the steep hillside above the river's northern bank. At the valley's narrowest point, a one-lane bridge—so delicate it seems made of filigree—spans the river in an arc so perfect that, mirrored in the still water below, it forms an unbroken circle. The United Nations has called the cast-iron bridge a "striking specimen of art," but its original purpose was prosaic: to speed raw materials into, and manufactured products out of, a hellhole of smoke and flame and filth called Coalbrookdale, the birthplace of the Industrial Revolution. Today it's called Ironbridge Gorge, and the pretty green valley it has become is home to an open-air museum so remarkable that it won a European Museum of the Year award.

The modern era began here, in this unlikely spot, through a curious collision of nature and man. Thousands of years ago, the River Severn flowed north, not south, toward what is now Liverpool. Near

The Severn River from Coalbrookdale's Iron Bridge

the end of the last Ice Age, however, its route was blocked by glacial cliffs and a vast lake formed. Eventually, a narrow ridge at the lake's southern boundary failed and the lake emptied, sending stupendous torrents of water southward to the sea, gouging out a deep ravine in the process and laying bare major deposits of coal and iron. And there things stood, until the early eighteenth century.

That's where man comes in. In 1707, Abraham Darby became iron-master of a small furnace at Coalbrookdale. Faced with a looming shortage of timber to make the charcoal that was central to smelting iron, Darby became convinced he could substitute the area's abundant coal for charcoal. After two years of experimentation, he succeeded.

Neither he nor Britain ever looked back. Almost overnight, the stretch of river valley from Coalport to Coalbrookdale became a seeth-ing industrial nether world, where sulphurous smoke turned day into night and the roaring fires of the blast furnaces turned night into day. Out of this inferno came the first iron wheels, iron rails and railroad ties, iron plates for ships, iron steam locomotive boilers, iron aque-ducts, iron-framed buildings, and, in 1779, the first iron bridge.

But the most momentous impacts of Darby's discovery were indi-rect. Freed from the tyranny of having to be close to sources of wood, foundries and related industries clustered where coal and iron were abundant—in the Midlands and north of England. In the mid-1700s, Britain was still an agrarian nation, its people scattered widely across a changeless pastoral landscape. Only 100 years later, more than half of the population lived in cities—teeming, stinking, disease-ridden cities that spread like viruses around the new industrial hubs.

By concentrating development in a few places in central England, the Industrial Revolution left many other regions to languish in a kind of pristine obscurity. Part of the reason so much of Britain's country-side is beautiful today is that in the nineteenth century many rural econ-omies simply collapsed.

🚗 A VOYAGE INTO THE INDUSTRIAL REVOLUTION

Distance: About 50 miles/80 kilometers
Roads: The A518 almost the whole way
Driving Time: Allow 2 hours
Map: Michelin Map #403

Much of Britain's early industrial heritage has already vanished. But in Ironbridge Gorge the Industrial Revolution survives. Here, spread over some six square miles, are communities, iron furnaces and steel foundries, tile and pottery factories, mines, and kilns, all caught in a time warp from sometime in the mid-1800s when the Industrial Revo-lution moved north and the gorge began a slow decline. "Discovered" by industrial archaeologists a few years ago, it has been rescued and carefully restored. Fascinating, fun, and not the least bit commercial, Ironbridge Gorge is perhaps the most unusual "museum" in Britain. Getting there from the White Peak region is easy. From **Ashbourne**,

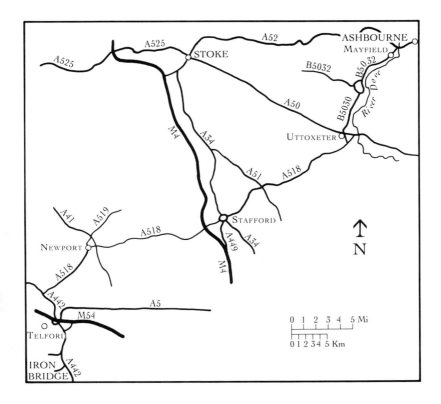

take the **A52** west in the direction of **Stoke-on-Trent**, but just after you cross the River Dove into Staffordshire (via the ominously named Hanging Bridge), turn **left** onto the **B5032** through the pretty stone village of **Mayfield**. (**Note:** If you decide to visit the pottery museum and showrooms of Stoke described in Diversions below, rather than visiting Ironbridge Gorge, stay on the A52.)

The B5032 follows the west bank of the Dove south through **Ellastone** and **Norbury** and then turns west toward **Cheadle**. But instead of heading west, stick with the river, now bordered by the **B5030** all the way to **Uttoxeter**, a pleasant market town with some of the half-timber buildings you'll see more of farther to the west. From the center of town pick up the **A518** and follow it southwest through Staffordshire, passing through **Stafford** and **Newport**, following signs for **Telford** in **Shropshire** (these days called "Salop," an ancient but unmusical tag; imagine A. E. Housman's masterpiece being called "A Salop Lad").

Just beyond **Donington**, turn south at a roundabout onto the **A442** in the direction of **Bridgenorth** (the A442 was recently improved and is a high-speed bypass of Telford center). Just a few miles beyond Telford, watch for signs to **Ironbridge** and follow minor roads through several roundabouts into the gorge.

Head first for the **Museum of the River and Visitor Centre**, just upriver from the iron bridge, following the red-and-white signs. There are five major sites in the Ironbridge Gorge complex—the **Museum of Iron and Darby Furnace** in Coalbrookdale, the **Iron Bridge** itself, the **Jackfield Tile Museum** and **the Coalport China Museum** downstream in Coalport, and the **Blists Hill Open Air Museum** up a tributary gorge above Coalport—as well as a half dozen lesser sites, including the ruins of the aptly named **Bedlam Furnaces**. The most intriguing of these sites is Blists Hill, a fifty-acre recreation of a Victorian community, complete with canal, gaslit streets, railway siding, period cottages, and a full complement of workshops and stores: butcher, baker, and candlestick maker, as well as bank, pharmacy, blacksmith, foundry and more. One of the best things about Blists Hill is that many of the shops are open for business—including the pub.

Plan on spending 45 minutes at the Visitor Centre, an hour or so at the Museum of Iron, perhaps 2 hours at Blists Hill (longer with lunch), and an hour or less at any of the other sites. The complex is open from 10:00 A.M. to 5:00 P.M. every day, year-round. You can walk to all the sites—a round-trip of roughly 5.5 miles (8.9 kilometers)—drive from one to the other, or take the "Park and Ride" shuttle bus that operates during the summer. If you plan to spend the day, the "Passport" admis-

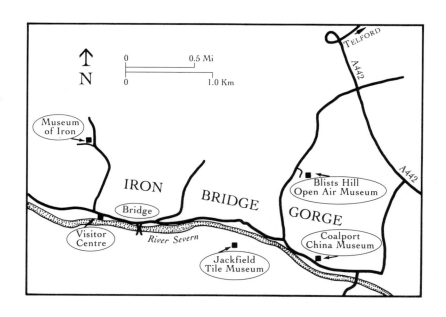

All the Victorian-age shops at Blists Hill are open . . . even the pub.

sion ticket to all sites is the best bargain (and it's valid indefinitely). For advance information, write the Ironbridge Gorge Museum, Ironbridge, Telford, Shropshire TF8 7AW.

ACROSS THE BORDER INTO WALES

Distance: About 45 miles/72 kilometers
Roads: The A5 almost the whole way
Driving Time: Allow 2 hours
Map: Michelin Map #403

For all Ironbridge's industrialism, the surrounding countryside is among the loveliest in Britain. To the south, the Shropshire hills climb to the long escarpment of Wenlock Edge, the remnant of a coral reef formed 425 million years ago, and to the lonely moors of Long Mynd. To the north, the Cheshire Plain, some of England's best farmland, spreads like a vast quilt to the old Roman city of Chester. And to the west, the hazy Welsh hills—your destination today—climb higher and higher to the wild fastness of Snowdonia.

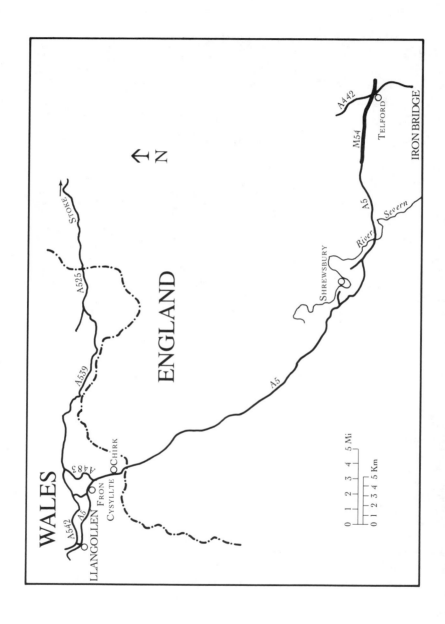

From Ironbridge, return to the **M54**, which skirts Telford (follow signs; the route will vary depending upon which end of the gorge you left your car), and head west toward **Shrewsbury** (the M54 becomes A5). Situated on a long lazy loop of the Severn, Shrewsbury (pronounced *SHROWS-bree*) is a lovely market town with many well-preserved medieval buildings and an ancient ruined castle, a pink sandstone relic of the incessant wars (between Celts and Romans, Celts and Saxons, Celts and Normans) that have raged along the Welsh border for millennia. If you didn't spend the entire day at Ironbridge, it's worth a visit.

From Shrewsbury, simply follow the **A5** north into a gradually rumpling landscape, crossing into **Wales** at **Chirk** (which has a superb early-fourteenth-century castle just west of town). It is a nearly seamless transition, marked modestly by a sign with the Welsh national emblem, a winged red dragon, and the salutation CROESO I CYMRU—"WELCOME TO WALES."

It wasn't always so easy. A few miles farther on is a more tangible boundary: **Offa's Dyke**, a 142-mile (227-kilometer) earthwork barrier that runs from the north coast almost to Bristol Bay and today is one of Britain's official Long Distance Paths. Built by the Saxon King Offa in the eighth century either as an administrative boundary or a defensive line (no one is sure which), it remains Wales's spiritual frontier. Crossing it was not encouraged; according to Saxon law, "Neither shall a Welshman cross into English land, nor an Englishman cross into Welsh land, without the appointed man from that other land who should meet him at the bank and bring him back again without any offence being committed." It didn't work; English and Welsh forces surged across the line dozens of times in the bloody centuries that followed.

North of Chirk the A5 turns west and enters the **Vale of Llangollen** (pronounced *thlan-GOTH-len*), a deep, green valley threaded by the silvery ribbon of the River Dee—or Afon Dyfrdwy (pronounced *AH-vun DUH-vr-dewy*), if you're Welsh and have a double-jointed tongue. Just beyond the village of **Fron Cysyllte** (pronounced *sus-UTH-teh*), watch for a minor road to the **right**. Turn **right** and follow it down into the valley for a view of the astonishing **Pontcysyllte Aqueduct**, engineering genius Thomas Telford's solution to how to get the **Llangollen Canal** across the valley of the Dee without stepping it down one side and up the other with time-consuming locks. There is something more than a little disorienting about seeing a boat drift across a narrow bridge 127 feet (39 meters) above the valley floor. On the other side, turn **left** onto the **A542** and follow it along the wooded northern flank of the pretty valley, with the sandstone cliffs of Ruabon Mountain looming above on the right, all the way into Llangollen. When you reach the fourteenth-century arched stone bridge over the Dee rapids, turn **left** into the center of town.

Man, boy, sheep, sheepdog—and the timeless rhythms of Wales

Llangollen ("The Church of St. Collen") is emphatically Welsh. There are no cute Tudor wood-and-plaster buildings (except for **Plas Newydd**, an eccentric reproduction); this is a stone-built market town, solid and purposeful, its houses topped with good Welsh slates as black as the "stovepipe" hats once worn by Welsh women. Along the street the language you hear is Welsh—for all its hard consonants, a soft, su-

The Eisteddfod Tradition

Popular as Llangollen's festival is, it is not a "real" *eisteddfod* (literally, a "sitting-down place"). Eisteddfodau (plurals in Welsh are formed by adding *au*) are competitions of Welsh music, song, poetry, and dance. They date from the twelfth century and celebrate the bardic tradition of poetry and song that flourished during that Golden Age. Unlike the international festival, a true eisteddfod is conducted only in Welsh. There are local and regional competitions year-round, culminating in the "crowning of the Bard" at the annual National Eisteddfod, the locale for which alternates between north and south Wales.

surrant tongue as whispery as the Dee itself slipping over its rocky bed. If the architecture and language weren't clues enough, you'd know you were in Wales just from the names on the shop awnings, which seem to be limited exclusively to Jones and Davies; Wales is notoriously short of surnames. But for all its "foreignness," Llangollen is a friendly place, and a marvelous gateway to Wales.

At the close of World War II, a Llangollen newspaperman, in a flight of romantic fancy for which the Welsh are famous, proposed that the town hold a concert and invite the world to sing. To his and everyone else's astonishment, they came—choirs from eleven countries that only two years earlier had been shooting at each other. They've been coming ever since; Llangollen is the home of the International Musical

Eisteddfod (pronounced *ice-TETH-vod*), a contest of singing and dancing that today draws thousands of contestants to the valley during the first week of July.

If you've missed the festival, there's still plenty to do in Llangollen. Begin by visiting the excellent Tourist Information Centre in the town hall. Then, as the afternoon draws to a close, choose from a 2-hour climb to the ruined medieval castle of **Dinas Bran**, perched above the town; a 2-mile (3.2-kilometer) stroll west along the canal towpath to the haunting ruins of thirteenth-century **Valle Crucis Abbey**; a horse-drawn **canal boat** trip high above the valley (summer only); or a ride upriver in the restored coach of the **Llangollen Steam Railway**. (Better yet, take the dinner train if it's running tonight; see Creature Comforts below.) For information on any of these options, write Tourist Information Centre, Town Hall, Llangollen, Clwyd LL20 5PD, Wales, U.K.

DIVERSIONS
Do "China" in a Day

If Ironbridge Gorge is the place for the inquisitive, **Stoke-on-Trent** is the place for the *acquisitive*—those who lust after English bone china. Stoke is the home of virtually every big name in "the China trade." Wedgwood, Minton, Royal Doulton, Spode, Coalport, Portmeirion—they're all here, and more.

Actually, there *is* no "Stoke-on-Trent"; the name is a twentieth-century creation precipitated by the amalgamation of six cities (Tunstall, Burslem, Hanley, Stoke-*upon*-Trent, Fenton, and Longton) known collectively as "the Potteries." The pottery industry emerged in this part of Staffordshire in the early eighteenth century, as a result of a felicitous combination of necessity, natural endowments, and entrepreneurship. Though the soil was too poor for farming, it was rich in pottery clays, and there was plenty coal for firing, lead and salt for glazes, and water for mixing. In the early 1700s, Thomas Whieldon established a pottery in Fenton, both to supply inexpensive storage vessels for the surrounding farming counties and to meet the burgeoning need for containers in which to infuse the leaves of the *Camelia sinensis* with water—tea, a hot new trend. There was demand, there was supply; what happened next was textbook economics. A young man named Josiah Wedgwood began working for Whieldon in 1754, then left to start his own pottery in 1759. Another of Whieldon's apprentices, Josiah Spode, left in 1770 to do the same. Thomas Minton worked for Spode, then spun off to create *his* own business in 1793. And so it went. Ambi-

*Bottle-kilns in Stoke-on-Trent, home of English bone china
(courtesy of the Gladstone Pottery Museum).*

tion, competition, and talent bred innovation—Spode combined ground animal bone, china clay, and Cornish stone, for example, and came up with "bone china." Soon all six towns were packed solid with brick factories, bottle kilns, and warehouses. It wasn't pretty, but it was—and still is—hugely successful.

For the whole story, head for the splendid **Gladstone Pottery Museum** on the **A50** Uttoxeter Road in **Longton** (open Monday through Saturday, 10:00 A.M. to 4:00 P.M.; Sunday 2:00 P.M. to 4:00 P.M.; closed Monday November through February). Then, with one of the city's detailed maps, cruise the factories, museums, and discount shops to your heart's content. Signs along the way are excellent. For a brochure, write the Tourist Information Centre, 1 Glebe Street, Stoke-on-Trent, ST4 1HP. (To pick up the itinerary again at Llangollen, head west on the **A525** through **Whitchurch**, then take the **A539** and **A542** into the Vale of Llangollen.)

CREATURE COMFORTS
Daily Bed

Because of the International Eisteddfod and its other, year-round attractions, Llangollen is well prepared for visitors. Several large hotels, a lot of guest houses, and a wide variety of B&B accommodations are located in and near the town. A little farther afield, there are farmhouse B&Bs along the A5 west of town. If you arrive without reservations, just head for the Tourist Information Centre in the town hall (open all year), and they'll find you a place for the night.

If you prefer to be a bit more farsighted, either consult the accommodation guidebooks listed in Further Reading, call your nearest British Tourist Authority office, or contact the Wales Tourist Board, Brunel House, 2 Fitzalan Road, Cardiff CF2 1UY, Wales, U.K., and ask them to send accommodation brochures featuring North Wales (they vary each year). For local information, write to the Tourist Information Centre, Town Hall, Llangollen, Clwyd LL20 5PD, Wales, U.K. In all Welsh accommodation guides, look especially for B&B listings that have received the "Dragon Award"—recognition from the Wales Tourist Board that they offer "particularly high standards of furnishings, decoration, facilities, comfort, and surroundings." Typically no more expensive than run-of-the-mill places, Dragon Award winners are your best bet throughout Wales.

One other option is a youth hostel in a recently refurbished half-timber manor house on Birch Hill, just east of town on the A5; write YHA Study and Activity Centre, Tyndwr Hall, Tyndwr Road, Llangollen, Clwyd LL20 8AR, or phone (0978) 860330.

Daily Bread

Llangollen has plenty of restaurants, hotel dining rooms, cafes, and pubs, so your choices for dinner are wider here than they're likely to be deeper into the mountains. When you peruse the menus, look for "Taste of Wales" features, designed to highlight the best food products from the country (Wales is, among other things, a major organic food producer for Britain).

For a more adventurous dinner, however, consider an evening in the dining car of the **Berwyn Belle**, one of the Llangollen Railway's steam locomotives. Twice each month from May through August (sporadically the rest of the year), the Belle pulls out of the station at 7:30 P.M., loaded with provisions for a gourmet dinner for roughly 100 diners, and chugs sedately up the Dee River valley for an impossibly romantic 3-hour sunset excursion. The price is reasonable, the scenery spectacular, and the experience unique. For information and reservations, write Berwyn Belle Bookings, The Station, Abbey Road, Llangollen, Clwyd LL20 8SN, or phone (0978) 860979 during office hours.

Castles, Kings, and Princes

LLANGOLLEN ◆ VALE OF CONWY
CONWY CASTLE ◆ CAERNARFON

◆ **A drive deep into Wales, then north to the coast**
◆ **Exploring the walled city of Conwy**
◆ **A walk around the castle of the Prince of Wales**
◆ **An optional visit to Bodnant Gardens**

*. . . in any country which has known invasion you will find
the older races in the mountains and the younger and
more vigorous races on the good, flat farmlands which they
have stolen from the original owners.*
——H. V. Morton
In Search of Wales, 1932

*T*he Welsh are the last true Britons. Driven from their homelands
by the Romans, harried by successive waves of Angles and Saxons,
harassed by Norman lords and Plantagenet kings, they have been dis-
placed but never quite defeated, made subjects but never fully submit-
ted. Withdrawing repeatedly to a wilderness so remote and brutal none
pursued them, they created a culture rich in literature and legend and
developed a streak of stubborn resistance as deep as their coal mines and
as wide as the vistas from atop the ancient Cambrian Mountains they
call home.

They do not call themselves "Welsh." *Weallas* is a Saxon word; it
means "foreigner." It is what the arrogant invaders called anyone whose
cries they could not understand as they slew them. In their own tongue,
they are the *Cymry*—"the countrymen"—and their ancient language has
been their bond and their hope for centuries. The English learned late
that you cannot subjugate a people unless you banish its language. They
can conspire in it in your very presence and leave you defenseless. They
can retreat into it and leave you isolated and mute. They can run circles
around you with it and leave you disoriented. They can live on it, be
nourished by it, and become immortal through it. And all this the
Welsh have done. Of all the remnant Celtic languages—Scots Gaelic,

Conwy, one of seventeen castles the English King Edward I built to contain the Welsh and discourage insurrection

Irish Gaelic, Manx, Cornish, Breton—only Welsh truly thrives, slipping into and out of the mist-cloaked mountains like a guerilla as the politics of linguistic colonialism ebb and flow from generation to generation.

Edward I never understood the power of language, but he did understand power. When he ascended the English throne in 1272, he inherited an England that had been in disarray for a century. Worse, he inherited a Wales that, under the leadership of "the two Llewelyns"—

LLANFAIRPWLLGWYNGYLLGOGERYCHWYRNDROBWLLLLANTYSILIOGOGOGOCH

Llan-vire-pooll-guin-gill-go-ger-u-queern-drob-ooll-llandus-ilio-gogo-goch.

Welsh Words

Like German, Welsh strings together shorter words to describe places. The key is knowing the short bits. The town *Llanfairpwllgwyngyllgogerychwyrndrobwllllantysiliogogogoch*, on the Isle of Anglesey, means "St. Mary's Church in the hollow of the white hazel near a rapid whirlpool and the Church of St. Tysilio near the red cave." Simple. For all its hard edges, it's a lilting language (perhaps one reason Wales produces such gifted singers, orators, and actors), but for outsiders it's neither easy to read nor "sing." A few hints: *ff* is pronounced like a single "f," while a single *f* is pronounced like "v." The *w* sounds like "oo," and the *y* like "i." The *dd* is a soft "th," as in "then." The way to make the sound of *ll* is to push the tip of your tongue firmly against the back of your front teeth and try to say "thl," letting the sound explode around the sides of your tongue and pop your cheeks. Another tip: the accent usually falls on the next-to-the-last syllable. Here are some common fragments:

aber	river mouth	*blen*	head of valley
adwy	pass	*bont*	bridge
afon	river	*bryn*	hill
allt	wooded hill	*bwlch*	gap
bach (or *fach*)	little	*caer*	fortress
ban	peak	*capel*	chapel
bedd	grave	*carn*	prominence
betws	church	*carreg*	rock

castell	castle	*is*	low
cefn	ridge	*isaf*	lowest
coch (or *goch*)	red	*llan*	church
coed	wood	*llyn*	lake
croes	cross	*llys*	palace
cwm	glacial valley	*mawr* (or *fawr*)	great
dinas	city	*melin*	mill
dol	meadow	*moel*	bare hilltop
du	black	*mynydd*	mountain
dwfr (or *dwr*)	water	*pen*	head
dyffryn	valley	*pentre*	village
eglwys	church	*plas*	hall
esgair	ridge	*pwll*	pool
fferm	farm	*rhaeadr*	waterfall
ffordd	road	*rhos*	moor
ffridd	sheepwalk	*rhyd*	ford
ffynnon	well	*tre* (or *dre*)	town
glan	shore	*ty*	house
gwern	swamp	*y*	the
gwyn	white	*yn*	in
gwynt	wind	*ynys*	island
hendre	winter home	*ystwyth*	winding

Llewelyn the Great and Llewelyn the Last—had used England's weakness to regain its geographic and cultural integrity. By 1267, Llewelyn II had secured authority over all other princes and barons in the region.

It was too much for the new king to swallow. Edward ordered Llewelyn II to London to pay homage; Llewelyn refused. Edward summoned him a second time, and a second time Llewelyn refused. Then Edward took hostage Llewelyn's bride, who was en route from France to marry him. Apparently not a romantic, Llewelyn refused a third time, and Edward declared war. In short order the tiny kingdom was surrounded and Llewelyn's forces were driven, as legions before them had been, into the wilds of Snowdonia. Llewelyn surrendered in 1277. Six years later he was killed during yet another insurrection.

In the twenty years following Llewelyn's surrender, Edward constructed a noose of seventeen castles around the Welsh coast—not to protect the country from outside aggressors, but to contain would-be Welsh rebels within the Snowdonian mountains. Designed by master craftsmen from Europe, they were state-of-the-art fortifications that could be defended by an astonishingly small garrison of only thirty men. The finest of these castles were Conwy, Caernarfon, Beaumaris, and Harlech, two of which are on our itinerary today.

🚗 CONWY AND THE COAST

Distance: About 45 miles/72 kilometers
Roads: Primary roads the entire distance
Driving Time: Allow 2 hours
Map: Michelin Map #403

This morning, head west on the **A5** in the direction of **Corwen** and **Betws-y-Coed** (pronounced *bet-oosuh-CO-ed*). Outside of Llangollen the A5 rises up the southern flank of the Dee River valley, providing sweeping views of the strange bleached-white limestone cliffs of Llantysilio Mountain that tower over the river beyond the foothills to the north. When the pastoral Dee turns south toward **Bala Lake**, the A5 climbs up the much narrower gritstone gorge of the **River Alwen** near **Maerdy**. The road clings precariously to the cliff edge until it gains the treeless, sheep-dotted moorland heights.

You know you're getting close to Betws-y-Coed when a road sign indicates zigzags for the next several miles and the A5 tips down into the narrow, twisting valley of the **River Conwy**. The trees close in around you, arching over the road and dappling the pavement with splashes of sunlight. Beautifully crafted (but very low) stone walls are all that stand between you and the foaming cataracts of the river below.

Don't turn left over the bridge and into the village of Betws-y-Coed—the closest thing to a tourist trap there is in Wales—unless you want to visit the National Park Information Centre (it's located in what once were the stables of the Royal Oak Inn). Instead, leave the A5 here and continue north on the **A470** through the lush **Vale of Conwy**. After just a few miles, the valley begins to broaden and flatten. The river wanders off to one side, then wanders back again, then quite suddenly widens and becomes tidal. Here, at **Tal-y-Cafn** (pronounced *tal-uh-KAvn*), is **Bodnant Garden**, one of the finest formal gardens in Britain and certainly the finest in Wales. Bodnant, now a National Trust property, was laid out by a Victorian builder in 1875 and is most famous for its blazing azaleas and mountainous rhododendrons. It also has brilliant daffodil meadows earlier in the spring and both rose terraces and perennial border gardens that flower all summer. The garden is open daily, 10:00 A.M. to 5:00 P.M., from mid-March through October.

Just a few more miles north, at the junction with the **A55**, turn left and cross the river's mouth. (Do not take the tunnel. Follow signs for Conwy.) Here two towns that could hardly be more different face each other across the sandy estuary. On the eastern shore basks **Llandudno**, a classic Victorian seaside resort—painted in the whites and creams of linen dresses and straw hats and trimmed in pastel shutters—built at the turn of the century as a playground for holiday-makers from the industrial Midlands. Ahead, on the western shore, **Conwy**, girded by its dark

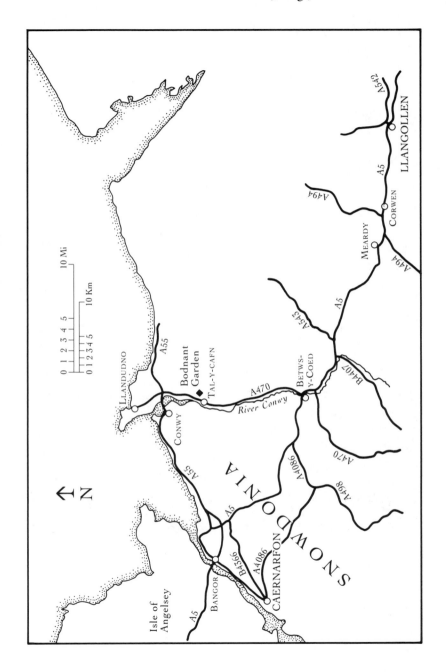

Swallow Falls, near Betws-y-Coed, North Wales

stone walls and anchored to the rocky headland by the eight massive towers of Edward's crenelated castle, glowers across the tidal flats at the frivolous development on the opposite shore. There is nothing frivolous about **Conwy Castle**.

When you reach the other side of the bridge (with Telford's graceful 1826 suspension bridge on your left), turn **left** through the town wall,

Castles like Conwy were so unassailable they could be defended by only thirty men.

beside the curtain wall of the castle itself, following signs for the car park and information center. The center has an excellent exhibition on Welsh history and a detailed explanation of Edward's castle-building strategy (it also can arrange for accommodations for you tonight, either here, if you're running out of daylight, or farther west in Caernarfon).

The castle itself, so imposing from the outside, is surprisingly domestic on the inside. There are, of course, the requisite machicolations for pouring boiling oil upon would-be attackers, narrow slits in the walls through which multiple archers could rain arrows on their opponents, and any number of other fearsome features, but Conwy also has the feel of a manor house, with a multistory great hall, complete with massive fireplaces, and a protected, almost cozy, inner ward in which the king's chamber and hall were located. Conwy is open Monday through Saturday 9:30 A.M. to 6:30 P.M. and Sunday 2:00 P.M. to 6:30 P.M. from mid-March through mid-October; Monday through Saturday 9:30 A.M. to 4:00 P.M. and Sunday 2:00 P.M. to 4:00 P.M. the rest of the year.

Conwy is said to be one of the finest walled towns in Europe. Compact but pleasantly laid out, it is bounded by 0.75 mile (1.2 kilometers) of almost unbroken stone walls, punctuated by twenty-two observation towers and punctured by three original gates. The walls run along the waterfront, then climb to the back of the city (from which point there are terrific views of the castle, the foothills of Snowdonia, and the river), then race downhill again to the castle's southwest tower. You can walk much of the wall.

🚗 TO THE SEAT OF THE PRINCE OF WALES

Distance: About 20 miles/32 kilometers
Roads: Primary road to Bangor, then secondary
Driving Time: Allow 45 minutes
Map: Michelin Map #403

From Conwy, follow the one-way traffic pattern through town and out the northwest corner of the city wall, following the **A55** in the direction of **Bangor**. The A55 runs along the shores of the **Bay of Conwy**, occasionally ducking through tunnels to penetrate rocky headlands or skirt quarries (indeed another tunnel has been constructed that carries the A55 underneath the Conwy estuary *and* the town of Conwy itself). Eventually the land flattens out, and there are sweeping

Caernarfon, the knot in King Edward's thirteenth-century noose of castles, is the grandest—and is where Charles became Prince of Wales in 1969.

views of the mouth of the **Menai Strait**, which separates the **Isle of Anglesey** from mainland Wales. As you approach Bangor, two more castles—Edward's **Beaumaris**, across the strait, and **Penrhyn**, a nineteenth-century sham on the mainland—are on the right side of the road.

Just before Bangor, bear **left** off the four-lane highway and, at the roundabout, take the first **left** onto the **A5** in the direction of Betws-y-

The First Prince of Wales

In 1284, soon after Llewelyn II's death, Edward I summoned the Welsh princes to Caernarfon to pay him homage. When they arrived, they petitioned him to appoint a "Prince of Wales" to rule them, one who spoke neither English nor French and whose character was unimpeachable—in short, a Welshman. To their astonishment, the king agreed. Then he withdrew, returning moments later with an infant in his arms: his son Edward II, born days earlier in the still-uncompleted castle—a Welshman, who spoke neither English nor French, and whose character was clearly unimpeachable. Outwitted, the Welsh leaders had little choice but to proclaim the king's son Prince of Wales on the spot. Welsh resentment festered until 1400, when a new leader, Owain Glyndwr, led another, again fruitless, rebellion. In 1536, Henry VIII (whose father Henry Tudor was of Welsh descent) signed an Act of Union formally joining the two feuding nations.

Coed. Immediately thereafter, turn **right** onto a secondary road, the **B4366**, signposted for **Caernarfon** and **Llanberis**. At the intersection with the **B4547** continue **straight** ahead in the direction of Caernarfon. This is a wonderful hilltop ride, with lush farmland rolling away from you on the left to the towering peaks of **Snowdonia National Park**, its dark slate clefts glistening in the warm light of the afternoon sun. Off to the right, the ground slopes sharply down to the shore and across the strait to the fertile fields of Anglesey, the granary of Wales. (**Note:** There are several farmhouse B&Bs along this scenic road. With Caernarfon only a few minutes away, any of them would make a good base for the night.)

When you reach a roundabout on the outskirts of Caernarfon, follow signs for **Town Centre** and do the same at the second roundabout. When you reach the little town square go around the green and turn left by the statue of David Lloyd George (the fiery Welsh former prime minister) and drive downhill to the car park on the waterfront, directly beneath the towering walls of **Caernarfon Castle**. If the castle is still open, late afternoon is a superb time to see it; the light of the setting sun brings out an inner fire from the alternating bands of brown and gray stone in the curtain walls and casts dramatic shadows across the broad lawns of the inner wards.

Samuel Johnson called Caernarfon "an edifice of stupendous majesty and strength." It is awesome. It was designed to be the knot in Edward's noose: a fortress, a palace, and the royal seat of government in Wales. If there is a coziness about Conwy Castle, there is none of it here. Caernarfon is about brute force; it is Edward I's will, cast in stone.

The entrance alone would have dismayed any attacker. There was a drawbridge over a deep moat flanked by two massive towers. The design for the gate had five doors, six iron portcullises, a right-angle turn, then an inner drawbridge. There were arrow loops in the walls and "murder holes" for oil in the roof.

The interior of the castle was the epitome of Middle Ages *luxe*; the lower ward (originally separated from the upper ward by yet another wall) housed both the great hall and the Eagle Tower. The largest of the castle's ten turreted towers, the Eagle Tower was the home and administrative headquarters for the king's governor of North Wales and the king's chambers when he was in residence.

The Eagle Tower is also where the castle's audio/visual program is shown. If you don't have time for the 50-minute guided tour (which leaves from the gatehouse every hour), see this program; it is an excellent condensed history of Wales and Caernarfon. Caernarfon Castle's hours are the same as Conwy's.

CREATURE COMFORTS
Daily Bed

If by the time you reach Caernarfon, you have neither booked accommodation from the Conwy Information Centre nor found an attractive B&B along the way, head for **Oriel Pendeitsh**, which is both the Pendeitsh Art Gallery and the Tourist Information Centre for the town. It's just a few yards from the castle entrance. In addition, if you're

The heights of Snowdonia tower over the coastal plateau near Caernarfon.

traveling "off-season" (from October 1 through Easter) and haven't already arranged accommodations in Dolgellau, the next stop on this itinerary, use Caernarfon's "Book-A-Bed-Ahead" service while you're in town; Dolgellau's Tourist Information Centre is only open "in-season."

To reserve a room in advance, consult the accommodation guides in Further Reading or use the brochures referenced in yesterday's Daily Bed section. For addresses and phone numbers of the half dozen youth hostels in the Bangor–Caernarfon–Llanberis area, see the YHA guide in Further Reading. For additional local information, write the Tourist Information Centre, Oriel Pendeitsh, Caernarfon, Gwyndd LL55 2PB, Wales.

Daily Bread

As both a major tourist stop and administrative center for North Wales, Caernarfon is well stocked with restaurants, cafes, and pubs. You'll have no difficulty finding a good place for dinner. As always, check with your hosts for the best local recommendations.

In the Wild Fastness of Snowdonia

CAERNARFON ◆ LLANBERIS PASS NANTGWYNANT PASS ◆ DOLGELLAU

- ◆ **A drive through Snowdonia National Park**
- ◆ **Optional climb or train to Snowdon's summit**
- ◆ **South through the Cambrian Range to Dolgellau**

The mountains shall erupt, the dragons will attack each other and tear each other to pieces. . . . The winds shall do battle with each other with a blast of ill-omen, making their din reverberate from one constellation to another.
——Merlin, the wizard

The remote mountain passes and peaks of Snowdonia are shrouded in mist and mystery, a breeding ground for legend, but the spirits that dwell here are not blythe. This is a land of fearsome giants. The Welsh call Snowdon's summit *Y Wyddfa Fawr*, the "great burial place." It is where Rhitta, a murderous giant who wore a cloak made from the beards of the kings he had slain, is alleged to be buried. Beneath the summit, in the icy waters of Glaslyn, lurks Afanc, a water monster. In Snowdonia dragons—red ones (for Wales) and white ones (for Saxon England)—are locked in perpetual conflict, demons hurl stones the size of houses from the misty heights, and invisible horses hammer the valley floors with their hooves, the thunder echoing off the towering cliffs. Stories are told of shepherds who come upon that most Welsh of legendary saviors, King Arthur, standing stock-still with his men in some remote mountain refuge, frozen in time, swords at the ready, awaiting the clarion call that will reanimate them to rescue Wales from the usurpers.

Maybe legends such as these are created to lend romance to the bleak history of a defeated people, or to give them hope. Possibly it's just medieval counterintelligence, designed to keep outsiders out. It certainly worked for some; for centuries travelers gave the region wide berth. Today, however, Snowdonia is one of Britain's most popular national parks and millions visit each year. Somehow, though, the mountains simply swallow them up; they vanish into the wild hills . . . like magic.

🚗 A DAY IN SNOWDONIA

Distance: About 55 miles/89 kilometers
Roads: Well-maintained, wildly scenic primary roads
Driving Time: Most of the day, depending upon stops
Map: Michelin Map #403

A leisurely schedule today, with plenty of time for slack-jawed gaping at Snowdonia's awesome scenery—and even a climb, if you and the weather are up to it. But first, if you did not have time to visit Caernarfon Castle yesterday, do it this morning; every visit to Britain should feature a castle, and there is none more spectacular (or better explained) than this one.

Then, follow signs from the center of Caernarfon to **Llanberis** and the **A4086**. The distance is a mere 7 miles (11 kilometers), but you might just as well be flying to another land entirely, the landscape is so different. The transition comes quickly, at **Cwm-y-glo**, where the verdant rolling fields of the coastal margin bump up against the hulking mass of the Snowdon range. Here the road slips through a gap and enters a long mountain-ringed valley. The little village of Llanberis is off to the right with the great pyramid of Snowdon towering above the village's chimney pots. At 3,560 feet (1,085 meters), it is the highest mountain in England and Wales. To the left, **Llyn** ("lake") **Padarn** shimmers beneath the shattered and terraced face of a vast mountain of slate, all that remains of the Dinorwic slate mine, which supplied roofing slates to the sprawling cities of the Midlands until it finally closed in 1969. Stay on the main road, which bypasses the village. Just ahead on the left is the entrance to the **Lake Padarn Country Park**, which is home to **Oriel Eryri**, an environmental interpretation center run by the Museum of North Wales, and to the Welsh Slate Museum. Just beyond the information center, on the right, is the **Snowdon Mountain Railway** depot (see Diversions below).

The geology of Snowdonia is as complex as any on earth. Snowdon itself is volcanic, but it's not a volcano despite its misleading shape. For all its impressive mass, it's only the broken and battered stub of a much larger formation. Some 400 million to 500 million years ago, molten rock rose from deep in the earth's core, found its way up through fissures in much older layers of sedimentary rock, then spread over the

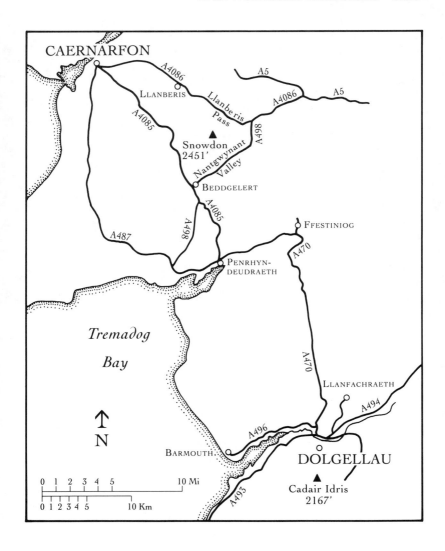

surface. Later, in a quieter era, more sediments were laid down. Then the whole area was compressed, uplifted, turned, twisted, faulted, and finally ground to bits by glaciers. That's why, as you drive east through the valley, one mountain may be a rounded dome (made of soft slates), while its neighbor may be a jagged mass of pinnacles (made of harder volcanics). The science notwithstanding, it makes for terrific scenery.

From Llanberis, continue east on the A4086. Beyond the tip of **Llyn Peris**, the road leaves the pleasant vale behind and the world around you quickly turns ominous and bleak. Meadows yield to rock-

Bleak, barren, wonderful—the Llanberis Pass, deep in Snowdonia National Park

strewn peaty ground cloaked in purple swaths of heather. Sheep pick their way across the steep slopes like mountain goats and tear hungrily at the meager clumps of edible grass that survive here. The road rises and falls along the right flank of the valley, then skitters across to the north side, with its vast scree slopes. Then the road begins climbing even more steeply, scurrying up the rapidly narrowing defile, first along one side, then the other, hurtling around house-size boulders that litter the landscape, leaping over a stream by means of narrow stone bridges, moving fast, as if in a hurry to escape unseen demons. The higher you climb, the more the walls of the **Llanberis Pass** close in. Shafts of sun slash through dark mists that appear suddenly on the cliff faces, rise, and then vanish. The mountains become menacing; huge blocks of stone, left behind by retreating glaciers, teeter high above the road, defying gravity. It is a breathtaking ride.

At the summit is **Pen-y-Pass**, with a youth hostel and a car park for two of the best paths to the top of Snowdon (see Diversions below). Here the A4086 tips over the lip of the pass and plummets down to a T-junction in the middle of a bleak moor at the head of two deep valleys. Turn **right** on the **A498** in the direction of **Beddgelert** (pronounced *beth-GEL-ert*) via the **Nantgwynant** (pronounced *nant-GOOIN-ant*) **Pass**. This is another splendid mountain road (one that can't seem to make up its mind whether it's one or two lanes), perhaps best seen in the late afternoon, with the sun glinting off the surface of

Slate Mining's Lasting Scars

The mountains of North Wales have produced minerals in abundance since the first century A.D., when the Romans began extracting lead. Coal, copper, iron, building stone, even gold have been blasted from Snowdonia, a place where bare rock often seems the only economic asset. When the housing boom brought on by the Industrial Revolution created an insatiable demand for roofing slates, Snowdonia's brittle rocks suddenly became valuable.

By the late 1800s some 16,000 people were employed in the mines. Some mines were on the surface, like the terraced mountainside facing Llanberis; others were deep within the earth, like the mines in Blaenau Ffestiniog. Several of the region's port towns and most of its little steam railroad lines owe their existence to the slate industry. But a three-year labor dispute at the turn of the century, the beginning of World War I, and the building slump caused by the Depression pushed the industry into a long and painful decline. By World War II, all that was left were a scarred landscape and, in some respects, an even more deeply scarred people: generations of exploited workers with limited skills and even more limited prospects. Most moved to South Wales to mine coal when the slate industry collapsed, only to be exploited yet again.

Llyn Gwynant far below. The narrow road clings to the steep eastern slope, with sweeping views across and down the length of the valley. The foothills are steep and thickly wooded, and the bare knuckles of the mountains rise high above them, with the ragged edges of Snowdon in the background. Far below, high cliffs plunge directly into the lake on one side, and on the other gnarled oaks grow along an emerald shoreline grazed by roving flocks of white-faced sheep. After slipping through a quiet mountain village, the road crosses the valley floor, here crisscrossed with dark stone walls, and then runs along the western shore of **Llyn Dinas** before reaching Beddgelert.

From Beddgelert, a former mining town that has become a walking and climbing center, head south in the direction of **Porthmadog**, following the banks of the River Glaslyn. The road ducks in and out of stands of weather-twisted oak trees, and the river clatters over huge boulders on the left, virtually a continuous cataract. Less than a mile from Beddgelert, turn **left** over the river following the **A4085**. The road climbs out of the river valley, then crosses a lumpy high mountain meadow edged with birch trees. At the village of **Penrhyndeudraeth** (pronounced *pen-rin-DIED-ra-eth*), turn **left** onto the **A487** and follow it up the estuary paralleling the tracks of the **Ffestiniog** (pronounced *fes-TIN-yog*) **Railway**, one of several restored "Great Little Railways of Wales."

Stay on the A487 until it dead-ends at a T-junction with the **A470**. Then turn **right**, skirt the eastern shore of **Llyn Trawsfynydd**, and follow the A470 up the pretty valley of the **River Eden**. The closer you get to **Dolgellau** (pronounced *dol-GETH-lie*), the narrower the river valley becomes. The bracken-coated hills on either side steepen, the little river quickens and is swelled by tributaries, and trees arch over the road forming a mossy green canopy. Then, the ravine ends abruptly and the broad valley of the Mawddach Estuary spreads out to the south. A few minutes later, the tightly clustered stone-built town of Dolgellau appears on the right, crouched in the shadow of **Cadair Idris**, a gigantic mass of volcanic rock rising to the sky to the south. Immediately after you pass the junction with the **A493** turn **left** onto a side road that parallels the A470 (which bypasses Dolgellau) and then **right** over the bridge into the heart of town.

Dolgellau seems too small—it's little more than a village, really—for a one-way traffic system, but the moment you enter it the reason becomes obvious. The streets and buildings were clearly laid out in another era, and even with traffic flowing one way, it's a tight squeeze in spots. Though its gray stone buildings are a bit austere at first glance, there is something uncommonly warm and welcoming about Dolgellau, even on a gray day. The way the town crowds around its little market square is cozy and protected, and the shops include a superb delicatessen-bakery (keep this in mind for a picnic lunch tomorrow). If you have not already made arrangements for accommodations for the next two nights (see Creature Comforts below), head for the Tourist Information Centre (open Easter through September) on the north side of the market square in a former Quaker meeting place.

DIVERSIONS
To Snowdon's Summit: By Rail or Foot— or Both

If you awaken this morning in Caernarfon to clear skies (a rare event), head immediately for Llanberis. Of the half million or so people who visit Snowdonia National Park each year, a fair number of them try to see Snowdon—at least from the bottom. Most are disappointed. When moisture-laden air sweeps in off the Atlantic (which is most of the time), Snowdon and its cousins force it upwards, where it cools and causes rain—as much as 200 inches (508 centimeters) annually. Most

Hardscrabble farming in the shadow of Snowdon, the highest mountain in Wales

days, Snowdon is wreathed in a turban of cloud, but when it's clear the view from the summit is magnificent. You can walk to the summit along any of several well-maintained trails . . . or go by train.

The **Snowdon Mountain Railway** is the easy way up. Opened in 1896, it is Britain's only rack railway; a stumpy little engine pushes a single coach (capacity fifty-nine) to the summit in just under an hour, then waits a half hour before beginning the return journey. If you're not much of a walker, that's the good news. The bad news is that, as the brochure states in typical British understatement, "clear, sunny days cannot always be guaranteed." If the summit is in cloud, don't bother; the experience won't be worth the cost. Also, at weekends in high season the little trains cannot accommodate the demand and waits are long. However, if a substantial queue has developed you can purchase a ticket for a specific train during the day, then go away and return a half hour before departure. The railway operates from March 15 through October; the first train leaves at 9:00 A.M. (8:30 A.M. in peak periods). Remember, it's cold up there, even in midsummer; dress accordingly.

Climbing the summit of the highest mountain in England and Wales only to discover a train station, tourists, and a busy cafeteria may not be your idea of a wilderness experience, but Snowdon is popular with walkers nonetheless. Cadair Idris is a far more rewarding climb (see tomorrow's itinerary), but if the weather is excellent today and the predictions for tomorrow are iffy, consider walking to the top of Snowdon (or walking down after taking the train up). Of the six most popular routes, two—the **Miner's Track** and the **Pyg Track**—make a varied and dramatic 5-hour round-trip and have the added advantage of starting at the 1,170-foot (357-meter) level at the Pen-y-Pass car park. Moreover, even if you don't feel driven to scale the mountain, the walk up the miner's track to Llyn Llydaw, a crystal tarn set in a cathedral of volcanic cliffs, is easy and delightful on a good day. The National Park has produced inexpensive but detailed walking brochures with interesting background narratives for each of the ascent routes; they're available at any Tourist Information Centre. In addition, the Ordnance Survey's Outdoor Leisure Map #23 "Snowdonia—Snowdon Area" covers all the routes as well (though without the narrative). Ordnance Survey maps are sold at information centers and at local newsagents. For more information, write to the Snowdonia National Park Authority, National Park Office, Penrhyndeudraeth, Gwynedd LL48 6LS, Wales.

CREATURE COMFORTS
Daily Bed

Graham and Diana Silverton are not your average Welsh B&B-keepers. In fact, they're not Welsh at all. Former English hoteliers, the Silvertons "retired" to **Llanfachreth**, an almost ridiculously scenic hamlet in a sleepy valley about 3 miles from Dolgellau. There they

The walls of Dolgellau aren't really "a mile high," but Cadair Idris, rising high above the handsome town, makes it seem so.

turned an early-seventeenth-century Welsh stone "longhouse"—where home and barn were under a single roof—into a small jewel called **Ty Isaf**, the "lower house." There are three bedrooms, small but handsomely decorated, but the real attraction of Ty Isaf appears when the sun goes down: after a complimentary drink with the Silvertons around a massive inglenook fireplace, guests are escorted into the dining room (the former dairy shed) for a four-course dinner (with several choices) that would be remarkable anywhere in Europe but is nothing less than astonishing in dour, Methodist North Wales, where one senses that such indulgences are shunned. Breakfast is similarly grand. Ty Isaf is only slightly more expensive than the average B&B, but even if you're traveling on a budget you have a ready-made excuse for staying here the next two nights: you'll need to stoke up before you climb Cadair Idris tomorrow . . . and, of course, you'll have earned a reward when you return tomorrow night. For reservations and directions, write Ty Isaf, Llanfachreth, Nr. Dolgellau, Gwynedd LL40 2EA, or phone (0341) 423261.

For other accommodation options, consult the Wales Tourist Board brochures in Further Reading. In addition, a youth hostel is romantically situated in a country house in the hills above Penmaenpool, just west of Dolgellau off the A493 (left up the lane after the Abergwynant Bridge); write Youth Hostel, Kings, Penmaenpool, Dolgellau, Gwynedd LL40 1TB, or phone (0341) 422392. For last-minute bookings, use the Tourist Information Centre in Dolgellau.

Daily Bread

If you're not staying at Ty Isaf, little Dolgellau has plenty of choices for dinner, from a modest cafe to the public dining rooms of several hotels. There is also a picturesque pub downriver at Penmeanpool, close to a wildlife refuge and nature trail.

But if the weather is warm and fair, you might consider a picnic dinner—if not this evening, then tomorrow. Stop in at the delicatessen just off the southeast corner of the market square and put together a picnic (your choices in the bread department will be better if you do this in the morning). There is a wine shop directly across the street. Then head for someplace dramatic—say, the beach at Fairbourne (on the A493 south) or the west-facing slope of the "Precipice Walk" (see tomorrow's Diversions section)—and watch the sun go down over the Irish Sea.

Ascending the "Chair of Idris"

DOLGELLAU ◆ CADAIR IDRIS

- ◆ A day climb to the summit of Cadair Idris
- ◆ An easy but still breathtaking "Precipice Walk"
- ◆ A rainy-day alternative exploration of old and
  new technologies

*Old Cader is a grand fellow and shows himself superbly
with everchanging light.*

——Charles Darwin

*T*here is an old saying that "the walls of Dolgellau are a mile high."
It is an exaggeration, but not an egregious one: the nearly vertical
north face of Cadair Idris does seem to leap directly from the back gardens of Dolgellau to the clouds. Nevertheless, the highest point of this
huge stone buttress is only 2,927 feet (892 meters).

Cadair Idris's powerful first impression comes from its spectacular
isolation. A huge plug of volcanic rock separated from the rest of Snowdonia by the Vale of Ffestiniog and the gentler mountains north of
Dolgellau, Cadair Idris rises directly from the shores of the Irish Sea
and is surrounded by dark green glens, deep rocky gorges, and the
broad and beautiful Mawddach Estuary. It can take longer to climb
Cadair Idris than Snowdon simply because there are so many distractions: glacier-cut hanging valleys vast and still as cathedrals, icy black
pools and foaming cataracts, frost-blasted boulder fields and rubble-
strewn scree slopes, meadows ablaze with wildflowers, and ridges rolling green as ocean swells to the hazy horizon. Each time you stop to
catch your breath the scene before you is so arresting, the sweep of each
new vista so panoramic, that you lose track of the trek and the time.

On a fine day there is no more rewarding walk in all of Britain. And
on a changeable day, with brilliant sun and impenetrable mists battling
for supremacy at the summit, the experience is positively mystical. Even
if you have to wait for good weather, climb Cadair Idris.

🏃 A DAY ON CADAIR IDRIS

Distance: 8.2 miles/13.2 kilometers; allow 2.5–3 hours for ascent—
time for descent depends on route taken
Difficulty: Moderately difficult for the first hour, easy on the summit
plateau, easy to difficult depending on descent route
Total Elevation Gain: 2,850 feet/869 meters
Gear: Sturdy hiking books, rain gear, an extra layer of clothes, camera,
extra film
Map: Ordnance Survey Outdoor Leisure Map #23

Begin with lunch. Purchasing it, that is. Head into Dolgellau and
put together a picnic at the delicatessen, then follow signs to the **A470**
and **A487** to **Machynlleth** (pronounced *Ma-HUN-cleth*). The A470
coils up the side of a wooded hill, eventually breaking out to open
moors that get wilder the higher you climb. At the lonely Cross Foxes
Inn, turn **right** onto the A487 and continue up a steadily narrowing
valley with the eastern arm of Cadair Idris on your right and the barren
hump of **Mynydd Ceiswyn** on the left.

Then, quite suddenly, a little less than 2 miles (3 kilometers) above
the inn, the road reaches the summit of the pass and pitches headlong
downhill through a gap so narrow and menacing it could do as a stand-
in for "the valley of the shadow of death." Towering ramparts of rock
loom high above the narrow road, blotting out all but a sliver of the
sky. A mountain stream hurls itself off the crags on the right, then turns
and rushes downhill beside the road. Huge chunks of cliff lay shattered
on the floor of the ravine below you, and occasional sections of wire
mesh attached to the sheer walls on your left do little to inspire confi-
dence. This dramatic defile is the **Bwlch Llyn Bach**, the "gap of the
little lake." The little lake itself, **Tal-y-Llyn**, shimmers in the morning
sun far below in a valley so flat, green, and pastoral it seems like a mirage from these rocky heights. When you finally reach the bottom of
the hill, just beyond the charming little Minffordd Hotel, turn **right**
onto the **B4405**, then right again beneath a canopy of trees and into
the public car park.

This is the beginning of the **Minffordd Track**, certainly the most
dramatic of the five routes to the top of Cadair Idris and the most visually varied as well. The walk begins at the back of the car park, by the
Nature Conservancy signpost. You cross over the little River Faw,
which feeds Tal-y-Llyn, walk up an *allee* of chestnut trees, then turn **left**
along a gravel path past a few derelict stone buildings. At a signpost just
a few yards farther on, turn **right** and begin a steep ascent up through
an oak wood beside **Nant Cadair**, a foaming cataract that splits, forms,
and splits again as it tumbles down its rocky bed beside the path. The
path soon becomes a series of steps, first wooden, then stone, built by
the Nature Conservancy to control erosion.

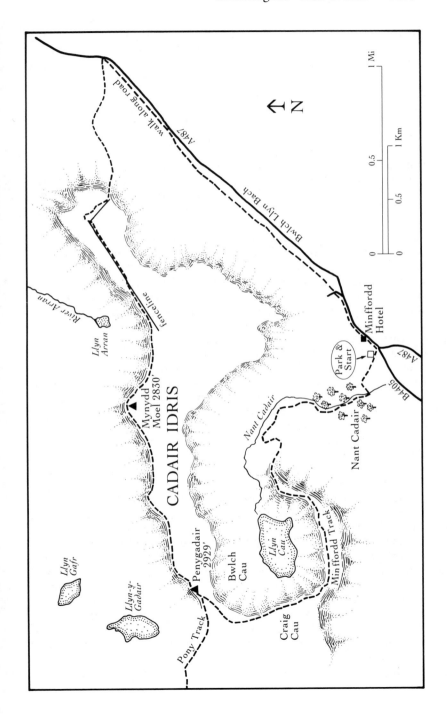

The wood itself, a protected relic of the woodlands that cloaked the flanks of Snowdonia for some 8,000 years, has a fairy-tale air about it. The trees are ancient, stunted, and gnarled, and their roots snake along the ground among the boulders in search of a soft spot through which to penetrate the earth. The ground is carpeted with an incredible array of mosses, some bright emerald green, others deep blue-green and looking like Lilliputian forests. Sunlight slips through the forest canopy and sends shimmery shafts through the misty air.

Above the wood, you pass through a gate in a stone wall and continue uphill along the gravel path, slanting to the right around the flank of **Craig Lwyd** and keeping to the left bank of the stream. Already, the prospect behind you is stunning: the patchwork valley floor presents a peaceful, domestic scene that contrasts sharply with the bleak moorlands high above.

Abruptly, the path levels out at the bottom of a broad glacier-scoured valley, and the stream races away to the right out of sight. Here and there, sheep pick their way among massive boulders, searching for what few bits of grass survive up here. In the absence of the roaring stream it is so quiet you can hear the low hum of bumblebees harvesting nectar from purple clouds of heather blossoms. The clear air, streaming in off the Irish Sea, is fresh, virginal.

Partway up the valley, on the right, the Nature Conservancy has fenced off a small section of peaty ground, presumably to determine what species would colonize the landscape in the absence of the sheep. In addition to heather and bracken, the test plot includes thorny gorse bushes covered in lemon yellow blossoms, bright lavender foxglove dancing in the wind, mosses and sedges of every description, and the tiny flowers of several other acid-tolerant alpine plants.

After a few more minutes of fairly gentle ascent, the footpath forks. Take the path to the left and begin the steep climb up the side of the crag. A few minutes later you reach your reward: a natural platform that reveals for the first time **Llyn Cau**—a sapphire blue glacial lake trapped in a vast and silent prison of rock whose walls rise 1,000 feet to the sky. The cliffs are deeply etched with cracks and gullies and bedecked with waterfalls. Sharp pillars of volcanic rock hang high above the diminutive tarn like swords of Damocles. Great gnarled blocks of stone lay scattered about the scree slopes beside the lake—the weapons of winter, rained down from the cliff faces by the insidious forces of frost. And soaring above it all—sometimes wreathed in cloud, sometimes etched against a brilliant azure sky—is the summit of Cadair Idris. It is said that if you spend the night beside the dark (and allegedly bottomless) waters of Llyn Cau, you will wake up blind, mad, or a poet. A monster is said to live beneath the surface. In this spectacular setting, neither legend seems improbable.

Higher still, the footpath gains the top of the ridge and what seems

Spend the night beside the waters of Llyn Cau, according to legend, and you'll wake up blind, mad, or a poet. Tough gamble.

like the whole of Mid-Wales is spread out before you to the south and east: the long patchwork valley from Tal-y-Llyn to the sea, the softly rounded Cambrian Mountains around Machynlleth, and the great gash of Bwlch Llyn Bach. From here, you can see that the ravine is actually part of a much longer rift, the Bala Fault, which stretches away to the northeast for miles, nearly to the English border. Ahead, the path climbs ever higher, circumnavigating the horseshoe rim of **Craig Cau**, a secondary peak, and picking its way gingerly along the vertiginous edge of the cliffs high above the tarn, so far below now that it looks like a gemstone caught in a onyx clasp.

Beyond Craig Cau, the path descends **Bwlch Cau**, then begins the final steep ascent to the summit plateau. A hundred yards or so from the summit, roughly at the point where the **Pony Track** (a popular easy ascent) joins from the left, the generally smooth face of the mountain becomes a vast field of frost-fractured granite blocks ranging in size from bricks to major appliances. The path picks its way through this moonscape, zigzagging this way and that, following a line of cairns; thankfully, you are screened from the wind sweeping in off the Irish Sea almost until you reach the summit cairn.

Cadair Idris means "the chair of Idris." Idris, according to Welsh legend, was one of the five giants who ruled the mountains of Snowdonia . . . or he may have been a seventh-century chieftain who resisted the Saxon invasion—history and myth are hard to separate in Wales. Whoever he was, he certainly had a knack for arranging furniture: from the "pillow" of his chair, the rocky summit called **Penygadair**, the view is simply stunning—far superior to Snowdon's. To the west, you can take in the whole of Cardigan Bay, from the Lleyn Peninsula on the north to the Pembroke Peninsula on the south. Beyond the bay, the Irish Sea stretches away to the blue haze of the mountains of Wicklow in Ireland. Far below the precipitous north face of the massif, the tranquil Mawddach River wanders lazily westward from Dolgellau to its estuary and the shining beaches of Barmouth. Farther north, all of Snowdonia spreads out like a giant relief map, with Snowdon, the Glyders, the Carnedds, and Foel-Fras stacked up, one behind the other. To the west and south, the Cambrian range rolls in great green waves to the English border and to the heights of the Brecon Beacons.

It's almost a shame to climb Cadair Idris on a perfectly clear day. In some respects the experience is more rewarding, and certainly more ethereal, on a day when the sky is busy with big, puffy cumulus clouds speeding in from the sea and washing over the summit plateau in dense, irregular waves. One minute you can see Snowdonia basking beneath a warm summer sky, the next you can hardly see your hand in front of your face, a moment later an uninterrupted view of the entire west coast of Wales, then nothing once again—it's like a slide show on a limitless screen.

The frost-shattered volcanic flanks of Cadair Idris

To descend Cadair Idris, choose one of several options. You may, of course, return by the same route as the ascent, secure in the knowledge that the world always looks different in the other direction. An easier descent is possible if you are willing to add a bit of ground transportation to get back to your car. The Pony Track, which you joined just below the summit, runs downhill, due west, to the bottom of the saddle between Cadair Idris and Tyrrau Mawr, then turns **right** and slips gently down the north flank of the mountain to the car park at **Tynant**, a few miles west of Dolgellau. There is no bus service to town there, and service from Dolgellau to Minffordd is limited, but you can call a cab from the public phone near the car park and be ferried over the pass to return to your car, or cadge a ride back to town from fellow walkers returning to the car park and call a cab from there (B & M Mini Cabs, Dolgellau, 0341-422346).

A more rewarding, if adventurous, return is to walk east along the summit plateau and descend into Bwlch Llyn Bach, the spectacular ravine through which you drove this morning. Though the Ramblers' Association uses this descent, most other walkers follow the more heavily beaten tracks. You are very likely to have this route all to yourself.

From the summit cairn, clamber over the rocks, past the stone shelter (where, many years ago, an old woman used to sell snacks to climbers), to the northern lip of the plateau and turn **right**, heading east downhill following a line of cairns. Where this path tips over the edge and descends the north face to icy Llyn-y-Gadair far below, stay on top and **continue** following the edge up to the summit of **Mynydd Moel**, at 2,830 feet (863 meters) only slightly lower than Penygadair. Continue east down the steep grassy slope, still keeping to the northern edge of the gradually narrowing plateau (the path is indistinct, but there are cairns). If anything, the view across North Wales from the eastern extremity of Cadair Idris is even better than the view from Penygadair; you can see more clearly the valley formed by the Bala Fault, partly filled by Bala Lake, and the full sweep of the Snowdonia range.

Eventually, near the narrowest point of this eastern finger of the plateau, high above little **Llyn Aran**, you reach a fence. Stay to the left of the fence until you reach a stile, then cross over and follow the right side of the fence toward a grassy hill straight ahead. The going here is easy, though a bit boggy in places.

When you reach another fence coming up from the right, cross another stile and turn **right**, following this new fenceline to the southeastern lip of the plateau, overlooking the breathtaking gash of Bwlch Llyn Bach. Then, descend on the clear path on the left side of the fence to the valley floor far below. This is a steep descent, with loose footing in one or two places, but the fence makes for convenient handholds, and the climb down looks more precipitous from the top than it actually is.

At the bottom of the cliff face, you continue east along a grassy foothill finger, then descend again—more gently this time—until you reach a gate by the A487. Turn **right** and walk downhill, being careful to stay on the berm whenever possible. In less than 0.5 mile (0.8 kilometer), you'll reach a stile on the right. Cross over the stile and turn **left**, following a bridleway down through the gap, with the highway above on the left and a pretty stream below on the right. After a bit less than 1.5 miles (about 2 kilometers), a gate takes you out to the road once again by the Minffordd Hotel. Beyond the hotel, turn **right** onto the B4405, then **right** again into the car park.

DIVERSIONS
The Precipice Walk

Don't be daunted; the rather breathless name given by Victorian tourists to this delightful 3-mile (5-kilometer) stroll is typical of the period but has relatively little to do with reality (the "Torrent Walk" just east of Dolgellau is another example of this florid genre). The "precipice" in question is a steep heather-clad slope, traversed by a level path tame enough for small children and sprightly grannies. But don't underestimate the payoff: probably no other short walk in all of Wales provides so much scenery for so little effort. If you choose not to climb Cadair Idris today and have a few hours free—especially toward sunset—"brave" the Precipice Walk.

From Dolgellau, take the bridge over the river and turn **right** in the

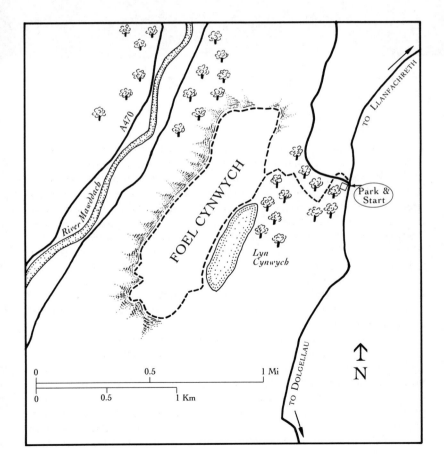

The view west from the Precipice Walk, near Dolgellau

direction of Bala. After just a few hundred yards, fork left onto a minor road signposted for **Llanfachreth** (there is also a sign for the Precipice Walk). Follow this road for about 2 miles (3.2 kilometers), twisting uphill and down through rocky meadows and dark woodlands, until the National Trust car park appears on the left. Park and turn **left** out of the lot onto a minor road. After perhaps 50 yards, fork **left** onto a path leading through a wood. On the other side, follow the path around to the **right**, past a small stone cottage, over a stile, and up a gentle hill. When you reach a meadow at the northern end of **Llyn Cynwych**, a small reservoir, bear **right** following a wall to the foot of **Foel Cynwych**, the hill the Precipice Walk circumnavigates. When the wall turns **right**, follow the path in the same direction and begin the counter-clockwise circuit.

Though the land is privately owned, the National Park Authority has installed small plaques along the path to explain the key features of each vista. The northern edge of the walk provides remarkably clear views up the valley of the River Eden to the Snowdonia range. Then, the path turns south along the west face of the hill, crossing the "precipice" section. Far below is the River Mawddach, and beyond, the western foothills of Cadair Idris. When the path curves around the southern edge of the hill you reach a little belvedere from which you can enjoy perhaps the finest view of the Cadair Idris escarpment in the valley and, off to the right, the Mawddach Estuary and the sea. Finally, the path curves around the hill one last time, skirts the reservoir, and returns to the wall where the circuit began.

A Rainy Day Alternative: Exploring Nineteenth- and Twenty-first-Century Technologies

When Atlantic depressions get stuck off the coast of Ireland, rain can be depressingly persistent and walking in it drudgery. You have two alternatives: (1) get a good murder mystery from the bookstore in

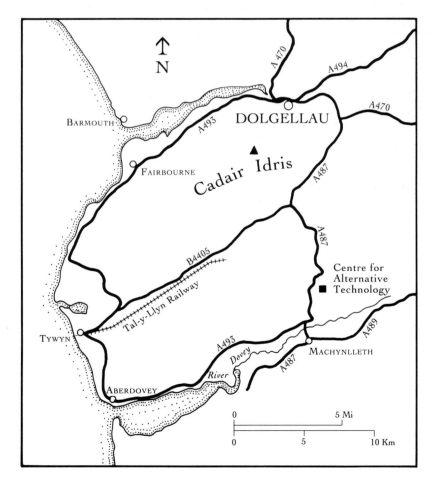

Dolgellau and curl up with a pot of tea or, (2) take a ride on the nineteenth-century narrow-gauge **Tal-y-lyn Railway**, then visit the **Centre for Alternative Technology**.

From Dolgellau, take the **A493** west toward **Fairbourne**, then around the western tip of the Cadair Idris plateau to the coastal town of **Tywyn**. Watch for signs for the steam railway. The Tal-y-Llyn Railway (open daily, Easter through September) was built in 1865 to haul slate from **Abergynolwyn** and was rescued by steam enthusiasts in 1951. The ride up the valley, with the little engine chugging and steam streaming past the antique coaches, is delightfully atmospheric. If the weather breaks, there are forest walks at two of the stops, Dolgoch Falls and Nant Gwernol.

Then continue south on the A493, through **Aberdovey** and up the valley of the River Dovey to the bridge to Machynlleth, but continue **straight** ahead instead of crossing the river, picking up the **A487** back in the direction of Dolgellau. After about 2 miles (3.2 kilometers), watch for signs for the Centre for Alternative Technology (open daily, Easter through September) on the right. The center is a sort of living demonstration project illustrating a wide range of sustainable development systems, including wind and water power, solar energy, organic display gardens, low-energy homes, and other environmentally friendly technology exhibits.

When you leave the center, regain the A487 and head north through Corris and Minffordd to return to Dolgellau.

CREATURE COMFORTS

The same as yesterday.

Traversing the "Desert of Wales"

MACHYNLLETH ◆ LLANDRINDOD WELLS
TEIFI VALLEY ◆ FISHGUARD

- ◆ **A journey into the heart of Mid-Wales**
- ◆ **Over the backbone of Wales on an old drovers' road**
- ◆ **Through the Teifi Valley to Pembrokeshire**

A mountainous wilderness extended on every side, a waste of russet-coloured hills, with here and there a black, craggy summit. No signs of life or cultivation were to be discovered, and the eye might search in vain for a grove or even a single tree.

——George Borrow
Wild Wales, 1862

There is a rippling ribbon of a road in Mid-Wales that traverses a landscape so lonely, a world so wild, that when you are in the midst of it the thought that the phrase "middle of nowhere" originated here is inescapable. Signs of humanity, such as they are—the wretched, roofless stone shell of a shepherd's cottage, a lonely stone bridge—offer cold comfort. Before the Forestry Commission began planting regimented rows of black-green conifers in patches on the hillsides, these moorlands were so empty they were known as "the Desert of Wales," a sodden Sahara of heather, bracken, peat, and stone devoid of settlement and occupied only by the hardiest mountain sheep. Even wildlife is sparse. Often the only thing moving on the barren ground is the dark shadow of a raven quartering the sky, ever watchful for the dead and dying.

Nothing quite so definitively embodies the spiritual divide between upland Wales and the gentle patchwork hills of England as does this old drovers' road over the Cambrian Mountains between Abergwesyn and

Tregaron. It is splendid in its isolation, breathtaking in its wild expanse. There may be no more exhilarating mountain drive anywhere in Wales. But go easy on the ale at lunch.

🚗 TO PEMBROKESHIRE BY WAY OF MID-WALES

Distance: About 175 miles/282 kilometers
Roads: Mostly good primary and secondary roads
Driving Time: All day, but with many stops
Map: Michelin Map #403

The Abergwesyn–Tregaron road is just one of the highlights today—a day of meandering south from the mountains of North Wales to the deeply etched coast of Pembrokeshire along an eastward-curving arc through the deep green valleys, "black-and-white" villages, and Edwardian spas of Mid-Wales. This morning, head south from Dolgellau on the **A470**, turn **right** onto the **A487** at the Cross Foxes Inn, drive through the **Bwlch Llyn Bach**, past the Minffordd Hotel, around the edge of the mining town of **Corris**, and continue south all the way to **Machynlleth**, near the mouth of the River Dovey.

Owain Glyndwr, the leader of the last Welsh rebellion, was named King of Wales in Machynlleth and held his Parliament here in 1404. But his reign was short-lived; within six years, the rebellion was crushed and Glyndwr was hounded into the hills by the English troops. In one of the enduring mysteries of Welsh history, he simply vanished, never to be heard from again.

Today, Machynlleth is a busy market town and the focal point for a relatively large number of artists and craftspeople who have settled in the Afon Dyfi (River Dovey) valley. It has a number of craft shops and galleries, perhaps the most notable of which is the Eagle's Yard Gallery, up a narrow passageway near the Victorian-era clock tower. Here, two nationally renowned artists—woodworker and furniture maker Roger Whitfield and textile artist Alison Morton—have their workshops.

From the center of Machynlleth, take the **A489** in the direction of **Newtown** and **Welshpool** for a few miles, then turn **right**, joining the **A470** and plunging deep into the hilly heart of Mid-Wales. This is the softer side of Wales: meandering streams form deep emerald green valleys, lush hedgerows replace the hard edges of the North's stone walls, oak groves cloak the hills, and wildflowers thrive along the roadside. Pretty as it is, Mid-Wales is still a hard place in which to eke out a living. Distant from nearly everywhere, with no major highways, industry is limited, and scenery notwithstanding, little of the land is arable. What Mid-Wales has in abundance is grass and water: consequently, wool is king here. Sheep cluster in lowland meadows and dot the hills all the

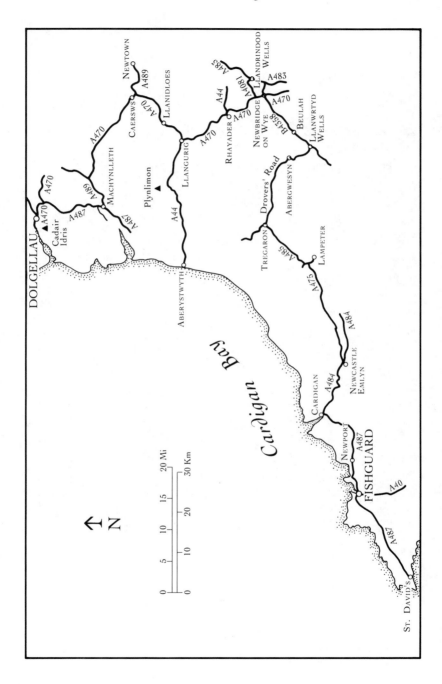

Water-driven, stone-built mill near Machynlleth

way up to the moortops. The streams and waterfalls that seem to fill every cleft in the landscape once supported dozens of old stone mills, both small and large. Many still remain, but have shifted from fulling (a process for shrinking and plumping wool fabrics) to flour milling and, farther south, to weaving.

At the roundabout outside of **Caersws** (pronounced *Care-SOOse*), follow signs for **Llangurig** and the A470. Go through Caersws and

Mid-Wales Sheep Farming

Powys, the county that occupies most of Mid-Wales, produces some 4 percent of the sheep in the entire European Community. Indeed many of Britain's best sheep breeds originated in Mid-Wales. And because the conditions vary sharply over very short distances here, the variety of breeds is enormous. There are black Welsh mountain sheep that thrive in the harshest moorlands and whose rich, dark wool is valued by hand-loom weavers. There are Beulah Speckled Face and Brecknock Hill Cheviots, which produce high-quality fleeces for fine fabrics, but can survive in only a few valleys. There are Clun Forest sheep whose thick forelock pompadours make them look like dwarf Elvis impersonators and whose long wool is so fine it's used for hosiery. And there are many others.

The principal tools of the shepherd's trade are a pair of strong legs for tramping the hillsides (though dirt bikes are increasingly popular), and three or four canny Border collies to herd the dim, edgy sheep. As you travel through Mid- and South Wales, keep an eye out for posters announcing sheepdog trials, contests in which these extraordinary animals compete in complicated herding tasks. The ability of a Border collie to control a skittish herd, often with nothing more than a steely gaze, is astonishing.

over a bridge, then turn **right** at a T-junction, again following the A470 and signs for **Llanidloes**. The road now winds south through the valley of the River Severn—the same Severn you encountered days ago at Iron Bridge Gorge. Off to your right, beyond the dark green hills of the **Hafren Forest**, is the 2,468-foot (752-meter) summit of **Plynlimon**, the highest mountain in Mid-Wales and the source of three great rivers: the **Rhiedol**, which flows west to the sea to **Aberystwyth** (pronounced *aber-UST-wuth*); the **Wye**, which seems to wander through much of Mid- and South Wales before finally reaching the sea below **Chepstow**; and the mighty **Severn**.

This valley is also where you begin seeing the architecture most characteristic of Mid-Wales, the "magpie" houses—half-timber farmhouses with bright white plasterwork and the timbers tricked out in jet black, like a magpie. Llanidloes is full of half-timber houses, many with lovely Victorian shopfronts (the ornate facade of Hamers butcher shop on Long Bridge Street is exceptional). Its best feature, however, is a 1609 timber-framed market hall that sits smack in the middle of the town's main intersection.

After Llanidloes, take the A470 south toward Llangurig. Llangurig isn't as charming as Llanidloes, though it does have a branch of the Craft Centre Cymru, an organization that displays a wide range of traditional Welsh crafts. At the roundabout outside of Llangurig, continue south on the A470, now paralleling the young River Wye, to **Rhyader**. Beyond the clock tower in the middle of Rhayader, stay with the A470 in the direction of **Builth Wells**. The Wye is quite wide here and wanders though a valley hung with pine plantations on the right and thick stands of oak on the left, beneath which the road runs. After about 6 miles (10 kilometers), bear **left** onto the **A4081** to **Llandrindod Wells**.

This spa town is a monument to the Victorian mania for "cures" of all sorts of ailments, real and imagined. It also contains some of the finest examples of ornate Victorian and Edwardian domestic and commercial architecture in the United Kingdom.

Llandrindod was little more than a lonely farmstead in the mid-1700s. That there was a sulphur spring in the area had been known for centuries, but largely ignored. But in the mid-1860s, the completion of the rail line connecting Shrewsbury and Swansea put the town on the map and soon entire families began arriving, first by the hundreds, then by the thousands, to "take the waters" (sixpence a day, all the sulphurous water you could drink). Almost overnight, an elegant spa town developed to cater to the whims of the visitors. Roads, squares, and parks were developed. Hotels and guesthouses were built to every taste and

Black-and-white "magpie" architecture is typical of mid-Wales.

income level. Shops and restaurants flourished.

After you cross the **River Ithon**, the road curves up to a round-about. Go around halfway, then turn **left** up the hill along Park Crescent, past a series of handsome storefronts. At the bandstand at the top of the hill bear **left** and follow signs for the Visitors Centre on Temple Street, just opposite Temple Gardens. You can pick up a walking tour brochure here, but even if you are running short of time (a good bit of challenging driving remains on today's itinerary) at least poke about town by car and take in the extraordinary architecture.

Much of the spirit of Llandrindod Wells is lodged in its buildings and shopfronts. There are grand hotels, such as the Metropole or Glen Usk, with mansard roofs and cupolas, forests of chimneys, and fanciful iron fretwork. Block-long cast-iron arcades are hung with bright flower baskets gracing handsome storefronts (such as the chemist and druggist in Park Crescent). Even mundane businesses like the Automobile Palace—a masterpiece of stone, brick, and tile—have elaborate housings. The Rock Park Spa itself is a curious confection of black-and-yellow brick with a huge iron-and-glass conservatory containing, among other things, a giant chessboard. And spread throughout the town are bandboxes and pavilions, formal gardens and grottos, and promenades that one senses were designed as much for flirtation as for exercise.

While Llandrindod Wells is delightful any time of year, you may want to time your visit for late summer, when the townspeople spend a week going about their business entirely in Victorian costume. For details, write the Festival Office, Old Town Hall, Llandrindod Wells, Powys LD1 5DL.

Leave Llandrindod Wells by the **A483** (past the Automobile Palace) and head south toward Builth Wells. In about 2 miles (3.2 kilometers), watch for a sharp **right** turn (on a bend) onto an unclassified road to **Disserth** and **Newbridge-on-Wye**. Disserth has a tiny thirteenth-century gray stone church in which Llewelyn II's body was hidden briefly after he was killed by King Edward's forces. The little road continues to a T-junction with the **B4358** from Llandrindod. Turn **left** here and continue into Newbridge to a second T-junction with the A470. The B4358 jogs **right** here for a short distance, then **left** over the River Wye toward **Beulah** and **Llanwrtyd** (pronounced *thlan-WUR-tud*) **Wells**. At the T-junction with the A483, turn **right** in the direction of **Llandovery**. At Llanwrtyd Wells (buy petrol if you have less than a quarter tank at this point), cross the bridge in the center of town and turn **right** at the church onto an unclassified road to **Abergwesyn** (pronounced *aber-GOO-ezin*).

Almost immediately the road becomes single-track, widening in some places, narrowing in others, following the dictates of the landscape. Ancient hawthorn hedges edge the road and there are one or two lonely farmsteads up on the slopes. The **River Irfon**—sometimes a torrent, sometimes a series of quiet pools—flows below on the right. Then, quite suddenly, the landscape flattens and a broad meadow opens ahead. When you reach Abergwesyn—little more than a clutch of cottages—turn **left** in the direction of **Tregaron**, following the route of an old livestock drovers' road.

Once you cross the cattle barrier (a grid of metal bars set into the pavement) outside of the village, you leave the civilized world behind. The road steepens, climbing higher and higher under a canopy of gnarled, ancient oak trees. Soon the valley becomes a canyon and the narrow road climbs up the canyon wall, careening around rocky outcrops and galloping along a lumpy roadbed. The steep slope seems to drop directly from your left fender to the furious river far below, and there is no barrier to protect you if your attention slips.

You are deep within **Abergwesyn Common** now, a National Trust property. Bracken and acid-tolerant grasses soften the texture of the land but do little to ease the bleakness. Ahead, the river cuts through a rocky chasm. The road—a thin sliver of modernity in a primitive landscape—dodges back and forth across the river several times, then squeezes between a cliff and a pair of old cedar trees and begins climbing (on a 1:4 gradient) up a series of switchbacks called the "Devil's Staircase." Then, after traversing a dark conifer plantation, it pitches downhill again, just as steeply, into a long valley, with trees draping the left flank and a wilderness of flaming yellow gorse and shiny green bracken cloaking the right. At the intersection at the bottom, keep to the **right** for Tregaron. Once again the road ascends the steep slope of a desolate valley, inching around peek-a-boo corners and bumping along roller-coaster ridges. The only sign of life anywhere is one lonely stone farmhouse far below by the river. After the next bridge, look to the right, across the valley, where a magnificent cataract flings itself over the lip of the moortop, then drops through a series of gossamer cascades into the valley far below.

Now the road zigzags through a series of lonely intersections (continue to follow signs to Tregaron), crosses another river, passes another waterfall, and climbs another hill into yet another forest until, at last, a sylvan valley opens up before you toward the west. Signs of habitation—a few farms, some tilled fields, livestock other than mountain sheep, clusters of stone cottages—appear as you draw closer to Tregaron.

From the center of Tregaron, cross the bridge and turn **left** onto the **A485** in the direction of **Lampeter**. The countryside here is soft, green, and domesticated—a far cry from the wilds of Abergwesyn Common. The scene is dominated by the **River Teifi**, which curves gently southwest to the sea from its source in **Cors Goch Caron**, a 4-mile-long (6.4-kilometer) wetland and nature reserve north of Tregaron. This is the land of **Ceredigion** (pronounced *Care-a-DIG-ion*), a 1,500-year-

Drovers' Roads

From the Middle Ages until the turn of the century, Tregaron was a major gathering point for livestock farmers throughout west-central Wales. After midnight on a given Sunday (herding was prohibited on the Sabbath), they put their livestock in the care of the drovers, the "cowboys" of Wales. Then, the drovers and their corgi dogs began herding the livestock east over the Cambrian Mountains (along the route you just took), bypassing roads to avoid paying tolls and to save the animals' hooves. For centuries they drove the animals all the way to London, later as far as Brecon, and, after the mid-1800s, to the rail station at Llanwrtyd Wells.

Cattle and sheep were the mainstay of the business, with one drover (and his dogs) for every 1,200 sheep, ten drovers for every 200 cattle. They also herded turkeys and chickens to market—typically tarring the birds' feet to protect them from the rugged terrain—and even pigs, their trotters outfitted with little leather booties.

Animals were not the only items entrusted to the drovers; they were commissioned by farmers to carry rents to landowners in London, pay local taxes, and purchase goods unavailable in western Wales. Given their multiple responsibilities, trustworthiness was crucial. Not surprisingly, many drovers later established banks. Lloyd's Bank, for example, was established by a drover from Llandovery.

old Celtic principality that stretches along the Welsh coast from the River Dovey at Machynlleth to the Teifi. Isolated from the rest of the world by the rampart of the Cambrian Mountains, it has remained thinly populated, pastoral, and unspoiled for centuries.

At Lampeter, stay on the west side of the river and switch to the **A475**, continuing down the valley toward **Newcastle Emlyn**. At a stop sign marking the intersection with the **A486**, turn **right** for a few yards, then **left**, continuing southwest on the A475. (The road here has some nasty curves, so take the warning signs seriously.) At **Aberaran**, just outside of Newcastle Emlyn, the A475 ends. Follow signs for the **A484**, which continues along the river toward **Cardigan**.

Just outside of Cardigan, watch for signs for the **A487** to **Fishguard** and take the new bypass over the river, with the city of Cardigan just off to your right as you cross the bridge. (**Note:** If you are traveling between November and Easter and need help with accommodations in the Fishguard area, drive into Cardigan and follow signs to the year-round Tourist Information Centre on Bath House Road; the Fishguard branch is seasonal.) At the roundabout on the other side of the bridge, the A487 climbs up to the coastal ridge and you are treated to a series of sweeping views of Cardigan Bay, with the **Preseli Hills** rising off to your left. The coastline here is deeply etched and most of the settlements nestle in the shelter of narrow valleys cut by streams as they tumble to the sea. **Newport**, a slightly touristy but well-kept village of stone houses and shops, is a good example.

The approach to **Fishguard** from this direction is especially dramatic. The A487 winds around a headland and drops sharply into **Aber Gwaun**, Fishguard's "Lower Town," a tiny fishing village gathered around a cove at the mouth of the **Gwaun River**. The road squeezes past the handful of stone cottages and fishing shacks arrayed along the shore, then climbs up the opposite headland and enters Fishguard's busy "Upper Town."

CREATURE COMFORTS
Daily Bed

The spectacular cliffs and beaches of the Pembrokeshire coast draw holidaymakers from all over Britain, so booking ahead for your two nights here is a good idea anytime in the summer. While there are lots of choices, the spirit of Pembrokeshire is captured nicely in two very different B&B establishments. Roy and Elaine Ayers's **Cefn-Y-Dre** ("the big house behind the town") is an ivy-draped early-nineteenth-century country house set amid pretty gardens on a hill above Fishguard. There are three charming rooms upstairs (one twin, two doubles). In addition, Roy, a painter and instructor who studied at the Royal Academy, has set up a fully equipped studio in the adjoining coach house to cater to visiting artists. Elaine is a skilled chef and puts on a splendid three-course dinner each evening (for which you must book ahead). Rates are competitive with other B&Bs in the area. From just north of the roundabout in the center of Fishguard, take Hamilton Street up the hill to the edge of town. Where the road turns sharply right, continue straight ahead, up a lane with a NO THROUGH ROAD sign, and a modest slate CEFN-Y-DRE plaque. For reservations, write Cefn-Y-Dre, Fishguard, Dyfed SA65 9QS, or phone (0348) 874499.

A completely different option is June and Mike Wynn's **Trewallter Farm**, a forty-one-acre organic farm a few miles south of Fishguard beyond **Mathry**, close to the coast. (Western Wales is Britain's largest center for the production of organic vegetables, fruits, and dairy products.) Their farmhouse accommodation is simpler than Cefn-Y-Dre, but the welcome from the Jersey dairy cow, the pig and piglets, the

The harbor of Fishguard, in Pembrokeshire

ducks, the chickens, and the guinea fowl is memorable. Two newly decorated rooms (one twin, one double) share a bath upstairs. From Fishguard's central roundabout, head downhill toward the ferry port of Goodwick and then take the A487 south. A few miles south of Mathry, watch for a sign on the right. For reservations, write Trewallter Farm, Mathry, Haverfordwest, Dyfed SA62 5JQ, or phone (0348) 837824.

In addition, between Fishguard and St. David's there are three youth hostels close to the coast; for addresses and phone numbers, consult the YHA guide listed in Further Reading. For other accommodation options, consult the other books in Further Reading, or the Wales Tourist Board catalogs referred to in earlier Daily Bed sections. For local information, write the Tourist Information Centre, 4 Hamilton Street, Fishguard, Dyfed SA56 9HL, and request local listings.

Daily Bread

In addition to a range of choices in Fishguard, there are a few excellent country pubs and restaurants in smaller villages south of town. Ask your hosts for their recommendations. The Wynns, for example, have a notebook of menus from restaurants in the area, with their candid reviews.

In the Footsteps of St. David

ST. DAVID'S HEAD ◆ PRESELI HILLS

- ◆ **A morning visit to St. David's Cathedral and the Bishop's Palace**
- ◆ **An afternoon walk around windswept St. David's Head**
- ◆ **An alternative drive among Pembrokeshire's most ancient archaeological sites**

(Pembrokeshire is) neyther perfect square, nor long, nor round but shaped with divers Corners, some sharpe, some obtuse, but in most places . . . bendinge inwarde as doth the Moon at her decreasing.

——George Owen, 1603

*F*rom the summit of Carn Llidi, a 600-foot knob of naked granite high above Wales's westernmost point, 5,000 years of Welsh history are spread out like an exotic feast upon a lumpy picnic blanket.

To the west, where the rugged cliffs of St. David's Head meet the angry Atlantic, you can just make out the weathered remains of an Iron Age fortress, defended from the mainland by a massive stone rampart, now crumbled and cloaked in heather and lichen. To the northwest, when the sun is low and shadows are long, the outlines of prehistoric field systems are visible, ghosting just beneath the emerald turf between the summit and the sea. Off to the northeast, the black volcanic skeleton of the southwest peninsula pokes through the smooth skin of the coastal plateau. To the southeast, tucked into the gentle folds of the valley of the little River Alun, sits St. David's Cathedral, a purplish gray medieval gem at the center of a cluster of white cottages gathered around its holy precincts like shelter-seeking sheep. And due south, just behind the gleaming strand of Whitesand Bay and marked by only a modest stone plaque, are the remains of a dark, narrow chapel dedicated to St. Patrick, who conceived on this site the dream of converting Ireland to Catholicism.

On a changeable day, with the wind breaking the sky into shards of gray and blue, the bright optimism of the early Christian saints and the dark visions of the pagan Celts coexist uneasily. Old and new, primitive and sublime jostle for the soul of Wales like the patches of sun and shadow that drift this way and that across the stony soil. And from this vantage point it is unclear, even today, which holds dominion.

IN THE HOLY HOLLOW OF ST. DAVID'S

It is said he was born at the height of a violent storm, and that a sweet freshwater spring gushed forth on the moment of his birth. It is said he lived only on bread, vegetables, and water, wore animal skins, walked barefoot, and stood for hours neck-deep in icy water while praying. It is said too that he could pull a plow as well as an ox and that he invented rugby, the Welsh national sport, by tossing boulders unearthed in the process.

He is the patron saint of Wales, St. David (*Dewi Sant* in Welsh), and little about him is certain. He appears to have been born at the beginning of the sixth century during the golden age of the Celtic saints, when devout and determined missionaries spread the Christian gospel from Wales to Brittany, Cornwall, and Ireland.

By A.D. 530—nearly half a century *before* Pope Gregory dispatched St. Augustine to convert England—David had established his monastery. Though his followers tried to hide the church they built in his name in a leafy hollow, marauding Vikings sacked it repeatedly. It was not until A.D. 1174, in the relatively peaceful period after the Norman invasion, that work began on a great cathedral in the same sacred swale. By then, David had been canonized by Pope Calixitus II and the cult of St. David was thriving. (In the curious calculus of medieval Catholicism, two pilgrimages to St. David's were worth one to Rome; three, worth one to Jerusalem.) Money flowed in, and in 1280 work began on a bishop's palace. The opulent final product, completed in the middle of the next century, would have appalled David and his pious, celibate, self-abnegating followers. It was richly decorated, topped with spires, and surrounded by a crenelated wall. Appropriately, perhaps, the palace didn't last; after the Reformation, Bishop Barlow stripped the palace's lead roofing and gave it to his five daughters for their dowries. But the splendid cathedral remains, and it is our first destination this morning.

From the center of Fishguard, drive downhill to **Goodwick** and turn **left** at the roundabout onto the **A487** in the direction of **St. David's**, 15 miles (24 kilometers) to the southwest.

Because it has a cathedral, St. David's is officially a city, but it's really just a small village of shops, holiday homes, guesthouses, pubs, and restaurants. Most of the pilgrims to St. David's these days are sun-worshippers on their way to nearby beaches. The cathedral is in the center of the village, but it is invisible, tucked away in a sheltering vale below the tiny triangular town "square." From the outside, the cathe-

The cathedral of St. David, nested in its secluded hollow, with the ruined Bishop's Palace in the foreground

dral is modest, even austere—a simple sandstone cruciform. But the interior is a revelation. The easily worked stone is richly decorated. Ten great piers march up the nave and splay upward to support an intricately carved roof of Irish oak. Curiously, the floor slopes sharply uphill toward the altar—allegedly to bring worshippers closer to God, but more likely because the bedrock below was unforgiving. Behind the altar, a casket holds bones believed to be those of St. David, discovered only in the last century during a restoration. It is an intimate cathedral, with that stolid permanence characteristic of the best of Romanesque architecture.

Cupped in the same natural bowl as the cathedral is the ruined bishop's palace, a romantic jumble of wall fragments, arches, and empty window frames. For the best view of the entire complex, walk up the leafy lane near the museum entrance to the hillside opposite the town. A road runs around the rim of the valley, and there are places along the wall from which to take pictures. Then follow the road back downhill, past the little duck-filled River Alun, and around to the stairs that lead back up to the square. The Tourist Information Centre on the square has a good exhibit on the history and landscape of Pembrokeshire (now incorporated in the Welsh county of Dyfed).

Then, have lunch in the village (or, better yet, shop for a picnic), and head back in the direction from which you came, on the A487. On the western edge of town, turn **left**, then **left** again onto the **B4583**, and follow signs to **Whitesand Bay**. There is a large car park above the beach.

☊ A CIRCUIT OF ST. DAVID'S HEAD

Distance: 4 miles/6.4 kilometers; allow 2–2.5 hours. The walk may be extended an additional 9 miles/14.5 kilometers, depending on route
Difficulty: Mostly easy; short climb to summit of Carn Llidi
Total Elevation Gain: 595 feet/181 meters
Gear: Walking shoes or sneakers will do; rain gear
Map: Ordnance Survey Landranger #157

A circuit of St. David's Head combines sweeping coastal vistas and ancient mysteries in roughly equal portions. It's hard to know which conditions are best for this walk—a warm summer's day with the perfume of wildflowers, the buzz of honeybees, and the distant delighted cries of beachcombing children filling the hazy air, or a screaming gale with herring gulls careening across an angry sky, rain lashing the ancient rocks, and the ocean heaving spume high above the cliffs, riming the heather and gorse that cloaks the coastal plateau. Of course, here on Wales's westernmost point, it's not uncommon to experience both in the same afternoon.

Begin at the steps in the northwest corner of the car park at Whitesand Bay and follow the well-marked footpath toward the end of the beach. It's an oddly disorienting beginning: On your left, surfers in neon-bright wetsuits ride long green cresting swells to the shore. On your right, a short sandy path weaves through the beach grass to a marker stone that says, UNDERNEATH LIES A CHAPEL DEDICATED TO ST. PATRICK, BUILT 6TH TO IOTH CENTURY, EXCAVATED 1921. Pembrokeshire is full of time warps like this.

That St. Patrick departed for Ireland from St. David's is almost certain. Historians believe he was a Pembrokeshire man, and St. David's had been a staging point on a trade route between England and Ireland

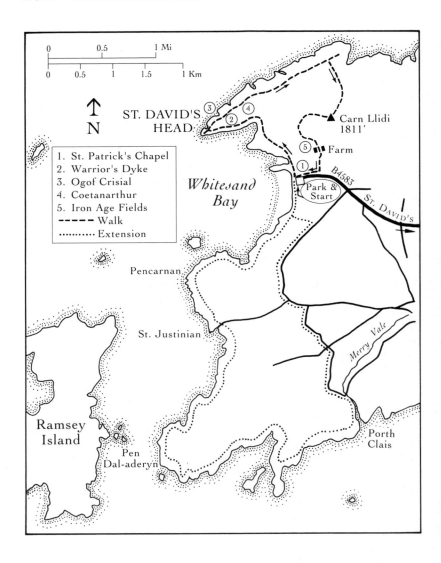

since the Bronze Age. By the sixth century, St. Patrick's missionary zeal would already have passed into legend and it was not uncommon for small cell-like chapels to be built along the coast where seamen could offer prayers to a favorite saint for a safe journey or give thanks for a safe return.

You're on the **Pembrokeshire Coast Path** now, a 160-mile-long (257-kilometer) maintained footpath that is the main artery of **Pembrokeshire Coast National Park**, Britain's smallest and longest na-

High above the Pembrokeshire coast at St. David's Head

tional park, established in 1952. The path soon reaches a promontory with the daunting Welsh name of **Trwynhwrddyn** ("the ram's nose"— pronounced *truin-HOR-theen*). Ahead is another, much smaller beach teeming with tidal pools and ringed with towering multilayered cliffs of purplish slate, yellow sandstone, and gleaming bands of quartz. The rock here has been uplifted so that the layers are nearly vertical, and the harder rocks march straight out into the deepening bay like a giant's handrail until they disappear beneath the waves.

Off to the right of the path, nearly buried in bramble and heather, you can just make out the outlines of Iron Age field systems, among the best-preserved in Britain. Large boulders form the base of the crumbling boundary walls, with smaller stones piled on top, as if the prehistoric farmers had simply tossed them there as they labored to increase the ratio of soil to stone in these unpromising fields.

The footpath now curves gently uphill, following the rim of the cliffs. The ground here is blanketed in wildflowers. There are great drifts of sea thrift, their clear pink blossoms bobbing on the breeze. Deeper pink campion flourishes close to the well-beaten path, as does yarrow, with its feathery leaves and foaming white blossoms.

Next, the path cuts across the base of the triangular point of **Penddedwen**, through acres of knee-high heather and yolk yellow gorse, and descends into the little valley at the head of **Porthmelgan Bay**. On either bank of the little stream, in a cleft sheltered from the wind, spearmint grows, its delicate flowers adding touches of lavender to the landscape.

Westward, the path climbs to **St. David's Head** itself. With its faintly weird volcanic outcroppings and incessant wind, this lonely outpost on the edge of the great beyond is fierce and unfriendly, so it comes as something of a shock to stumble upon unmistakable signs of settlement. The first sign is **Warrior's Dyke**, a 75-foot-wide (23-meter) Iron Age ditch and stone barrier that runs 200 feet (61 meters) from cliff to cliff across the base of the headland. With a height archaeologists estimate at 15 feet (5 meters), it would have been a formidable defense. Beyond the wall, poking through the wiry sea grass, is the second sign: the foundations of a small 2,000-year-old settlement. Though the primitive huts shelter in the lee of a massive ledge, there is nothing inviting about this site. Exposed to raging Atlantic gales, battered by the perpetual thunder of the surf below, and bereft of either soil to grow food or water to drink, life in this stronghold would have been brutal at best.

But what a view they had. From the huge slabs of rock at the westernmost tip of St. David's Head—rock more than 600 million years old—the seascape is stunning. The Romans called this place Octopitarium Promontarium, "the promontory of the eight perils," and the perils are all too obvious. On the western horizon, the rocky islets known as the **Bishops and Clerks** rise like hungry teeth from the foaming green sea. Closer in, anchored in a riptide-wracked sound between **Ramsey Island** and the mainland, are the vicious pinnacles of **Carregtrai**, **Carreg-gareiliog**, **Gwahan**, **the Horse**, and the aptly named **Bitches**—seamen's nightmares all. Behind you, the coastal margin climbs sharply upward to the naked, knobby crest of **Carn Llidi**. The whole panorama is breathtaking.

Return now to the main path, bear **left**, and continue up the exposed northern coast. Just beyond the dyke, you climb another headland and pass **Ogof Crisial**, "crystal cave," a narrow gash in the cliff veined with a yellow quartz known locally as "St. David's Diamonds." Just beyond the head of this gash, watch for a side path to the **right** that picks its way across the rock-strewn headland, eventually leading to **Coetanarthur**, "Arthur's Quoit," a 5,500-year-old New Stone Age burial chamber. The primitive quoit, typical of chambers that litter the west coast of Wales, consists of a thick 12-foot-long granite slab supported by one upright stone (three or four originally). The entire construction would once have been covered with earth, but time, wind, and water have long since removed the shroud.

The coast path now continues along the cliff edge to another headland, marked by a cairn. This side of the peninsula is completely carpeted with bell and ling heather, occasionally interrupted by splashes of blue bellflowers and yellow primroses. Ignore the first path branching off to the right and continue north on the coast path. When you reach a broad, grassy path angling away from the cliffs, turn **right** and follow it uphill along the right side of a stone-walled enclosure. From here, the climb up Carn Llidi is moderately steep but short, only a few hundred feet.

From Carn Llidi's frost-fractured granite summit there are spectacular views of much of southwest Wales. To the north, the coastal plateau stretches to Strumble Head, with its white lighthouse tirelessly blinking four flashes at ten-second intervals. Beyond, on a clear afternoon, the mountains of Snowdonia hang above the curve of Cardigan Bay like violet clouds. Inland, the Preseli Hills slope up from the coast, their smooth flanks broken by a line of dark granite tors like the erosion-exposed, fossilized ribs of some great, long-buried beast. To the south, beyond St. David's, St. Bride's Bay sweeps in a broad green arc, first left along Newgale Sands, then right, out to St. Ann's Head and the nature reserve on Skomer Island. At your feet, to the west, St. David's Head thrusts itself into the churning sea. From this height, with the sun low on the western horizon, the islands in Ramsey Sound look like ships anchored in a sea of shimmering mercury. Beyond Ramsey Island, South Bishop lighthouse warns ships away from the Eight Perils and beyond that, 18 miles (29 kilometers) from land, Small's Light, the world's most remote manned lighthouse, keeps its lonely watch—a very small light in a very large sea. Finally, far to the west, the Wicklow Hills of Ireland appear and disappear like a blue mirage at the very edge of the earth itself.

The route down is easier than the way up. Pick your way across the granite slabs to the **west** of the summit and descend to the ruins of a World War I hydrophone station (an updated "warrior's dyke"), then follow concrete steps around the side of the hill. Where the steps end, a clear path leads downhill between walled fields edged with blackberry bramble and soon reaches a farmyard. Continue downhill along a lane and eventually regain the B4583. Turn **right** to return to the car park at Whitesand Bay.

If the day is still young and your enthusiasm still high, consider extending this coast walk to the gentler side of the peninsula, south of Whitesand Bay. From the southern end of the car park, follow the coast path above the beach, around the headland of **Pencarnan**, to the tiny port of **St. Justinian**. The port is named after the saint who, according to yet another legend, made Ramsey an island. Apparently finding life at St. David's monastery insufficiently austere, Justinian walked to Ramsey over a land bridge, then severed the isthmus with his axe, leaving the Bitches behind as fragments. But Justinian's followers found life too hard and, somewhat uncharitably, cut off his head. At that point, Justinian, now thoroughly annoyed, picked up his head, walked across the water to the mainland, and had himself buried in the chapel (now a ruin) near the little port that bears his name. You no longer have to

walk on water to get to and from Ramsey Island, the home of the largest breeding colony of gray seals in Wales and one of several island
nature reserves in the Pembrokeshire National Park. Weather permit-
ting, boats to Ramsey leave from the lifeboat station at Porthstinian at
10:00 A.M. and 11:00 A.M., from Easter through September, returning
again at 3:15 P.M. Boat tours around the island depart at 11:00 A.M.
and 2:00 P.M.
    From Pencarnan, the path continues around the peninsula, finally
turning east at **Pen Dal-aderyn**. Following the ragged clifftop, you
soon reach **Porth Clais** and the mouth of the little River Alun. At the
head of the cove are two lanes. The one branching right follows the
river up "Merry Vale" to St. David's. The one to the left zigzags across
the peninsula and connects with several public footpaths that will return you to Whitesand Bay.

🚗 AN ALTERNATIVE AFTERNOON
AMONG THE ANCIENTS

Distance: About 60 miles/97 kilometers (returning to Fishguard)
Roads: Many minor country lanes
Driving Time: The balance of the afternoon
Map: Ordnance Survey Landranger #157 and #145

    The strange and often lonely landscape of Pembrokeshire is littered
with ancient sites, some prehistoric, some early Celtic, most in quite
spectacular locations. If a walk around St. David's Head isn't in the
cards this afternoon, head for the back roads and drive into the misty,
distant past.
    From St. David's Cathedral, return to Fishguard by the **A487**, bear
left at the roundabout in Upper Town, toward Cardigan, but turn
right immediately onto the **B4313**, signposted for **Cwm Gwaun**. The
B4313 runs high along a ridge with wide views across the open land to
the rocky heights of the Preseli Hills away to the left. Ignore the first
left turn, opposite a pub, and continue along the ridge for another mile,
then bear **left** downhill to Pontfaen. Cross the river, the **Afon Gwaun**,
and follow the narrow road upriver along the left bank.
    The lush wooded valley of the River Gwaun would inspire superla-
tives in any location, but here amid the bleak, windblown moorlands of
the Preselis, it is a small miracle. Cwm Gwaun was cut deep into the
surrounding plateau by torrents of glacial meltwater during the last Ice
Age and it has been maintained ever since by the little river that drains
the moorlands far upstream. In the spring, the gently twisting valley is
carpeted with primroses and bluebells, and daisies and buttercups
sparkle in the emerald watermeadows in midsummer. Oak and syca-
more trees arch overhead, dappling the roadbed. It has a queer, fairy-

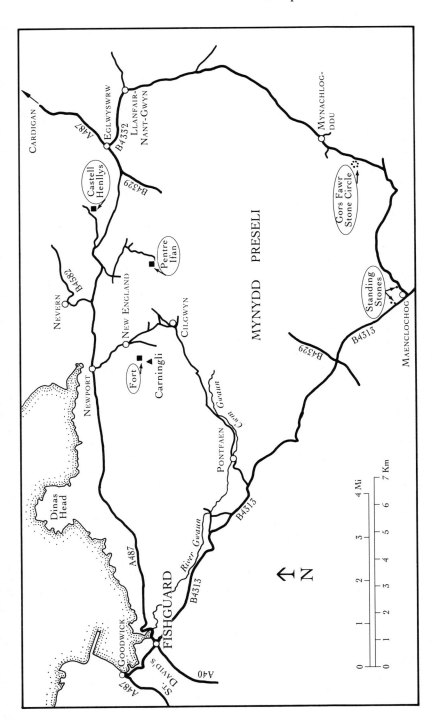

land quality; driving through the vale, you half expect to come upon a knot of elves dancing in a sunlit glade.

Continue up the Cwm Gwaun until the road crosses the river and climbs uphill. At the intersection at the top, turn **left** in the direction of **Trefdraeth** (Welsh for Newport). At the next junction, turn **left** again for Newport and climb high onto **Carningli Common**.

With its eerie, isolated standing stones and Iron Age hill fort, Carningli is well worth a brief detour. A little more than 1 mile (1.6 kilometers) from the tiny hamlet of **Cilgwyn**, at an intersection curiously named **New England**, watch for the public footpath across acres of heather and gorse to the hilltop. The views from the rock-strewn summit are magnificent. At your feet, the little town of Newport sits above the estuary of the **Afon Nyfer** (River Nevern), which wanders down from the east through gently rolling hills. To the northeast, Cardigan Bay sweeps away into the distance beyond **Cemaes Head**. To the southwest, the rocky coast bulges at **Dinas Head**, curves in toward Fishguard Bay, then out again to **Strumble Head**, and on to St. David's Head. Behind you to the south is the long, smooth profile of **Mynydd Preseli**—bleak, barren, uninhabited.

From New England, continue into Newport. Turn **right** into Market Street, then **right** again at the next block to rejoin the A487 heading toward Cardigan. About 1.5 miles (2.4 kilometers) out of town, watch for a **left** turn onto the **B4582**, signposted for **Nevern**. The road dips downhill into the valley of the Afon Nyfer, passes an ivy-covered, flower-bedecked old pub, skips over a medieval stone bridge, then curves around into **Nevern**. Tiny Nevern, long a stop on the pilgrims' route to St. David's, is home to two extraordinary monuments, both on the grounds of its little parish church. The first is the **Vitalianus Stone**, carved with inscriptions in both Latin and the ancient Celtic Ogham tongue and thought to have been erected in the fifth century as a memorial to a Celtic soldier in the employ of the Romans. Near one corner of the church is the second monument, the 13-foot (4-meter) **Great Cross of St. Brynach**. (A contemporary of St. David, St. Brynach was, according to legend, in the habit of communing with the angels on Carningli). Dating from the tenth century and one of only three in Wales, its intricate carving has a strong Irish influence—more evidence of the common religious heritage of Celtic Wales and Ireland. (While in Nevern, you may also want to take in a demonstration of traditional farmhouse cheese-making at Nevern Dairy—see Creature Comforts below.)

Leaving Nevern, backtrack to the A487 and turn **left**. After 1 mile (1.6 kilometers), take the first **right** up a narrow hawthorn-lined lane. At the first intersection, turn **left** and, after another mile, take the first **right**, continuing uphill. Bear **right** at the first fork and **left** at the second, and stop at the little car park signposted for **Pentre Ifan**.

The Stonehenge Connection

The flanks of the strange, stubby Preseli Hills contain dozens of megaliths—standing stones, stone circles, and stone rows—built 4,000 to 5,000 years ago by a people who clearly held this landscape to have mythic power. But in 1921 a discovery was made that suggested this power extended far beyond Wales, deep into prehistoric England. In that year, the geologist H. H. Thomas concluded that the massive stones that form the inner ring of Stonehenge were "bluestones," a coarse volcanic rock found only in the Preselis. How did they get there? Archaeologists theorize that the 4-ton stones were hauled overland on rollers, then rafted across Bristol Bay and up the rivers of western England, then rolled again to their final resting place on Wiltshire's Salisbury Plain. Technically feasible, it would have been a stupendous undertaking nonetheless. Geologists, on the other hand, think the stones were carried to England more prosaically, by glaciers—yet there is no other evidence of the glacier. And so, like so much about Stonehenge, the mystery remains.

Pentre Ifan, erected between 3000 and 4000 B.C., is said to be the finest Neolithic dolmen quoit burial chamber in Wales. Situated on a windy slope high above Cardigan Bay, Pentre Ifan is an aesthetic as well as an engineering marvel. The massive, 16-foot (5-meter) capstone is perched more than 7 feet above the ground, supported almost delicately by several tapered megaliths. Several more upright outlier stones stand silent vigil nearby. The whole complex originally would have been cov-

Massive, yet delicate—Pentre Fan, the finest neolithic burial quoit in Wales

ered by an earth and stone cairn some 120 feet (37 meters) long pointing downhill.

Retrace your route now back to the A487 and turn **right** in
the direction of Cardigan, but turn **left** almost immediately thereafter for **Castell Henllys**, an Iron Age settlement nestled in a wooded
valley just off the highway. The site, privately owned, has been
reconstructed to provide a sense of life some 2,000 years ago, com-

plete with round thatched huts, stables, a forge, and farming and crafts typical of the period.

Return to the A487 and turn **left**. At the tongue-tying village of **Eglwyswrw** (pronounced *egg-loose-OO-roo*), turn **right** onto the **B4332** and, after about 1.5 miles (2.4 kilometers), turn **right** again onto an unclassified road through **Llanfair-Nant-Gwyn**, heading south toward Mynydd Preseli. Ignore the turn to the left toward **Crymych** and continue straight ahead. The narrow road climbs steeply up the bleak eastern flanks of Mynydd Preseli and soon reaches a plateau. At the village of **Mynachlog-ddu** (pronounced *mun-ACH-log-thee*), turn **right** at the T-junction, then **left** at a fork. Less than a mile ahead, Preseli's best stone circle, **Gors Fawr**, materializes on the right where the plateau widens. Like so many megalithic monuments, little is known about why Gors Fawr and the several standing stones scattered about this windswept tableland were erected. Still, it is a moving, if mute, testimony to human commitment that so much manpower and effort should have been devoted to so mysterious a task.

From Gors Fawr, continue south on the same minor road until you reach a T-junction (near **Llangolman**) and turn **right**. Follow this minor road west along the foot of Mynydd Preseli to **Maenclochog**, and turn **right** onto the **B4313**. Then, simply follow this road northwest (past more standing stones) all the way back to Fishguard and home.

CREATURE COMFORTS
Daily Bed

The same as yesterday.

Daily Bread

One of the joys of picnicking in Britain is the opportunity to sample local foods. Here in Pembrokeshire, put **local farmhouse cheeses** on your shopping list. Partly because of the growth the organic farming movement here, partly because milk production quotas have forced dairy farmers to produce higher-value products, and partly because Pembrokeshire just seems to attract farm families with an entrepreneurial spirit, small farms in southwest Wales today produce more than thirty different kinds of cheese. They range from the mild, crumbly Caerphilly (the best-known) to tangy cheddars, buttery Goudas (from a farm run by a relocated Dutch couple), and several goat cheeses. Some are plain, some flavored with herbs, still others lightly smoked. A small dairy in Nevern that produces cheddar welcomes visitors (open 9:00 A.M. to 5:00 P.M., Monday through Friday all year and Sunday July through September). You can get a list of other cheese makers from any Tourist Information Centre.

Across "Little England West of Wales"

FISHGUARD ◆ LAUGHARNE
CARREG CENNEN ◆ BRECON

- ◆ **A drive along the medieval "Lansker Lines"**
- ◆ **A detour to Dylan Thomas's boathouse home**
- ◆ **An exploration of the most romantic castle in Wales**
- ◆ **An afternoon visit to the Brecon Beacons Mountain Centre**

In Wales there are jewels
To gather, but with the eye
Only. A hill lights up
Suddenly; a field trembles
With colour and goes out
In its turn; in one day
You can witness the extent
Of the spectrum and grow rich
With looking . . .

—R. S. Thomas
Selected Poems 1946–1968

You come upon it as in a dream. One moment you are twisting and turning down high-hedged lanes between meadows gilded with buttercups. The next, you round a bend and there—high above you upon a pillar of stone—is Carreg Cennen Castle.

It is an eagle's aerie of a castle, a forbidding fortress rising to the sky from the summit of a sheer limestone cliff hundreds of feet high. As you approach, your imagination races ahead, summoning roiling black clouds, crackling bolts of lightning, and a howling wind. The scene demands tempest and tumult: the crash of armor, the thunder of horses' hooves, the sizzle of arrows slicing the air, the cries of dying men.

There are some 400 castles in Wales, but many have about them a

Carreg Cennen, Wales's most romantic castle, seems to have grown out of the limestone cliff upon which it perches.

kind of museum-piece preciousness. Not Carreg Cennen. Broken and battered by centuries of sieges, Carreg Cennen carries its wounds nobly, like an aging war veteran. It is a magnificent relic, but only one of many high points in today's drive across South Wales to the Brecon Beacons National Park.

🚗 DRIVING EAST ALONG THE "LANDSKER"

Distance: 120 miles/193 kilometers, not including side trips
Roads: The A40 most of the way; some side trips on minor roads
Driving Time: All day
Map: Michelin Map #403

Trace a line on your road map across Pembrokeshire from Newgale (near St. David's) eastward to Amroth (near Tenby). Then look carefully at the map. Towns north of this line have decidedly Welsh names: Croes Goch, Maenclochog, Llandysilio, and the like. Towns to the south, on the other hand, have very different names: Newgale, Wolfsdale, Castlemartin, Pembroke, and Templeton, to name just a few. You've just discovered "Little England West of Wales."

When the Normans moved into Wales, more than two decades after conquering England in 1066, they arrived by ship and came ashore in the protected deep harbors of south Pembrokeshire. Gradually, they moved north and east, building castles as they went: first, simple ones of earth and wood, and later—at Pembroke, Manorbier, Tenby and other towns—massive stone fortifications. Having driven the Welsh from the land, the Normans were obliged to import Flemish and Anglo-Saxon workers to till the rich soil. Soon the manorial settlement pattern they had already established in England emerged in this remote corner of Wales as well: tightly clustered villages, open field systems, and tall churches sturdy enough to serve defensive as well as devotional duties. But the colonization stopped roughly 15 miles (24 kilometers) inland, at an unofficial east–west frontier called the Landsker, or "land scar." To the north was "the Welshry," a bleak, thinly settled landscape of bogs and moors. To the south were the lush farmlands of "the Englishry." Language subjugated landscape; Pen-fro (which means "land's end" in Welsh) was Anglicized into Pembroke; Dinbych ("little fortress") became Denbigh, and later Tenby. Soon, virtually every hamlet south of the Landsker had an English name; the speaking of Welsh was frowned upon, even banned. Today, fewer people speak Welsh here than anywhere else in Wales.

The **A40** follows the Landsker line fairly closely between **Haverfordwest** and **Carmarthen** and is your principal route east this morning. If you have been staying in Fishguard, the A40 runs due south across open moorland and pastures to Haverfordwest, but the coastal route from St. David's, the **A487**, is more attractive. Coming out of St. David's, the road clings to the coastline, then dives down into a narrow cleft in the cliff side to enter the little village of **Solva**. A picturesque jumble of brightly trimmed, whitewashed eighteenth-century cottages, Solva was a thriving fishing village and lime shipping port until the be-

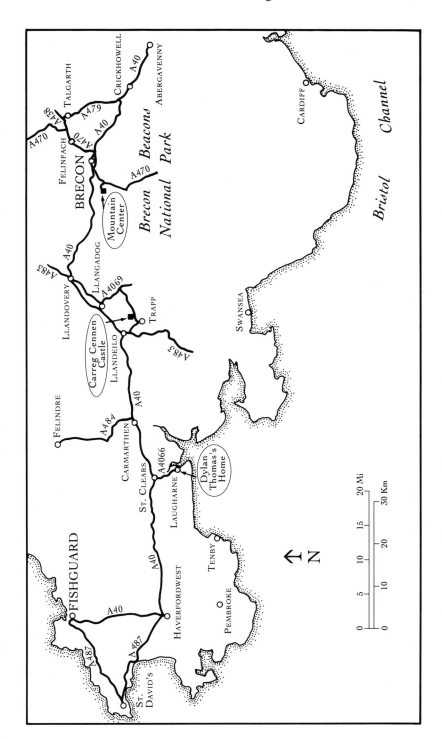

ginning of the century. Today, its tiny dogleg harbor is as likely to be filled with yachts as fishing boats, and the schooners are long gone.

After scooting across the little River Solva via a one-lane bridge, the road climbs back up the steep opposite bank and runs along the high coastal plateau again. A few minutes later, it curves sharply to the right and drops down to **Newgale Sands**. Its absence of sand notwithstanding (the beach is composed entirely of rounded rocks piled by winter storms into stony gray dunes that drift right to the roadside), Newgale offers panoramic views of St. Bride's Bay. Off to the right through the blue haze is St. David's Head and Ramsey Island. Around to the left is the **Marloes Peninsula**, with **Skomer Island** off its tip. The floor of the bay is sloped perfectly for producing long, rising combers. When the surf is up, regardless of the weather, dozens of brightly wet-suited surfers and kayakers bob on the white-capped surface studying the swells.

Beyond the beach, the A487 climbs up to high ground again, over Keeston Hill, and then descends into **Haverfordwest**, the capitol of Pembrokeshire before the county was combined with Cardigan and Carmarthen to form Dyfed in 1974. Haverfordwest is a linguistic reminder of Pembrokeshire's pre-Norman invaders; it is a Norse name— *haver fjord*, or "corn inlet"—as are many other place names in this area, including Solva, Skomer, and Skokholm Island, names the Normans do not seem to have been able to erase.

From Haverfordwest, continue east on the A40, following the Landsker line toward Carmarthen, a distance of some 30 miles (48 kilometers) over fertile, rolling hills. From **St. Clear's**, the A40 becomes a high-speed, four-lane divided highway all the way into Carmarthen. (See Diversions for side trips from St. Clear's to Welsh poet Dylan Thomas's riverside home in Laugharne, or to the mills and craft shops north of Carmarthen.)

East of Carmarthen, the A40, following the course of a Roman road, enters the long, lovely valley of the **River Tywi**. It is a serene landscape of vivid green meadows edged with neat hedgerows and bisected by the lazily looping river, but it is also strategic. Plunging deep into the heart of Mid-Wales, the Tywi Valley was the scene of repeated battles between the Welsh and the Normans and their successors. Four great castles—Carmarthen, Drsylwyn, Dinefwr, and Llandovery—are sited at narrow spots along the valley. With histories that date from the Norman invasion and even earlier, they played key roles during the struggle between Edward I and Llewelyn the Last for control of Wales in the thirteenth century, and in Owain Glyndwr's rebellion in the early fifteenth century. Of these epic battles, however, little remains but ivy-hung ruins.

On the western edge of **Llandelio**, turn **right** onto the **A483** and drive south over the river and through **Ffairfach**, keeping an eye peeled for signs to the **left** to **Carreg Cennen Castle**. Unquestionably the most romantic castle in Wales, Carreg Cennen was probably built originally in the twelfth century, though fortresses existed on the site even before the Romans. During the thirteenth-century struggle between King Edward I and Llewelyn the Last, the castle changed hands repeatedly. Edward I's forces seized it during the second campaign against Llewelyn in 1282, but they were surprised and overthrown by Llewelyn the Last's brother the same year. Next, the Earl of Gloucester seized it and added to the fortifications. In 1287, Lord Rhys ap Maredudd captured both Carreg Cennen and Dryslwyn Castle for the Welsh in one day, but the Normans prevailed again shortly thereafter. The existing castle was completed during this period, but it fell to the Welsh again after a year-long siege during Owain Glyndwr's rebellion in the early 1400s. During the War of the Roses the castle was surrendered by the Lancastrians, and in 1487 some 500 men were dispatched to demolish the fortress. Thankfully, they didn't get very far.

From the castle towers there are spectacular views east across the pristine green valley of the **Afon Cennen** to the brooding bulk of **Black Mountain**, the huge mass of red sandstone that is the western anchor of the **Brecon Beacons National Park**. Behind you, the soft hills of Mid-Wales and Pembrokeshire drift northwestward into a pastel blue haze. Invisible beneath you is Carreg Cennen's biggest surprise: a steep, 200-foot (61-meter) underground tunnel, carved into the limestone cliff, that leads to a cavern and spring far below the castle. The castle is open Monday through Saturday 9:30 A.M. to 6:30 P.M. and Sunday 2:00 P.M. to 6:30 P.M.; from mid-October to mid-March the castle closes at 4:00 P.M.

From the castle car park, retrace your route a few hundred yards and take the second **left**. This narrow road drops down to the River Cennen at **Trapp**, a hamlet that is little more than a pub, phone box, and a tiny schoolhouse. After crossing the river, bear slightly **left** at the pub and drive up the long, increasingly barren flanks of Black Mountain. Ignore a turning to the right partway up the hill and continue to the first **left**. Turn here, and follow this single-lane road northeastward, high on the slope of the mountain. There are wonderful views back down into the valley and across to the castle, high on its white limestone perch, but be careful of the incredibly stupid sheep grazing the grassy berm or ruminating stubbornly in the middle of the lane. Cars seem to be an infrequent and easily ignored interruption up here. Follow this lane, ignoring all turns, for about 6 miles (9.7 kilometers), until it dead-ends at the **A4069** on the windswept flanks of Black Mountain. Here turn **left**, and head downhill toward **Llangadog**. The road here follows a lovely mountain stream and passes in and out of tunnels of trees, the road surface sequined with sunlight here and there where the canopy thins and light penetrates. Some 4 miles (6.4 kilometers) later, in the

The Beacons tower above the fertile farmland around Brecon.

center of Llangadog, turn **right** and continue on the A4069 up the valley of the River Tywi to **Llandovery**. At the intersection with the A40, turn **right** and continue east in the direction of **Brecon**.

The A40 climbs steadily now, following a tributary stream of the Tywi. Beyond **Halfway**, the pastoral farmlands of the lower valley give way to open moorland. The mountains finally release you at **Sennybridge**, and the road descends into the broad green valley of the **River Usk**. After a few more miles, the A40 bends around to the right and the Brecon Beacons rise up to the clouds before you.

The A40 bypasses the center of Brecon, the nucleus of the Brecon Beacons area, swinging around its southern edge through a series of roundabouts. At the first roundabout, leave the A40 and head south on the **A470** toward Cardiff. After perhaps 3 miles (4.8 kilometers), at **Libanus**, watch for a minor road on the **right** signposted for the

Brecon Beacon Mountain Centre. Turn in here and follow the minor road uphill for about 1.5 miles (2.4 kilometers). With photo displays, audiovisual programs, and a wide range of books, brochures, and maps, the center is the best introduction to the Brecon Beacons National Park. Afterward, backtrack to the A40/A470 roundabout and enter Brecon. With plenty of accommodations nearby (see Creature Comforts), shops and restaurants, and the largest livestock market in Wales (a noisy, fragrant, bustling affair held every Friday in the marketplace on the north side of town), Brecon is an ideal base for the next two nights.

DIVERSIONS
Pilgrimage to Dylan Thomas Country

Off and on, up and down, high and dry, man and boy,
I've been living now for fifteen years, or centuries, in this
timeless, beautiful, barmy town, in this far, forgetful,
important place of herons, cormorants, castle, churchyard,
gulls, ghosts.

—Dylan Thomas
Quite Early One Morning

He called it "Llareggub" in what subsequently became *Under Milk Wood*. And if you have a working knowledge of the lower reaches of British slang and can read backwards, you know all you need to know about what the poet Dylan Thomas really thought about the town in which he spent the last years of his short, tempestuous life. The *real* "Llareggub" is **Laugharne** (pronounced *Lorn*), a town he seems to have loved and despised in roughly equal measure, and it is a place of pilgrimage for lovers of his muscular narrative poetry. The side trip begins at St. Clear's. Turn off the A40 and head south on the **A4066** through gently rolling farmland, with the River Taf winking between the trees off to your left. After a bit less than 10 miles (16 kilometers), you reach Laugharne, a simple town composed principally of slate-roofed Georgian and Victorian houses gathered around the ruins of **Laugharne Castle**. As it enters town, the A4066 first becomes King Street, and then Market Street, passing Brown's Hotel (Thomas's favorite pub) and slipping gently downhill toward the water. The boat-house Thomas called home, well marked, is below a lane called Cliff Walk (also "Dylan's Walk"). Brightly whitewashed, it stands on stilts, heron-like, above the mud flats of the broad estuary of the Taf and Tywi rivers—"the two-tongued sea" of *A Child's Christmas in Wales*. It is an incongruous spot, a place of peace and beauty that contrasts sharply with Thomas's boisterous, often angry work. The property is managed by the local tourism council and is open daily from Easter through October, 10:00 A.M. to 6:00 P.M.

The Mills and Craftworkers of Southwest Wales

The hills and valleys of southwest Wales are filled with handsome old stone mills and the workshops of a wide range of craftworkers. Local Tourist Information Centres carry a variety of free brochures to guide you to these mills and shops, among them *Crafts in Dyfed*, and *The Pembrokeshire Craftsmen's Circle*. One of the most interesting concentrations is around the little town of **Felindre**, near **Llandyssul**, roughly 12 miles (19 kilometers) north of Carmarthen on the A484. The heart of this group is the **Museum of the Welsh Woolen Industry**, with a working woolen mill, the museum, and the workshops of several independent craftworkers. Other mills and workshops are nearby. The museum complex is open year-round Monday through Friday, 10:00 A.M. to 5:00 P.M., as well as Saturday from April through September.

CREATURE COMFORTS
Daily Bed

One of the most active and quality-conscious regional farmhouse B&B associations in all of Britain is **Brecon Farm and Country Holidays**, a group of eight farms all within roughly 15 minutes of Brecon. All are warm, friendly, and comfortable and five of the eight also serve hearty evening meals. Two have received the highest commendation from the Wales Tourist Board, the Welsh Dragon award. The irrepressible Meudwen (pronounced *MY-dwen*) Stephens presides over **Upper Trewalkin Farm**—and, more significantly, its kitchen, as Mrs. Stephens is a formidable chef who has done Welsh cooking demonstrations on behalf of the Tourist Board as far away as London and Paris. Upper Trewalkin, the sheep farm she and her husband, David, operate, is northeast of Brecon near Talgarth. The setting is glorious; beyond Mrs. Stephens's lush garden, the hills rise like great green ocean swells to the heights of the brooding Black Mountains in the hazy distance.

Equally high in the hills is Theresa and Goronwy Jones's **Trehenry Farm**, a mixed livestock and grain-producing farm above Felinfach, just a few miles northeast of Brecon on the A470. Mrs. Jones has three bedrooms, each with private bath, and her dinners are in the best farmhouse tradition (and must be reserved in advance). As with all Tourist Board award winners, it is wise to book in advance for the two nights you will spend here. For reservations and directions, write Upper Trewalkin Farm, Pengenfforde, Talgarth, Brecon, Powys LD3 0HA, phone (0874) 711349; or Trehenry Farm,

Felinfach, Brecon, Powys LD3 0UN, phone (0874) 754312.

For a *Brecon Farm and Country Holidays* brochure, as well as other information on accommodations in the national park, you can write directly to the Brecon Tourist Information Centre, Watton Mount, Brecon, Powys LD3 7DF, between April and October, or to the Wales Tourist Board in Cardiff during the off-season (see Useful Addresses).

In addition, youth hostels are located just east of Brecon at Groesffordd and just south of Brecon in Libanus. For addresses and phone numbers, see the YHA guide in Further Reading. Other accommodations options are covered in the books and brochures listed in Further Reading.

Daily Bread

If dinner at a farmhouse B&B doesn't work out, the roughly triangular area formed by the towns of Brecon, Talgarth, and Abergavenny hosts a wide array of inns, hotels, and restaurants. As always, ask your hosts for their suggestions and keep an eye out for TASTE OF WALES signs on the door, generally a reliable indication that the owners approach cooking with imagination and a dedication to fresh local ingredients.

Meudwen Stephens's farmhouse B&B in the Brecon Beacons National Park

High in the Brecon Beacons

PEN-Y-FAN ◆ LLANTHONY VALLEY HAY-ON-WYE

- ◆ A day hike to the highest mountain in southern Wales
- ◆ An alternative drive through the Black Mountains to Llanthony Priory and the Vale of Ewyas
- ◆ A short walk high above England on the Offa's Dyke Path
- ◆ A visit to "The Town of Books"

So it must have been after the birth
of the simple light
In the first, spinning place, the spellbound horses
walking warm
Out of the whinnying green stable
On to the fields of praise.

———Dylan Thomas, 1946

*T*hey rise like tidal waves of stone, the massive Brecon Beacons. Up from the murky depths of the dark Welsh coalfields they surge, smooth and peaty brown, steadily gaining elevation and momentum until, high above Brecon, they crest and freeze—their motion arrested, their muddy mass petrified, their blunt menace suspended in perpetuity, as if by a spell. Beneath the crests, the sheer northern faces of the Beacons drop more than 2,000 feet into the deep green valley of the River Usk. Lush and undulating foothills ripple away to the north, eventually losing themselves in the topographic chop of Mid-Wales. Away in the blue-green misty distance, east and west, other wave-mountains hang on the horizon, their northward flow frozen forever.

The five peaks of the Beacons (so-named because they were used for signal fires long ago) form the heart of the 519-square-mile (1,344-square-kilometer) **Brecon Beacons National Park**, but there are three other distinct mountain ranges in the park. Just west of the Beacons is **Fforest Fawr**, a range of heather-covered hills that once was a royal hunting ground for the princes of Brecon. On the eastern and western fringes of the park are, respectively and confusingly, the **Black Mountains** (which are not black) and **Black Mountain** (which is neither black nor a mountain, but a long green ridge). These four ranges are remnants of an immense bed of red sandstone laid down in a vast, muddy delta nearly 400 million years ago. Later, subterranean shifts tipped the mass upward to the north. Then, during the last Ice Age, glaciers attacked the exposed northern edge, scouring the cliffs, scooping out depressions later filled with crystal-clear rainwater and snowmelt, and gouging deep U-shaped valleys. Wherever you go in the park, the soaring scarps of the Beacons are an inescapable part of the background—glowering in the rain, shining in the morning sun, or sharply etched by the shadows of late afternoon.

Despite its accessibility from the population centers of Cardiff and Swansea and, for that matter, London, the mountains, valleys, villages, and farms within the heart of the Brecon Beacons have somehow preserved the unhurried grace and gentle beauty of a simpler era. Depending upon weather and whim, today's itinerary presents several ways to enjoy this peaceful place.

⚲ A DAY ATOP THE THREE PEAKS

Distance: About 6 miles/9.7 kilometers; allow 4–5 hours
Difficulty: First half hour and final hundred yards before summit are steep and demanding; balance of walk moderate
Total Elevation Gain: About 1,900 feet/580 meters
Gear: Sturdy walking shoes/boots, rain gear, lunch, camera
Maps: Ordnance Survey Landranger #160; *Walks in the Brecon Beacons*, a brochure published by the National Park Service and available at park information centers

Wreathed in mist or basking in the sun, the rounded contours and vertiginous edges of the Beacons are irresistible lures for walkers. Beneath the swooping scarps, the rolling farmlands are an earthy patchwork: acid yellow with rapeseed, smoky blue with barley, emerald green and pin-dotted with sheep, and rust red where the furrows are fresh. To the east are the brooding Black Mountains. To the south, beyond the deep, narrow coalfields, the Bristol Channel shimmers, smooth and silvery, in the afternoon sun. Far to the west, beyond Fforest Fawr and Black Mountain, you can see almost to Pembrokeshire. And northward across Mid-Wales, the landscape, dappled by racing cloud shadows, crumples upward all the way to Cadair Idris and the heights of Snowdonia.

The smooth-flanked Beacons, cloaked in soft bracken and heather, are deceptively benign, like a genial grandfather with an unpredictable mean streak. If anything, the three main peaks of the summit plateau— **Pen-y-Fan** (2,907 feet/886 meters), **Corn Du** (2,863 feet/873 meters), and **Cribyn** (2,608 feet/795 meters)—are *too* accessible. One ascent, beginning high on the A470 pass between the Beacons and Fforest Fawr at the Storey Arms, is so high at the outset (more than 1,400 feet/426 meters) that the summit can be reached in an hour. Yet despite its benign appearance, Pen-y-Fan warrants care; heavy rains and impenetrable mists can sweep in from Bristol Bay in what seems like moments and the temperature can drop precipitously, even in midsummer. That caution aside, our route to the top today is deeply rewarding, a classic ridge walk with real but perfectly achievable physical challenges, magnificent vistas, and an easy, rather pastoral descent.

This morning, stop in Brecon and put together a picnic lunch. Then drive **west** through the center of town, cross over the River Usk, pass St. David's Church, and then turn **left** onto **Frwdgrech Road**. After ducking under the A40 bypass and passing a small industrial site, the road crosses a little bridge and immediately branches three ways. Take the **left** fork, and drive steadily uphill through a generally wooded landscape, paralleling a stream called **Nant Gwdi**. At another junction of small lanes, roughly 1.5 miles (2.4 kilometers) from the fork, steer **straight** ahead toward the looming bulk of Pen-y-Fan, following signs to the Cwm Gwdi Camp. Soon the road steepens and narrows further, crosses a cattle grid, and passes a military training site composed principally of Quonset huts, on the right. Park in the car park on the left just beyond the military site.

The walk begins on the east side of the car park, where a clear path clambers down into a mossy gully filled with gnarled old trees and threaded by a whispering mountain stream. You cross the stream by a simple plank bridge, then follow an irregular flight of earth-and-wood steps up the opposite bank. Here the path weaves through a quiet grove of birch trees before breaking free to a steep slope outfitted in bright yellow gorse bushes and delicate heather. By any of several lush green passages through the gorse and heather, continue climbing upward, slanting slightly to the **right** toward an obvious lateral path below the brow the hill above you. As you ascend to this path, the gorse gives way to a profusion of bracken fern, the bane of hill farmers throughout Britain because sheep refuse to eat it.

The lateral path skirts the scree slopes of **Allt Ddu** (1,844 feet/562 meters), one of many north-trending spurs or finger ridges left behind by the glaciers that cut the scarps. After perhaps half an hour, you finally reach the top of the spur. The view backward over Brecon is lovely, stretching across the undulating central valley to the heights of the Cambrian Hills of Mid-Wales. Ahead, looming above

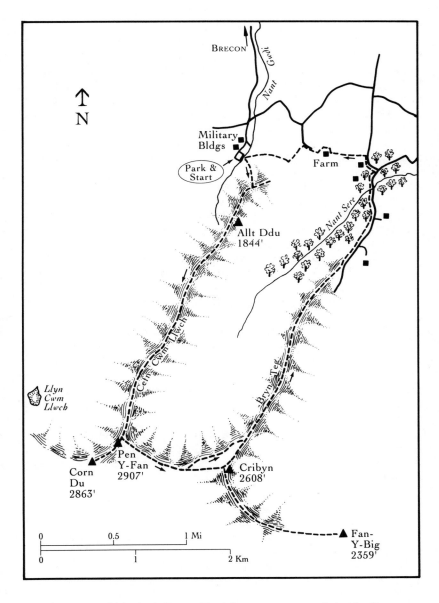

you, barren and bleak, is Pen-y-Fan, first among equals in the Beacons. To the left rises Cribyn, looking more like a pyramid than a mountain. Just beyond Cribyn to the east, and only marginally lower, is the delightfully named summit **Fan-y-Big**. Radiating from each of these sentinel summits are rank upon rank of spurs, like flying buttresses supporting some vast Gothic cathedral.

It is profoundly quiet atop the Allt Ddu spur. A tractor toils mutely in a rocky field far below; dust rises but no valley sounds reach you. Birdsong is absent too, the birds no doubt finding the leafy hollows and lush meadows near the River Usk more hospitable than these exposed high ridges. The air is crisp and completely still, the dark plateau ahead acting like a vast windscreen against the prevailing southerlies. The only sounds up here are the desultory complaints of the sheep that graze the steep slopes, poking about among the moorland shrubs and sedges for tender green morsels, finding few, and rocketing off in crazed flight when surprised by a lone walker.

Ahead, the spur narrows to a knife-edged ridge called **Cefn Cwm Llwch**. In the yawning chasms to the left and right, weird mini-climates generate fast-rising mists that climb the nearly vertical walls of the escarpment and then, just as rapidly, dissipate. The path before you—now crisp and clear, now indistinct in the mist—rises gradually toward Pen-y-Fan. The mountain's sheer sandstone face is creased by dozens of horizontal bands, and cascades of reddish gravel spill down from the weathered ledges like dusty cataracts.

A few hundred yards beneath the summit, the footpath steepens markedly and deteriorates to a tiring mix of shifting sandstone pebbles and unreliable rocks and slabs. When you finally haul yourself over the lip of Pen-y-Fan, a stiff southern breeze smacks you full in the face—a welcome change on a muggy summer's day. As you catch your breath, the irresistible first impression of the summit plateau is that it must be the home of a hopelessly unruly child; in every direction, the ground is littered with building blocks of red sandstone, perfectly rectangular and ranging in size from dominos to bricks.

The difference between the northern and southern approaches to Pen-y-Fan and its neighbors is striking. The southern flanks and spurs, smooth and furred with grass and heather, dip gently downhill, eventually losing themselves in blue-green conifer plantations far below. To the south, a chain of reservoirs sparkles like a jeweled necklace in the sunshine.

But it is the northern panorama that tugs at your attention. To best appreciate it, turn right when you reach the top of the plateau and continue uphill a few yards to the true summit of Pen-y-Fan. Here, great slabs of sandstone—more resistant to erosion than the layers below—jut out over the abyss and present perhaps the most spectacular (if somewhat unnerving) picnic site in all of Wales. Beneath your feet the mountain simply drops away to oblivion, as if cleaved from the earth by a giant's sword. To the west, the slightly lower summit of Corn Du looms above a tiny teardrop of a lake called **Llyn Cwm Llwch**, cupped in an amphitheater of stone carved by a passing glacier. Beyond the lake, the limits of civilization are so clear it looks as if a chalk line had

The knife-edge ridge between Pen-y-Fan and Corn Du in the Brecon Beacons

been drawn around the base of the mountains. Above the line, the ground is unforgiving, the prospects for life bleak and barren. Below the line, the scene is a soft and harmonious blend of farm and field, woods and valleys.

The descent begins with an ascent. From Corn Du, backtrack up to the top of Pen-y-Fan and then follow the well-worn cliff-edge path east-ward down the steep slope to a saddle between Pen-y-Fan and Cribyn. Here the main path immediately begins scrambling uphill to Cribyn's summit. But watch instead for a path to the **left** that tips over the edge of the cliff and slips laterally across the steeply angled face of Cribyn. This is a wonderful traverse, a narrow indentation in the nearly 45-degree slope of Cribyn's pyramid flank—dizzying, breathtaking, but quite safe.

After you curve around to Cribyn's north face, turn **left** and take the gentle path descending a long spur called **Bryn Teg**. The peaty, grass-covered slope is as springy as a mattress and fatigue vanishes—but watch for the needle-like leaves of sedges that tell you where the boggy places are.

Almost exactly an hour after leaving Corn Du, you reach the end of the spur, marked by a stone cairn, and begin a steeper—but still easy—descent to the valley below, following a broad, grassy green aisle be-tween high banks of bracken fern. Finally, this sloping, sheep-dotted meadow ends at an old stone wall. Go through the gate by the National Trust marker, and bear **left** down a narrow farm track edged with stone walls and hawthorn hedges and bristling with blackberry bramble. Sur-faced initially with fist-size cobbles that are hard on tired ankles, the track soon becomes a paved lane. After a bit less than 1 mile (1.6 kilo-meters), the road enters a bosky glen and skips across an old stone bridge arched over a busy mountain stream called **Nant Sere**. Then, af-ter climbing uphill out of the glen, the road forks. Take the **left** fork and walk up this lane past a modern farmhouse on the left. A hundred yards or so farther on, watch for a wooden stile on the **left**, nearly obscured by a dense bed of nettles. Turn off the road here, go over the stile, and follow the fenceline to your right. Ignore the gate in the fence partway up the hill; continue to the head of the field and go through an older gate under some trees. Walk **straight** ahead after this gate, keeping a line of trees on your left and heading toward a small wood. The foot-path crosses the left corner of this wood, through a dark green passage, and emerges on the other side in a field with a farm up ahead. Follow the obvious path toward this farm, and go around the **right** side of the first sheds you encounter. Pass through a gate into the farmyard, turn **right** at the horse stalls, and walk through the farmyard out along the farm's access road. Then, after a few more yards, turn **left** up a sunken lane surfaced with rubble stone and go over the stile in the fence straight ahead. Walk uphill through a field, following the tree line and keeping the sunken lane on your right. At the end of this field, pass through yet another gate, walk up a few feet, and turn **right**, continuing around the base of Allt Ddu, the steep hillside you ascended earlier today. When you reach the stream, in its leafy ravine, turn **left** and follow the left bank uphill under the trees until you reach the narrow plank footbridge at which you began this walk. The car park is just above.

🚗 LLANTHONY PRIORY AND THE VALE OF EWYAS

Distance: 32 miles/51 kilometers (from Brecon)
Roads: Mostly minor roads, narrow but scenic
Driving Time: About 1 hour
Maps: Michelin Map #403; Ordnance Survey Landranger #160 and #161

The Black Mountains, on the eastern edge of the national park, are less assertive than the Brecon Beacons, but possess a subtle beauty of their own: soaring ridge lines, soft edges, narrow pastoral valleys, and ancient hamlets. For centuries, they were part of Wales's bulwark against outsiders, a solid 20-mile (32-kilometer) wall of stubborn red sandstone and high moorlands that, if they did not actually repel invasion, at least discouraged it.

But the Black Mountains also have a secret. A narrow sliver of a valley, deeply serene for so rugged a region, twists right through the mountains' heart. Accessible only by a sinuous one-lane road, the secluded **Vale of Ewyas** has a Shangri-la quality. Only minutes from the busy market town of Abergavenny, it nonetheless has a palpable remoteness that distances it both in time and space from the rest of the region, a peacefulness that lifts the spirit. Perhaps as a result, it also is home to the skeletal remains of a beautiful and little-visited priory of great antiquity.

If scaling the Brecon Beacons doesn't suit you this morning, head for Abergavenny . . . but take the back road. Just beyond the easternmost roundabout of the **A40** bypass around Brecon, turn **right** onto the **B4558**, signposted for **Talybont**. This pretty lane crosses over the River Usk and then parallels the **Monmouthshire and Brecon Canal** as it heads downstream. The "Mon and Brec" was created in 1812 (by the joining of two shorter canals) to improve the flow of coal and limestone northward from South Wales and agricultural goods southward. A splendid piece of engineering, it runs southeast through the Usk River valley, sometimes level with the river, sometimes high above it. Its industrial roots notwithstanding, the canal is a lovely companion as you travel south on the B4558, its sun-dappled surface winking through the trees that line the towpath. Below Talybont, just beyond

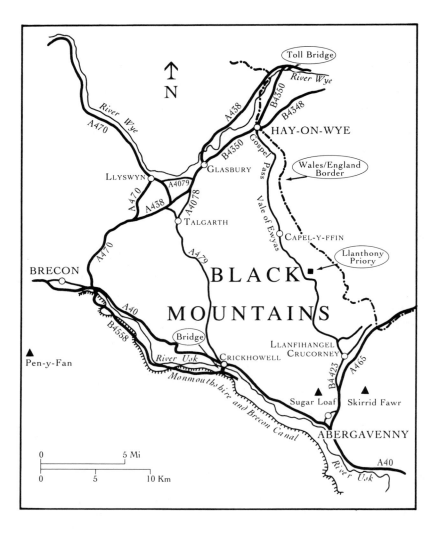

the drawbridge, the canal tunnels through a hillside to avoid going around or over it, then drops through a short flight of locks before reaching **Crickhowell**. Here, turn **left** over Crickhowell's arched stone bridge (which, curiously, has twelve arches on one side and thirteen on the other) and, at the intersection with the A40, turn **right** toward Abergavenny.

Abergavenny, in the shadow of the twin peaks of **Sugar Loaf** (an extinct volcano) and **Skirrid Fawr**, is a handsome market town, a centuries-spanning hodgepodge of buildings cleverly knit together by dozens of window boxes, resplendent in summer with petunias, geraniums, lobelia, and alyssum. It also has a maddening one-way traffic flow system that seems designed explicitly to keep you from ever seeing the center of town. But persist; if you plan to take the half-day walk from Llanthony Priory (see below), this is a good place to shop for a picnic lunch.

From Abergavenny, follow signs for the **A465** toward **Hereford**. After just over 4 miles (6.4 kilometers), however, watch for a **left** turn onto the **B4423**, signposted for **Llanfihangel Crucorney** and **Llanthony**. Then, after the Skirrid Inn (built just forty-four years after the Norman Conquest and Wales's oldest inn) turn **left** again, following signs for Llanthony.

Soon you are snaking up a narrow glacier-carved valley with the fast-flowing River Honddu on your right. In a little more than 1.5 miles (2.4 kilometers) from the Skirrid Inn, two hills swoop down to the river, and road and river squeeze through a gap. On the other side, a lush green valley, narrow as a knife blade, appears—first curving left, then swinging right—hemmed in on both sides by the high ridges of the Black Mountains. The steep western slopes of the valley are thickly wooded, while the somewhat gentler eastern slopes are managed much as they were in feudal times, with small farms scattered along the valley floor, meadows on the lower flanks of the hills, and common grazing land above the 1,000-foot (305-meter) line. The road, bounded on both sides by high hawthorn hedges dense with wildflowers, wanders up the valley for 4.5 miles (7.2 kilometers) before skipping over to the right bank of the river. Just ahead, opposite a farm sheltered by a grove of chestnut trees, watch for a lane sloping uphill to the right to **Llanthony Priory**.

"Llanthony" is a corruption of the Welsh *Llan-Ddewi-Nant-Hodni*, or "the Church of St. David on the River Honddu," and tradition has it that St. David founded a hermitage on this remote site in the sixth century A.D. Six centuries later, William de Lacy, a retainer of the Norman lord of Ewyas, and Ernisius, the court chaplain, discovered the remains of the hermitage and set about reestablishing it. By 1108 a new church had been consecrated and by 1120 an Augustinian priory (the first in Wales) was established. The priory was abandoned in 1135 because of a Welsh uprising, but the monks returned in 1175 to begin construction of the present priory. After the Dissolution, in 1538, the monks were pensioned off and, gradually, the priory deteriorated.

The remains of Llanthony Priory hint at what must have been a structure of stunning scale and beauty in so remote a place. It is situated on a curve in the narrow valley, with the ridges of the Black Mountains swooping up on both sides. Apart from the occasional farm building it is quite alone in its splendid setting. Even today, whether shining in the sun or softened by mist, the soaring fragments of the long arcaded nave, the intricately carved Gothic arches, and the crumbling crenellations of

The haunting ruins of Llanthony Priory in the remote Vale of Ewyas

the central tower are wildly romantic. Less romantic, perhaps, but welcome nonetheless, is the tiny pub located in the low-ceilinged cellar of what once was the prior's house and now is a small hotel. It must be the only priory in Britain with its own pub.

If the weather is clear, spend a couple of hours walking along the ridge high above the priory. It is a generally easy walk with a spectacular bonus: a positively vast view deep into England from the ridge top. Afterward, pick up the driving itinerary to continue north up the steepening vale.

⫞ ALONG THE OFFA'S DYKE PATH HIGH ABOVE ENGLAND

Distance: About 3.5 miles/5.6 kilometers; allow 2.5 hours
Difficulty: Ascent to ridge top moderately steep but gradual; balance of walk easy
Total Elevation Gain: 1,024 feet/312 meters
Gear: Walking shoes or sneakers, rain gear, lunch, camera
Map: Ordnance Survey Pathfinder #1063

To begin, walk out of the priory car park, with the little stone parish church of St. David's on your left. Go over a stile beside the gate on the other side of the access road, then turn **right** up a gravel track, with the priory ruins on your right. At the top of the gravel lane are a gate and another stile. On the other side, the waymarked footpath parallels the eastern boundary wall of the priory grounds, then crosses another stile in a hawthorn hedgerow and turns **left** up the hillside along the edge of a field. At the top of the field, the path turns **right**, now following the field's upper edge, just inside a wire fenceline that marks the boundary of **Wiral Wood**. At the opposite corner of the field, turn **left** over a stile and up a well-worn track that climbs into the cool, dark wood.

The path emerges from the wood over yet another stile to the left of a metal gate, and then climbs up along the margin of another meadow, heading for the moorlands above. Ahead, high above the ridge line, glossy black ravens drift on the updrafts; if you are lucky, you may also discover a harrier hawk hanging on the wind, tense and motionless, scanning the ground for prey.

At the next stile, you leave the cultivated lower slopes and enter the steep, bracken-choked commons. Another waymarker guides you **left**, slicing diagonally uphill (do not take the level path). Then, about half-way up this hillside, beside a group of hollies, the path switches **right** and continues its now steepening climb through the bracken. Ahead, the path picks up a ruined stone wall and runs along its uphill side. It is profoundly quiet here, high above the valley—as if you were taking in some wide-screen nature film without a soundtrack. Occasionally, the

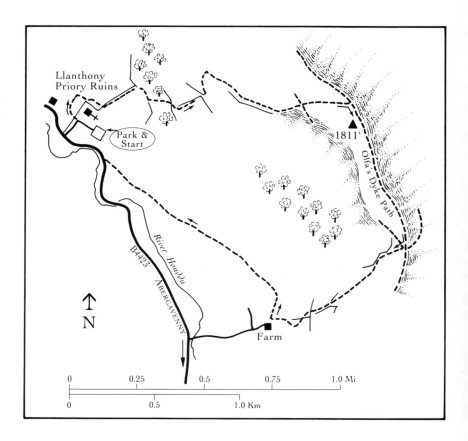

silence is broken by the echoing cries and whistles of a distant shepherd guiding his Border collies as, together, man and dogs drive a flock of skittish and stubborn sheep down off the moortop for shearing.

After a few more minutes of climbing, the stone wall disappears and is replaced by a rough track up a shallow gully. Continue uphill along this grassy swale in the same slantwise direction, keeping an eye out for clumps of sedge that mark boggy spots where springs seep from the fractured rock.

The summit of the ridge announces itself quietly, by a subtle change in vegetation. The drifts of glossy-leafed bilberry that have adorned the higher slopes disappear as you reach the plateau, replaced by acres of bronze-green, lavender-flowered heather stretching away in all directions. Soon you reach a clear intersection of three paths: one to the left, one slanting off to the right, and the third forging **straight ahead**. Take the latter.

Then, quite suddenly, you reach the edge of the plateau, and before you, spread out like a giant, rumply quilt, is what seems at first to be the whole of England, billowing away to the hazy eastern horizon. This high bluff is the Welsh border, and in few places is the barrier between the two countries more assertive, the gulf more graphic, than on this precipice. Behind you, the somber Black Mountains; before you, the luxuriant hedgerowed fields and meadows around Hereford. Farther afield, the **Malvern Hills** rise to the northeast. Beyond them, the gradually leveling plain of the Severn River spreads north and south. And farther east still, the sharp edge of the Cotswold Escarpment climbs to the puffy clouds.

At roughly the point at which this spectacle appears, turn **right** onto a well-worn path toward an Ordnance Survey pillar ahead on the next rise. You're on the **Offa's Dyke Long Distance Footpath** now. Created in 1971 by the Countryside Commission, the path stretches from the Severn estuary on the south coast of Wales to the Dee estuary on the north coast, paralleling the dyke for 60 of the path's more than 170 miles (274 kilometers).

From the Ordnance Survey marker (1,811 feet/552 meters), continue walking south along the eastern edge of the bluff, sloping gently downhill. Here the ridge narrows sharply, to the point that the plateau is barely wider than the path itself. To the east, the ground drops off precipitously to the valley far below. To the west, the slope is more gentle. At this point you reach an intersection of several paths. One climbs steeply uphill from the valley to your left, reaching the ridge top at an east-facing slab of sandstone that makes a good picnic site. Another comes uphill diagonally from behind you to your right. Turn sharply **right** onto this path and follow it for just a few yards, until you can see a well-made stone wall downhill on your left. Then turn **left** and walk downhill through the springy heather, past several depressions, called "butts," dug by grouse hunters for cover. When you reach the wall, bear **left** and pick up an obvious path leading downhill along the left side of the wall.

Not as sweeping, perhaps, as the east-facing vista from the ridge top, the view west from this path is splendid nevertheless. The ridge arcs away to your left, high above the curving and impossibly green floor of the Llanthony Valley. Ahead to the southwest, the distinctive cone of Sugarloaf punctuates the skyline. And directly ahead, across the narrow valley, the main mass of the Black Mountains plateau lumbers off toward the western horizon.

Partway down the hill, the stone wall you've been following makes a right turn. At this point the path diverges from the wall, bearing slightly **left** and downhill toward a farm. Off to the right now, Llanthony Priory once again appears, rising ghost-like above the trees along the valley floor. From this viewpoint it's easy to imagine the priory as it was in its heyday and to appreciate the stark contrast between

The view across the Welsh border into patchwork England, from the Offa's Dyke Path

its graceful form and ordered proportions and the wild disorder of the mountains that surrounded it. It must have been an astonishing vision to pilgrims approaching from this direction.

Eventually, beneath a grove of trees, you reach a steel gate. Go through the gate (securing it again after you do) and continue downhill between two lines of wire fencing. The ground here, beyond the reach of grazing sheep, is rich with wildflowers—especially dainty daisies and a profusion of bright magenta foxgloves. At the end of the fenceline, beneath an ancient clump of hawthorns, cross over a stile and continue downhill, now to the right of a fenceline, eventually picking up a deeply rutted tractor track. Immediately above the farmhouse, turn **right** onto a well-worn farm lane. From here on, you simply forge straight ahead to the north along the clear path, through a succession of small meadows, over several stiles, beneath two oak trees of amazing antiquity, over two or three watercress-choked streams, until you can hear the River Honddu, clattering over the sandstone ledges in its bed as it rushes downhill to the south. When you reach the road, carry on straight ahead for a few yards, then turn **right** up the access road to the priory.

🚗 OVER THE GOSPEL PASS TO THE "TOWN OF BOOKS"

Distance: About 10 miles/16 kilometers
Roads: A pulse-quickening but scenic one-lane road
Driving Time: About 30 minutes
Map: Michelin Map #403; Ordnance Survey Landranger #161

From the priory access road, turn **right** and continue up the valley. The road loses its "B" classification at this point, and it soon becomes clear why. This is the quintessential British country lane—narrow with occasional passing points, hemmed in by high hawthorn hedges, twist-

One of the wild ponies that wander the "Gospel Pass" above Hay-on-Wye

ing and turning, with visibility seldom more than a few yards. One has the distinct impression that the British invented disc brakes to ensure that heart-stopping sudden encounters with oncoming cars on such "roads" would not become unpleasant scenes. As the road snakes up through the narrowing valley, it skips over the River Honddu from time to time and slips through tiny hamlets and past wildflower-strewn meadows grazed quietly by horses from a nearby pony-trekking center.

Beyond **Capel-y-ffin**, the road finally hoists itself out of the valley and ascends the high, empty moors atop the Black Mountains. This windy no-man's-land, virtually the only route through the Black Mountains, is the **Gospel Pass**, and it doesn't take a lot of imagination to guess why earlier travelers gave it such a name. Dodging weathered outcrops of purplish sandstone and dense thickets of flaming yellow gorse, the thin black strip of pavement seems as out of place in this lonely landscape as footprints on the moon. But then, as you reach **Hay Bluff** (2,220 feet/671 meters), the northern edge of the plateau, the ground falls away to a breathtaking panorama. Far below, the rich farmlands of the Wye River valley spread from the broad plain west of **Leominster** on the right to the narrower bottomlands east of **Talgarth** on your left. In the distance, the patchwork fields give way abruptly to the heather-clad mountains of Mid-Wales.

Immediately below, almost out of sight, is **Hay-on-Wye**, the town that reinvented itself to become the world's largest used-book store. To get there, head downhill for a couple more miles, through a leafy valley, bearing left occasionally and following signs to Hay. Just before the T-junction next to the castle, turn left into the public car park. The Tourist Information Centre is in the Craft Centre, adjacent to the car park.

Like many minor market towns in rural Britain, Hay-on-Wye was dying a slow death in the early 1960s. That was before Richard Booth discovered, almost by accident, that there were profits to be made in selling second-hand books, cheap. He had a simple, if eccentric vision: turning Hay into the world's largest used-book store. Buying books by the truckload from estate sales and private libraries wherever he could find them, Booth gradually filled one after another of the town's empty and forlorn shopfronts. (He also bought the town castle, declared independence from Britain, crowned himself king, and made his horse prime minister, but that's another story.) Soon book lovers were beating a path to Hay's doorstep.

Today, Hay boasts more than two million volumes, and the number of booksellers is, well, voluminous. There are bookshops in barns, in the old cinema, wedged into nooks and crannies in the castle, in sheds, out on the sidewalks, and in shopfronts of all kinds. There are quietly elegant bookstores that smell of wood polish, leather, and paper and that display rarities behind locked glass cabinets. There are dusty, cavernous, inexpressibly chaotic bookstores with books cascading from

Many of Hay-on-Wye's bookstores occupy the premises of businesses long gone; this one was a butcher's shop.

ramshackle shelves that sag under the sheer weight of words. There are bookstores specializing in children's books, in military history, in science, in the environment, in erotica, in the occult, in bibles, in performance art, in poetry—even in American Indians. You can buy books of great antiquity and value, beautifully illustrated and handsomely bound. You can buy books by the pound. You can even buy books by the foot—old leatherbound books on completely useless subjects that

The first among equals of Hay-on-Wye's bookstores

look good on shelves. It is, in short, a book lover's paradise.

When you've had enough of the world of words, turn **left** out of the car park, then **left** again at the T-junction. At the YIELD sign a few yards ahead, turn **right** and then bear **left** downhill following the **A4350** east. In a few minutes you come to a charming little toll bridge over the River Wye (the toll is 50p). On the other side, turn **left** onto the **A438** and follow it west along the river past the villages of **Three Cocks** and **Bronllys**. Then pick up the **A470** toward Brecon and home.

DIVERSIONS
Big Pit

If bad weather argues for a day indoors, consider delving into the real heart of South Wales—by going underground. Just a few miles southwest of Abergavenny, on the **B4248** between the villages of **Blaenafon** and **Brynmawr**, is **Big Pit**, a 200-year-old mine that was still producing the coal and iron for which South Wales was long famous as recently as 1980. Today it's a museum. Former coal miners kit you out in miner's helmets and lamps, then take you 300 feet down the mine shaft to the labyrinth of tunnels deep within the mine. You tour the coal face, the even older ironstone workings, the rail lines, the stables for the animals that hauled the coal cars and the engines that replaced them, the underground workshops, and more. It is an extraordinary experience. Aboveground there are first-rate exhibitions on mining history and the life of nineteenth-century Welsh mining families.

CREATURE COMFORTS
Daily Bed

The same as yesterday.

Daily Bread

For a pastoral alternative to conventional dining spots, you may wish to consider an evening on the Monmouthshire and Brecon Canal, aboard the *Lord William De Braose*—a traditional 57-foot canal boat that has been converted to a cruising restaurant. The restored narrowboat departs each evening from Govilon Wharf, on the canal near Abergavenny, and runs through lovely scenery along one of the longest lock-free sections of any canal in Britain. Set menus are offered at three price ranges and the boat can accommodate thirty-nine diners in the summer (thirty-two in winter). For information and reservations, write Abbott's Restaurant, 16 Monk Street, Abergavenny, Gwent NP7 5NP, or phone (0873) 3792 or 3668.

East to England

MONMOUTH ◆ TINTERN ABBEY
CHEPSTOW ◆ BURFORD

- ◆ **South to the Wye River Gorge and Tintern Abbey**
- ◆ **Across the Severn Bridge to England and the Cotswolds**
- ◆ **An afternoon walk to an Iron Age monument high on the Cotswold Escarpment**

O sylvan Wye! thou wanderer through the woods,
How often has my spirit turned to thee!
———William Wordsworth, 1798

*T*he River Wye—that most Welsh of rivers, born on the heights of Plynlimon, swelling and strengthening as it muscles through the Cambrian Hills of Mid-Wales—turns sluggish and uncertain when it reaches the border near the end of its southward run. Here the clear, fresh water of a thousand Welsh mountain streams mingles with the salt tide of the English sea, clouding the river's bloodline. Trapped between the towering, tree-clad cliffs of the Wye Gorge, with England on one bluff and Wales on the other, the river wanders anxiously back and forth across the valley floor, as if suddenly unsure of its loyalties.

The scene of this border drama is among the most picturesque in Britain. Indeed, it is where the complex eighteenth-century aesthetic doctrine of landscape perfection called "the Picturesque" was born. Its creator, William Gilpin, used the Wye River valley as the prime example of a landscape in which the form, proportion, texture, and color of the works of nature and man existed in profound visual harmony—as they do to this day. Rugged limestone bluffs loom high above the swooping river, their steep walls densely draped with oak, beech, and ash. Salmon flourish in the brackish river, resting briefly in quiet pools and eddies as they struggle upstream to spawn. Cows and sheep graze meadows dazzling with wildflowers. Carefully crafted stone walls partition pastures into a pleasing mosaic.

And on one broad bend in the river, rising like a spirit from the valley floor, is Tintern Abbey. With its great ruined arches curving heavenward like fingers peaked in prayer, Tintern Abbey has a haunting beauty that has inspired poets like Wordsworth and painters like Turner for centuries. Silent and serene in its secluded setting, it is an enduring monument both to faith and to the folly of men—of medieval abbots who flaunted their great wealth, and of a king who believed he could dominate a religion by dismantling its buildings.

There are few more pleasant ways to take your leave of Wales than by way of the Wye.

RETURNING TO OLDE ENGLAND

Distance: About 150 miles/240 kilometers
Roads: Mostly primary roads and motorway; narrow lanes at end
Driving Time: All day, with stops
Map: Michelin Map #403

From Brecon, follow the **A40** southeast through Abergavenny toward **Monmouth**. About 15 minutes east of Abergavenny, the road passes the romantic rose-tinted ruins of **Raglan Castle**, moldering incongruously in the middle of a modern farm on the north side of the highway. Pass Raglan and continue east on the A40. After passing through a tunnel, you approach Monmouth, situated at the point where the **River Monnow** empties into the Wye (hence "Monmouth"). An ancient town of blood-red sandstone, Monmouth has had strategic significance for all of Wales's invaders, from the Romans to the Normans. Its castle was built soon after the Norman Conquest and is used even today by the Royal Monmouthshire Engineers. At the first roundabout at the edge of town, continue **straight** ahead and watch for a turn to the **right** following signs for the **A466** and **Chepstow**. The road crosses the River Wye, then bears right, following the river's eastern bank.

The drive south is one of the most pastoral in Britain. Sometimes riding high above the valley, other times clinging to the riverbank, the road ducks in and out of dark tunnels of foliage, the ground dense with bluebells in the spring. Off to the right, the sparkling River Wye appears and disappears through the trees as it snakes across the valley floor. At **Bigsweir**, the A466 skips across the graceful span of a bridge built by Thomas Telford, then turns south again along the western bank of the river.

Eons ago, this section of South Wales was a broad coastal platform. But just before the last Ice Age, the platform was uplifted and the river found itself with new work to do to reach the sea. Exploiting weak

Roofless, windowless, but its spiritual strength undiminished—Tintern Abbey

spots and rifts in the limestone bed, the river has steadily carved itself a new course, digging deeper and deeper into the rock by dissolving it, rather than eroding it, and gradually widening its bed. It's doing so even today. The river loops this way and that on its southward course, imperceptibly eating away at the valley floor and at the limestone ramparts that tower above it on both sides.

One of the biggest of these loops is at **Tintern Parva**. The river and road bend east around a promontory, then curve sharply west again. Ahead, only yards from the riverbank, is the soaring, roofless ruin of Tintern Abbey. Tintern was founded in 1131 and was one of the first Cistercian foundations in England. The Cistercians favored a monasticism of seclusion and demanding manual labor, which led them to remote sites and, eventually, to great wealth. They cleared woods, drained marshes, and developed new agricultural lands with extraordinary zeal and determination. By the late thirteenth century, for example, Tintern Abbey had established satellite farm estates, called *granges*, over a wide area and owned some 3,000 sheep. That level of

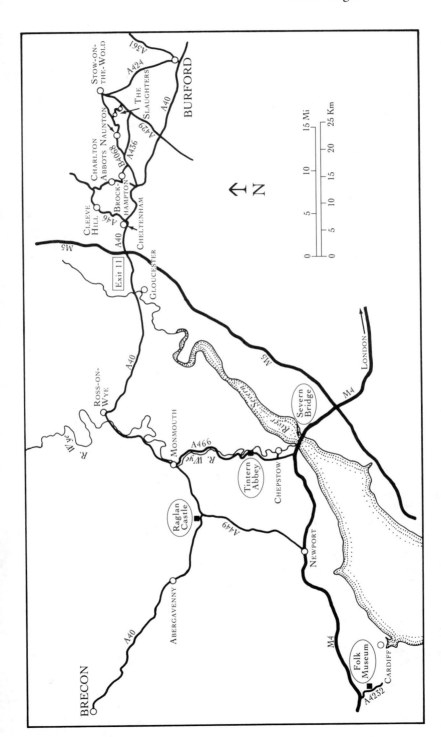

prosperity made it possible for the original church to be rebuilt, and construction continued from the mid-thirteenth through the mid-fourteenth centuries. At its zenith, the abbey and its many monastic buildings covered nearly thirty acres.

In the end, it was the abbey's fortune that caused its fall. While Henry VIII claimed the Dissolution was designed to weaken the hold Rome had over the crown, the real reason was economic. He wanted the abbeys' wealth, and what Henry wanted, whether it was wealth or wives, he usually got. Unlike many other abbeys, however, Tintern was so distant from centers of population that it escaped being used as a source of ready-made building stones. Its lead roof was stripped, but much of the great abbey remains: the entire main structure, its arches intact, the intricate stone tracery of the vast west window, the long nave, the bell tower supported by its massive piers, and the foundations of many monastic buildings. The abbey is open from 9:30 A.M. to 6:30 P.M. Monday through Saturday, and 2:00 P.M. to 6:30 P.M. Sunday, mid-March through mid-October; it closes at 4:00 P.M. mid-October to mid-March.

From Tintern, continue south on the A466 toward Chepstow, climbing up the wooded western slopes of the Wye valley. After the little hamlet of **St. Arvans**, pass the Chepstow racecourse and, at the roundabout, turn **left** onto the **B4293** to enter Chepstow, with its nar-

Chepstow Castle, whose rectangular keep is the oldest stone building in Britain

row medieval streets and commanding castle high above the Wye. Less than a year after the Battle of Hastings in 1066, William the Conqueror gave his friend William FitzOsbern the task of pacifying the *Marches*, or "frontier," of Wales. FitzOsbern's first act was to construct the great rectangular keep at Chepstow, on a cliff above a ford across the Wye on the main coastal route west. Believed to be the first stone castle in the country (earlier fortresses were made of earth and wood), the keep is the oldest datable secular stone building in Britain. Superbly strategic, the castle was expanded continuously for nearly six centuries, seeing duty through the civil war before being abandoned in the late seventeenth century. Britain's first castle is also the last castle on this itinerary, and well worth a visit (open daily, same hours as Tintern Abbey).

From the center of Chepstow, return to the A466 and follow signs for the **M4** and the **Severn River Bridge**, joining the motorway at exit 22, heading east.

From the toll booth on the eastern shore of the Severn estuary, continue on the M4 for about 5 miles (8 kilometers), then take the **M5** north for a fast 30 miles (48 kilometers) to **Exit 11**. The motorway roughly parallels the River Severn, but the most obvious feature of the landscape is the high ridge on your right as you drive north. This is the **Cotswold Escarpment**, the edge of a 640-square-mile (1,656-square-kilometer) slab of limestone that runs some 60 miles (100 kilometers) from Bath almost to Stratford-upon-Avon and defines both the western boundary and much of the inherent character of that most pleasant of English regions, the Cotswolds.

Leave the motorway at Exit 11 and, at the roundabout, follow signs for the A40 east to **Cheltenham**. After two more roundabouts, you enter Cheltenham, a gorgeous spa town nestled beneath a curve of the high escarpment. With block after block of elegant Regency townhouses, Cheltenham's architecture is a treat for the eyes—but keep one eye peeled for road signs for the **A46** north, in the direction of **Winchcombe**. (On the other hand, if you are in the mood for a bit of chic urban dawdling, follow the "i" signs to the Tourist Information Centre on the Promenade, a flower-lined boulevard in the city center.) On Cheltenham's northern fringes, in the village of **Prestbury**, the A46 turns north along the foot of the limestone ridge. Then, at **Southam**, it abandons the bottomland and turns to climb the steep slopes of the scarp. Stop for a few minutes in the hillside village of **Cleeve Hill** and take a short walk south along the well-marked **Cotswold Way**, another of Britain's official Long Distance Footpaths, for one of the finest views in Britain. On a good day, the panorama from **Cleeve Cloud**, the escarpment's aptly named 1,083-foot (330-meter) summit, sweeps from the Malvern Hills across the rich farmland to the northwest, to as far away as the Sugar Loaf, on the western horizon above Abergavenny.

Directly below, Cheltenham sprawls away from its neat Regency center. It is a view that seems to have been appreciated for millennia; there are traces of Iron Age earthworks directly above Cleeve Hill and along the western edge of Cleeve Common. The common itself is a wide, breezy knoll carpeted in green, flecked with wildflowers, and echoing with the songs of skylarks—and the thundering hooves of racehorses as well, for this is a favorite "gallop" for the horses and jockeys who compete at the racecourse below you at Prestbury.

When you've seen enough, return to the car and continue uphill toward Winchcombe for another 2.5 miles (4 kilometers); just before Winchcombe, turn **right** onto an unclassified road signposted for **Charlton Abbots**. The narrow lane climbs steeply for about a mile, then turns sharply left along the forested slope. At an obvious parking area, stop and walk uphill through the wood on a footpath well marked for **Belas Knap**.

The folds and knolls east of the Cotswold Escarpment are littered with the remains of civilizations long gone. There are Roman villas (the site of one, in fact, is just below the car park), Bronze Age and Iron Age settlements and fortifications, and even well-preserved burial sites from the Stone Age. Of the latter, Belas Knap is the most remarkable of some seventy scattered about the central Cotswolds. The footpath from the road climbs a short distance to the hilltop, then turns left to follow the fence bordering the delightfully named Humblebee Wood. After only a few hundred yards you come to a stile in a hawthorn hedge, on the other side, like a giant sleeping beneath a grassy coverlet, is the Belas Knap Long Barrow. Belas Knap was built by New Stone Age settlers some 5,000 years ago as a burial chamber. Some 180 feet (55 meters) long and 60 feet (18 meters) wide, it consists of four burial galleries, in which the remains of thirty people have been identified, and an elaborate—and false—"entrance." The false entry, perhaps designed to discourage grave plunderers, and the roofed galleries are crafted of thin, carefully shaped and fitted limestone slabs that reveal a remarkable level of masonry skill. The site itself, were it not for the present woodland, would have commanded a spectacular view west over the Severn plain. To this day, no one knows why these primitive settlers undertook such a monumental task—estimated to have required more than 15,000 man-hours of labor—to house the bones of so few individuals. Ancient and slightly eerie, Belas Knap is an evocative reminder that those quaint medieval villages tucked so scenically here and there among the hollows of the Cotswold hills are relative newcomers.

From the car park, continue in the same direction you were traveling on the narrow lane, passing through Charlton Abbots. At **Brock-**

The mill at Lower Slaughter—arguably the prettiest village in the Cotswolds

hampton, turn **left** in the center of the village and, when you reach the intersection with the **A436**, turn **left**. Soon thereafter, where A436 forks to the right, continue **straight ahead**, joining the **B4068**, signposted for **Stow-on-the-Wold**. This pleasant minor road wanders across high rolling farmland on its way to the tiny village of **Naunton**. After you cross the bridge over the little **Windrush River** at Naunton, continue up the hill and take the second turn to the **right**, signposted for **Upper Slaughter**. The narrow lane slides gently downhill into perhaps the most unspoiled village in the Cotswolds. Straggling along iris-edged banks of the little **River Eye**, Upper Slaughter is the epitome of the "heart of England": the ancient limestone cottages glow in the afternoon sun, rambler roses and clematis climb up and over stone walls, and colorful cottage gardens buzz with bumblebees fat with contentment. It is the kind of scene in which you would not be surprised to find Miss Marple bustling along the lane, her birdlike eyes darting this way and that, capturing subtle clues to the private passions one always suspects are bubbling beneath the surface of such tranquil villages.

From Upper Slaughter, cross the River Eye and start uphill. Almost immediately, turn **right** into a narrow lane and, at the next intersection, turn sharply **right** again, descending back into the river valley to **Lower Slaughter**. Park along the main road near the little bridge opposite the hotel. This is Upper Slaughter's fancy sister, a bit heavy on the makeup and slightly overdressed, but stunning nonetheless. Smartly turned out cottages hung with window boxes bursting with begonias and cascades of deep blue lobelia line each side of the River Eye, which is guided through the village along a channel neatly edged in stone. Wider here than in Upper Slaughter and spanned by a couple of simple white bridges, the river is really a millrace for an old flour mill that rises picturesquely beside its massive wooden water wheel at the northern edge of the village. Their murderous-sounding names notwithstanding, the Slaughters have an innocent history. The name comes either from a family called Slaughter who lived here in the sixteenth century or from the Saxon word *slohtre*, or "marshy place." No one is sure which, but butchery seems out of the question.

When you've finished wandering around Lower Slaughter, continue on the same road as before until it reaches the busy **A429**. Here, turn **left** and head north for a bit more than 1 mile (1.6 kilometers). At the intersection with the **A424**, turn sharply **right** and head south to **Burford**, less than 9 miles (14 kilometers) ahead and your home for the night.

The approach to Burford is splendid. The A424 runs along a high ridge with sweeping views of the surrounding wolds, then pitches downhill and bends sharply **left**. At a mini-roundabout, follow the A424 around to the **right** and over a fourteenth-century one-lane bridge spanning the impossibly pastoral Windrush River. On the other

Along the winding Windrust River, Burford

side, the town of Burford climbs steeply before you, its broad main street lined on both sides with a nearly seamless procession of stone houses, shops, and inns, their crooked stone roofs climbing uphill to the sky. Sweep away the cars and replace them in your mind's eye with horses and carriages, and you need change nothing else to experience a small but wealthy market town of the mid-1700s. Charming and less touristy than other Cotswold market towns, Burford is well furnished with small hotels, inns, restaurants, and pubs, and is the perfect base for exploring the region.

DIVERSIONS
The Welsh Folk Museum

If, before you cross back into England, you want just a bit more of Wales, visit the superb **Welsh Folk Museum** just outside of Cardiff at **St. Fagans**. One of Europe's foremost open-air exhibitions, the Welsh Folk Museum sprawls over 100 acres of parkland. While there are excellent introductory historical and cultural exhibits in the entrance pavilion, the real attraction is the museum's wide range of traditional buildings, moved here from all over Wales. Working in the restored buildings are bakers, weavers, woodcarvers, blacksmiths, leather workers, coopers, and other traditional craftspeople, who bring the buildings, and the nation's history, alive. One of the most intriguing sites is a row of outwardly identical miners' cottages, each decorated to represent a different period in two centuries of Welsh mining history. From **Chepstow**, take the **M4** west to Exit 33, then follow the **A4232** south and watch for museum signs. The museum is open from 10:00 A.M. to 5:00 P.M. daily from April through October, and Monday through Saturday, November through March.

CREATURE COMFORTS
Daily Bed

Burford has been catering to travelers for hundreds of years, and along High Street and Sheep Street you can choose from among six centuries' worth of atmospheric little hotels and inns, all with twentieth-century amenities. Accommodations (and prices) range from pleasant to posh. Burford and its environs also offer excellent B&B options. If the Tourist Information Centre in the Brewery building (now a wine shop) on Sheep Street is open, check their bulletin board for the brochures and business cards of nearby B&Bs. Many superb old limestone cottages and homes in the Cotswolds have been rescued from deterioration by families who have subsidized the cost of restoration by offering bed and breakfast. One of the most notable is **Dower House**, on Westhall Hill in Fulbrook, overlooking Burford. Though at first it looks medieval, Dower House was actually built in 1810, but its honey-colored limestone walls, carved stone mullions, leaded windows, steeply pitched gables, massive oak door, and polished stone floors were designed to match the sixteenth-century manor house next door. Diana and David Westall have spent nearly a decade restoring the house, funded in part by the proceeds of the sale of a 1933 Alvis touring car David restored. The walls throughout are covered with William Morris wallpapers and the house is filled with antiques. There are three double rooms in the front of the house (one with a massive carved four-poster bed), and another double with private bath is in the west wing. Breakfast is the usual, made unusual in good weather by being served in the sunny Victorian conservatory. Prices are extremely reasonable and Burford is just a short walk downhill. To get to Dower House from Burford, go back over the little Windrush River bridge and turn **right** at the mini-roundabout onto the **A361**. A few hundred yards up the hill, turn sharply **left** onto a narrow lane marked NO THROUGH ROAD.

Dower House is up the hill on the right with three distinctive front gables (look for the 1933 Lagonda, David's latest project). For information, write Dower House, Fulbrook, Burford OX8 4BJ, or phone (099382) 2596. Reservations are a must.

One caution is in order: Burford is the perfect distance from London for a quick weekend break and Londoners love it, so if you plan to arrive on a Friday or Saturday (or anytime in midsummer) reserve ahead. The closest youth hostel is on the market square in Stow; for reservations write: Youth Hostel, Stow-on-the-Wold, Cheltenham, Gloucestershire GL54 1AF, or phone (0451) 30497. For more accommodations information, write the Tourist Information Centre, The Brewery, Sheep Street, Burford 0X8 4LP, or phone (099382) 3558.

Daily Bread

With the exception of a small cafe (which closes early), dinner options in Burford are its hotels and pubs. That said, the range is wide, from multicourse extravaganzas at the Bay Tree Hotel on Sheep Street to simple but imaginative fare at the warm and friendly Mermaid Inn on High Street.

But, in keeping with the architectural theme, the most intriguing meals are to be had downriver at **the Swan**, a splendid pub in a restored water mill astride the Windrush in the tiny hamlet of **Swinbrook**. From Burford, drive over the bridge, turn **right** at the mini-roundabout, and drive uphill. In **Fulbrook**, where the A361 bends to the left, go **straight ahead** instead, up a narrow country lane that rides high above the river valley. After about a mile, the lane drops down into village of Swinbrook. At the T-junction, turn **right** and curve down to the river. The Swan stands alone at the bridge. For a change of scene after dinner, return to Burford by driving across the bridge. Turn **right** at the first intersection, around the riverside cricket pitch, and then just follow your nose upstream right into the center of town.

A Day in the Cotswolds, A Night in Greenwich

BURFORD ◆ BIBURY ◆ CHEDWORTH ◆ LONDON

- ◆ **A leisurely drive through the Coln River valley**
- ◆ **A visit to a Roman villa at Chedworth**
- ◆ **An alternative bicycle ride around Bourton-in-the-Water or Burford**
- ◆ **Two fast routes to London**

How often have I paused on every charm,
The sheltered cot, the cultivated farm,
The never-failing brook, the busy mill,
The decent church that topped the neighboring hill...
——Oliver Goldsmith, 1770

*B*urford is at its best at the extremes of the day: late in the afternoon when the setting sun burnishes the gold of its ancient stone walls, and just after dawn, before the twentieth century imposes its noisy imperatives on the High Street. If weather permits, rise early this morning and watch the town awaken.

Begin at the medieval bridge over the Windrush, as the mist rises from the water meadows and the resident pair of swans sail silent as ghost ships over the smooth green surface of the stream. Turn down the first narrow alley on the left to the tall iron gates of the Church of St. John the Baptist. This great Norman church, one of the finest in the Cotswolds, is a monument to the wealth generated by the "Cotswold Lion," the sheep breed that defined quality in wool for centuries. So completely did the people of medieval Burford depend on sheep that the churchyard is crowded with tombs topped with limestone replicas of woolpacks.

Then, with the rising sun streaming through the trees, walk down the churchyard walk, between lavender plants as fragrant as incense, and out the side gate past the fifteenth-century almshouses, with their elf-size doors. Wander up the back lane, curving first left, then right, under fruit trees and past closely packed cottages with gardens chaotic with color—magnificent old roses, masses of single-blossom hollyhocks, bushy daisies, jewel-tone lupines, and towering delphiniums ranging from vibrant cerulean to a fragile robin's-egg blue. At Whitney Street, turn right and follow it for a block to the High Street. Before, above, and below you along the wide, sloping street, the continuous (though wildly crooked) pitched stone roofscape of Burford blazes with the full force of the morning light.

Burford ("the *burh*, or borough, by the ford") was established as an independent borough around 1200 (though its history can be traced to mid-seventh-century Mercia) and thrived as a trading center throughout the Tudor period. Indeed, most of the buildings along the High Street are Tudor, though many have newer facades, and their continuous, narrow, front-to-back plots are virtually unchanged from the plans laid out by the thirteenth-century burgesses. Early in the morning, before the traffic picks up, you can feel the gentle pulse of the awakening village. Someone will already be bustling about at the bakery across the street and up the hill. They'll be scrubbing the sidewalk in front of the Mermaid Inn too. If it's market day, deep purple cineraria, bright red geraniums, and cut flowers will already be displayed for sale under the arches of the Tolsey, the town's sixteenth-century courthouse, right next to the iced trays of the traveling fishmonger. Nip into the bakery, grab something sinful, and watch the day begin.

🚗 ABROAD IN THE HIDDEN COTSWOLDS

Distance: About 35 miles/56 kilometers
Roads: Mostly minor roads and narrow lanes
Driving Time: Till early afternoon
Map: Ordnance Survey Landranger Map #163

The Cotswolds—perhaps England's most beloved region—are a curiously contradictory landscape, at once windswept and spacious and, in its sheltered clefts and vales, intimate and cozy. To a great extent, this split personality is an accident of nature. The Cotswolds consist of a vast, lumpy bed of fine-grained limestone. This limestone, which, depending on the light, can glow a rich apricot or fade to ashen gray, is easy to fashion into building blocks and carve into decorative stonework. It is everywhere: in the stone walls that race across the hills (*wolds*), in humble cottages and grand manor houses, in parish churches (and St. Paul's Cathedral), and in the Georgian and Regency townhouses of Bath and Cheltenham. Even the lichen-crusted roofing

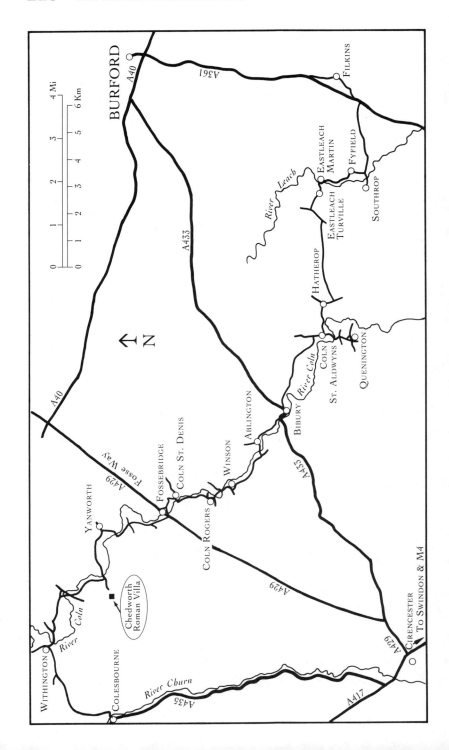

"slates" are not slate at all, but slabs of limestone. But this stone does more than decorate the landscape, it determines the patterns of settlement as well. Except for Stow, virtually every hamlet, village, and town in the Cotswolds is in the folds, not on the wolds. The reason is water. Limestone drains quickly, so the high rounded hills are dry. Settlements are strung along the banks of the region's few reliable rivers and along "spring lines"—places on hillsides where springs emerge.

The result is an up-hill-and-down-dale sort of place, a landscape of wide airy vistas and close-knit villages that Mark Twain once said was "too beautiful to be left out of doors." The celebrated towns of the Cotswolds—Broadway, Chipping Campden, and too-cute-for-its-own-good Bourton-on-the-Water—are lovely, especially after the tour buses leave. But the real beauty of the Cotswolds, the places that possess what John Masefield called "the inward peace that beauty brings," are the out-of-the-way villages. To capture that inner grace, you need to get off the main roads, charming though they may be, and seek out the single-track lanes. Go on foot or by bicycle (see Diversions), or simply follow one of those life-giving little rivers from hamlet to hamlet, water meadow to millrace. Study the precise artistry of a mortarless stone wall, or a dovecote. Get down on your knees and count the varieties of wildflowers and herbs flourishing in a well-managed meadow (meadows take managing, they don't just happen). Listen carefully to the ebb and flow of conversation, gossip, and news in a small village pub, impenetrable as the vernacular may be. Here, in the end, are the real Cotswolds, and the real Britain.

We end the day today in London—or, more precisely, Greenwich—but we begin with some of the hidden places in the Cotswolds. From Burford, drive up the steep hill to the big roundabout. Go around halfway and turn south on the **A361** toward **Lechlade**. About 4 miles (6.4 kilometers) south of the roundabout, turn **left** onto a lane signposted for **Filkins**. Just before you enter the heart of this pretty little village, look for a large stone barn on the right with a small **Cotswold Woolen Weavers** sign. Here, in a handsome grouping of restored farm buildings, artisans have established an exhibition on the Cotswold wool industry and a busy mill full of clattering Victorian weaving machinery in which visitors are welcome.

Then, continue through the village (note the walls of upright stone slabs, unique to Filkins), past the Lamb Inn, and out to the A361 again. Turn **left** onto the A361 and, almost immediately, turn **right** for **Southrop** and **Fyfield**, driving across an open landscape of fields and meadows edged with thick hawthorn hedges and fringed with frothy cow parsley and bright pink campion. Before reaching Southrop, turn **right** at a signpost for Fyfield and **Eastleach**. At the T-junction at Fyfield, turn **left** toward **Eastleach Martin** and, across the **River Leach**, its sister village, **Eastleach Turville**. The two pretty hamlets are

Rack Isle and the weavers' cottages in Bibury, along the River Coln

joined by a narrow bridge and an ancient stone "clapper" footbridge. Just beyond the pub in the center of Eastleach Turville, bear **right** in the direction of **Hatherop**. At the next T-junction, turn **left**, then, almost immediately, turn **right** onto yet another lane, signposted for Hatherop and **Coln St. Aldwyns**. This road takes you up over the divide between the rivers Leach and Coln (both tributaries of the Thames). At the next T-junction, turn **right** into Hatherop, then **left** in the center of the village to drop downhill between the high stone walls of a large estate with sheep and cows grazing the parkland between clumps of ancient beech trees. Below, the **River Coln** zigzags across the valley floor.

Coln St. Aldwyns, named after a hermit saint called Ealdwine, is a delightful collection of sturdy Cotswold cottages fronted by pretty gardens. At the central T-junction, detour **left** down the hill to the river, passing the old mill, in the direction of **Quenington**. When you get to the large green, bear **left** past a pub called the Earl Grey and drive to the bottom of the hill to explore a classic Cotswold combination of manor,

manor house, farm, and mill by the river. Then, retrace the route back to Coln St. Aldwyns and go straight up the hill out of town in the direction of **Bibury**. At the top, turn **left** over a hill (along a short stretch of **Akeman Street**, a Roman road) and back to the river valley again, with a splendid view of an old manor house (now a hotel) and the rest of the roofs and chimney pots of the village of Bibury spread out across the valley.

At the T-junction with the **A433**, turn **left** downhill and around to the right to Bibury, one of the Cotswolds' most beautiful villages. Bibury has a multitude of charms, but perhaps its most intriguing feature is Rack Isle, a tiny wildflower- and reed-filled nature reserve cupped in a lovely swale, with the village's much-photographed weavers' cottages strung along one edge. Rack Isle harks back to the seventeenth century, when the village's weavers hung freshly fulled (washed and plumped) fabric there on racks, called *tenters*, to dry (the origin of the phrase "on tenterhooks"). Today, fat trout lounge in the placid Coln, which flows around the isle; mallards and other well-fed wildfowl paddle contentedly along the surface; and larks sing in the reed beds. It is an altogether delightful spot—despite the crowds.

At the Swan Hotel, where the main road turns left, continue **straight ahead** instead, with the Coln (and a trout farm) on the left. From here, it's less than a mile to **Ablington**, quieter and less "done" than Bibury, but with its own timeless riverside beauty. Here, just beyond the two stone lions guarding the local manor's gate, bear **left** over the river toward **Winson**. As you approach this hamlet, watch for a sign that reads WINSON VILLAGE ONLY and turn **right**, plunging down a narrow lane that curves toward the river, past lovely limestone cottages overrun with flowers, and then climbs back to the main road again. The valley opens up a bit as you approach **Coln Rogers**, a village almost entirely taken over by a vast horse farm. Stop in Coln Rogers for a moment and wander down the lane toward the river to visit the squat little parish church—over 1,000 years old and one of the few intact Saxon churches in England.

Now the road continues upstream to **Coln St. Dennis**, the last of "the Colns." At the fork beyond the village, bear **left**, arriving almost immediately at **Fossebridge** and the **A429**. Take a quick look at your road map. With few exceptions, the A429 runs ramrod straight for some 80 miles (129 kilometers) from **Cirencester** to **Leicester** and beyond to **Lincoln** (though it loses its number, and sometimes its pavement, along the way). There are two clues here: straightness and the "cester" in these names. *Cester* is the Roman word for "fort," and straight is how Romans liked the roads they built between them. The clues tell you that you've reached the **Fosse Way**, one of several Roman roads—so well engineered that their routes and even their beds are still in use—that converge on Cirencester.

Turn **left** onto the A429, cross the river, and then turn **right** onto another minor road, signposted for **Yanworth**. Once again, follow the River Coln, now meandering lazily across the floor of a broad, peaceful valley grazed by jet black Angus cattle. After passing straight across a four-way intersection, the road crosses the tiny river and climbs up the opposite hillside to a T-junction. Here, turn **left** in the direction of **Withington**, and dip back down into the Coln valley. Cross the river, and at the fork in the road, stay **left**, climbing up the forested hillside to **Chedworth Roman Villa**.

Cirencester (then called Corinium) was Roman England's second city, after London, and the Romans and their most prosperous Romano-British allies often maintained country villas in addition to their town homes. Indeed, Ordnance Survey maps for this area are littered with "Roman Villa (remains of)" notations. The remains are usually disappointing—except for Chedworth. Built sometime in the second century A.D. and occupied through the fourth, the villa was discovered in 1864 by the local gamekeeper, who noticed that rabbits burrowing in the hillside were excavating mosaic tiles as they built their warren.

The Chedworth villa is remarkably well preserved, thanks to a land-

In tiny Winson, along the River Coln

slide that covered it with earth. The site includes farm buildings and workshops and a handsome country house that had all the usual Roman luxuries: elaborate baths, under-floor heating systems, glazed windows, brightly painted walls, and beautiful mosaic floors. The west wing of the house has an elaborate mosaic with the four seasons depicted in the four corners of the room. The complex and its museum, operated by the National Trust, are well worth a stop; open 10:00 A.M. to 5:30 P.M., Tuesday through Sunday, from March through October; 11:00 A.M. to 4:00 P.M., Wednesday through Sunday, from November through early December.

🚗 EAST TO LONDON

Distance: About 110 miles/177 kilometers
Roads: Mostly primary roads and motorway
Driving Time: 3–4 hours, depending on traffic
Map: Michelin Map #404

From Chedworth Roman Villa, descend the hill and turn **left** in the direction of Withington, continuing **straight ahead** at the next intersection, past a lovely small manor house and barn. At the T-junction at Withington, turn **left**, passing a picturesque riverside pub called The Mill (a good stop for lunch), then cross the river and climb into the village. At the center of Withington, turn **left** and follow signs for **Colesbourne**, branching **left** again at the fork outside of town. This minor lane ducks in and out of small woods, then slips down the side of another valley. At the T-junction, turn **right** into Colesbourne, on the banks of the **River Churn**.

At Colesbourne, turn **left** onto the **A435** and follow the Churn downstream to Cirencester. As you approach Cirencester, turn **left** onto the **A417** (another Roman road, called the Ermine Way) and take it around the eastern fringes of the city. When it turns east, continue southeast instead, following signs for the **A419** toward **Swindon**. As you approach Swindon, watch for signs to the **M4** motorway and take another bypass around the east side of this industrial city. Then simply take the M4 east toward **London**.

If you've made your own plans in London, stay on the M4 and, when it ends, continue straight ahead on the **A4** to central London and Hyde Park. If your trip has reached its end and you're bound for the airport, Heathrow is right on the M4 just beyond the junction with the **M25**. If Gatwick is your destination, leave the M4 at the M25 junction and follow the M25 around to the south, switching to the **M23** south, well signed for the airport.

This itinerary, however, heads for **Greenwich**, just downriver from the city, only minutes from the heart of things by train, yet possessing

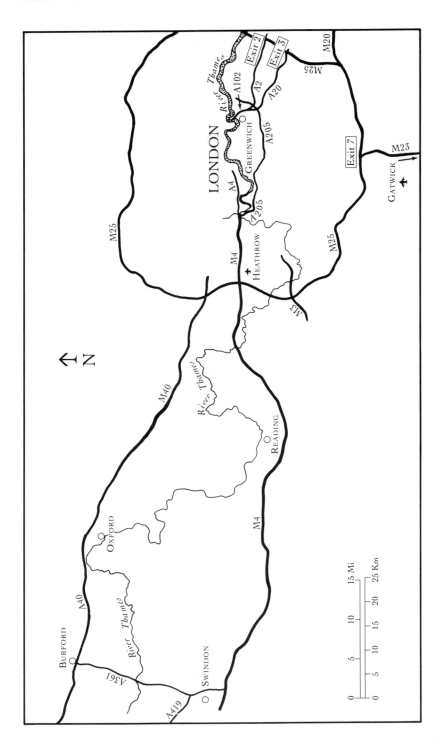

the charm of a village. To get there, go to the end of the M4, then follow signs (carefully) for the **South Circular** (sometimes called the Inner Ring Road), technically the **A205**. This route, a precursor to the M25, swings around through London's southern suburbs, then back up to the river, just east of Greenwich. Before you get that far, however, leave the A205 at the **A102** and follow signs for the **Blackwall Tunnel**. Then, just before you reach the tunnel, exit for Greenwich. In moments, you'll be cruising through the parkland adjacent to the Greenwich Maritime Museum. At the T-junction in the middle of the town center, look for the sign for the Tourist Information Centre, to the right, for guidance on accommodations and sightseeing.

DIVERSIONS
Walking and Cycling in the Cotswolds

If this day dawns impossibly sunny, consider spending the morning exploring the Cotswold countryside at a leisurely pace, by walking—or pedaling—from village to village. London is only two to three hours away, so you'll have plenty of time to get there later.

There are several walking options. Many Tourist Information Centres in the Cotswolds have developed their own local walking tour itineraries, complete with annotated maps. Alternatively, you can simply follow either of two Cotswold walks described in detail in *The Best of Britain's Countryside: Southern England*. Finally, you can contact the Cotswold Warden Service, County Planning Department, Shire Hall, Gloucester GL1 2TN, phone (0452) 425672, and ask for details on their program of **guided walks**. An official "Area of Outstanding Natural Beauty," the Cotswolds have a team of voluntary wardens who lead walks from many locations several times a week throughout the year. Even if you do not make arrangements in advance, duck into the Tourist Information Centre in Burford for a seasonal brochure of the walks being offered.

Cycling is, if anything, an even more delightful option. The web of narrow lanes that weaves through the Cotswolds, though not as flat as East Anglia, makes for some of the most pleasant cycling in Britain. The Oxfordshire Tourism Office has created a well-signed **Cotswold Cycle Way** that runs through the eastern Cotswolds quite close to Burford, and Gloucestershire is in the process of doing the same for the west. Check the Burford Tourist Information Centre for information on the Cotswold Cycle Way. For Gloucestershire routes, contact Gloucestershire Tourism, County Planning Department, Shire Hall, Gloucester GL1 2TN. Bicycles can be hired at the Golden Pheasant Hotel, The High Street, Burford, phone (099382) 3223, and nearby at Teagues, High Street, Bourton-on-the-Water, phone (0451) 29248. The number of bicycles is limited at both locations, however, so reserve in ad-

If the weather is fine, abandon your four wheels for two!

vance or check early in the morning. Rates are reasonable. Then, armed with an Ordnance Survey map of the area (available at any newsagent's or bookstore) and recommendations from the hire agent, plunge off into the heart of England. (Later, to reach London, drive east from Burford on the A40 to Oxford, then take the M40 to the city.)

CREATURE COMFORTS
Daily Bed

This itinerary assumes you'll want to spend a day or two at the end of your trip sightseeing in London. One of the most delightful cities on earth, London also has attained the dubious status of being one of the most expensive on earth. There's nothing wrong with being extravagant, so long as price and value match. Increasingly, however, this relationship is distant, at best, in many London hotels, even the "modest" ones.

You shouldn't have to sink a substantial hunk of your travel budget on a hotel room in London (your eyes will be closed most of the time you're in the room anyway). Below is a list of three attractive alternatives.

STAY IN THE SOUTHERN SUBURBS. If you look closely at your map (the "Greater London" inset of Michelin Map #404) you'll notice, south of the M25, a web of thin black lines interrupted by little white rectangles. The lines are railroads, the rectangles stations. The accommodation guides in Further Reading list a number of B&Bs, inns, and hotels in villages near these rail lines. You can stay the next two nights south of the city, take the train into the city in the morning after the rush hour (thus saving with a day excursion ticket), then come home after dinner or theater in town. The money you save on lodging will far outweigh the cost of the train ticket and a day of not using your car—not to mention the annoyance of driving and the cost of parking in the city.

STAY NEAR YOUR AIRPORT. Whether you are flying out of Gatwick or Heathrow, consider staying at an airport hotel. You can return your car today and take an inexpensive day excursion train (from Gatwick) or the Tube (from Heathrow), ride into the city tomorrow morning, then return in time to pack tomorrow evening knowing you won't have to deal with the hassle of getting to the airport. You'll already be there.

STAY IN GREENWICH. This charming urban village—the focal point of tomorrow's itinerary—is only 15 to 20 minutes by train from Charing Cross Station in central London and a delightful 30 minutes by the new RiverBus from Charing Cross Pier. In travel time, that's as close to the heart of things as Kensington. Accessible, more affordable, and possessing formidable attractions of its own, Greenwich is an excellent alternative to staying in pricey central London. To arrange accommodations, you can write the Tourist Information Centre, 46 Greenwich Church Street, Greenwich SE10 9BL for suggestions, or call them a day or two in advance at 081-858-6376 and use their booking service. There is also a private B&B booking service called Welcome Homes at 6 Turnpin Lane, Greenwich SE10 9JA, phone 081-853-2706. In addition, a branch of the moderately priced Ibis hotel chain has been opened right in the center of town (call your travel agent for information). Finally, not in Greenwich, but in nearby Rotherhithe, in the heart of the rejuvenated Surrey Docks, is a brand-new youth hostel; address inquiries to Youth Hostel, Island Yard, Salter Road, London, SE16 1LY, or phone 071-232-2114. For other London youth hostels, see the YHA guide in Further Reading.

Note: Remember to confirm your return flight reservations tonight or tomorrow morning; call London Directory Enquiries (142) for the phone number of your airline (airline reservations and information offices are generally open only during regular office hours).

Exploring the "London River"

- ◆ How to get around on (or near) the river
- ◆ A walking tour of historic Greenwich
- ◆ Along the "reborn" Thames by boat and light rail
- ◆ Getting around in central London

Then Commerce brought into the public Walk
The busy Merchant; the big Warehouse built;
Rais'd the strong Crane; choak'd up the loaded Street
With foreign Plenty; and thy Stream, O THAMES,
Large, gentle, deep, majestic King of Floods!
—James Thomson, 1726

The River Thames, swollen by rains that fall in distant English hills, laden with silt from remote English fields, flowing placidly through centuries of English history, comes to life near the end of its long journey as it twists through central London. What London was and is—the archetypical international metropolis—it owes in large part to its river, its throbbing commercial aorta. To know London, you must know the "London River," as its watermen have called it for generations.

Its name is Celtic, *Taom-Uis* ("the pouring forth of the water"), and long before the coming of the Romans, the Celts had built a settlement on its marshy banks called Llyn-Din ("the fort by the pool"). When the Romans did arrive, in A.D. 43, they set up housekeeping on some gravel knolls on the north bank and adopted the Celtic names, calling the river Tamesis and the site Londinium. From that point on, the histories of each were one and the same. One by one, the conquerors came, borne upriver and into English history on the Thames's tidal surge: Vikings, Angles, Saxons, Jutes, Danes, and Normans.

By the Middle Ages, London had become the known world's preeminent trading port. At the Pool of London, just below London

Bridge, the Hansea and the other European merchant guilds set up shop along wharves that lined both banks. By 1594, more than 40,000 watermen were officially employed on the river, ferrying goods, piloting vessels, keeping the crowded docks humming. It was said that you could cross the river from bank to bank on the decks of ships and never get your feet wet. As commerce and congestion grew, the docks spread downstream. And east of the city's gritty East End, where the muddy river curves south and then north again in a huge 4.5-mile (7.2-kilometer) oxbow, a marshy expanse known as the Isle of Dogs became the largest shipping complex in the world, with some 700 acres (283 hectares) of protected water and 55 miles (88.5 kilometers) of docks.

By Dickens's day, the docklands had become a seething microcosm of humanity. Watermen, lightermen, stevedores, dockers, barrow boys, sailmakers, and, later, steamfitters thronged the quaysides. Seamen from the four corners of the earth swarmed the streets of Wapping. A "Chinatown" grew in Limehouse. A hundred languages clashed with impenetrable Cockney English and competed with the screeching gulls, clanging bells, snapping sails, and screaming steam whistles of Victorian maritime London. The heady scents of tar and hemp and foundry smoke mixed with spices from the Moluccas, coffee from the Americas, and tea from China and India. The British empire was expanding, the East India and West India companies thriving, and the Industrial Revolution booming, sucking in new raw materials from around the globe and pumping out new manufactured products for an eager world.

And then it was over. The Blitz, which killed 29,000 Londoners, damaged 80 percent of the city's buildings, including much of the strategically vital docklands. The docks were rebuilt and as late as the 1950s were handling some 50 million tons of cargo a year, but the end was near; deeper-draft vessels and the container ship revolution moved commerce far downstream and left the docklands behind. By the 1970s, the city had turned its back on the river and the Isle of Dogs had become a wasteland of rusting cranes and rotting docks. The shells of massive warehouses sat, windowless and roofless, amid acres of rubble.

Today, this too has changed. After decades of neglect, it finally dawned on London that there was a gold mine out its back door: a river now clean enough that salmon had returned, vast areas of valuable river frontage, and glorious stone and brick commercial buildings ripe for reuse.

It's not been an easy rebirth; the London Docklands Development Corporation, created by central government in 1981 with sweeping powers, initially ran roughshod over the neighborhoods along the river, seizing land by eminent domain or squeezing working-class families and long-established businesses out through rising land values and taxes. When these social issues finally were ironed out, an economic slump brought some of the most ambitious development projects to a standstill. The architecture in the new Docklands runs the gamut from sensitive re-use to unabashed post-modernism, a sort of circus for the eye. Controversial, yet vibrant, the docklands and the rest of "the London River" have been reborn.

GETTING AROUND ON (OR NEAR) THE RIVER

A day along the Thames is a trip through London's history. The reach of river between Westminster and Greenwich includes the Houses of Parliament, St. Paul's Cathedral, the Tower of London, St. Katherine Docks, Butler Wharf (and Terence Conran's Design Museum there), Tobacco Dock, Canary Wharf, West India Quay, Greenwich, and—not incidentally—such venerable riverside pubs as the Prospect of Whitby (thought to be London's oldest), the Mayflower, the Barley Mow, and the Trafalgar, among many others. The best place to begin is Greenwich. If you aren't already staying there, you have several route alternatives.

BY BOAT. From April through October, **riverboats** run from **Westminster Pier** (next to the Westminster Underground station) to Greenwich every 30 minutes from 10:30 A.M. to 4:00 P.M., with a somewhat more restricted schedule in winter. (An added benefit is a cheeky running narrative on the sights from the captain—if he's in the mood.) Depending upon tides, the trip takes about 45 minutes. For more information, call 071-930-4097.

Sleek, zippy **RiverBuses** leave **Charing Cross Pier** (near the station) every 20 minutes from 7:00 A.M. to 8:00 P.M., Monday through Friday, year-round, and take only 30 minutes to reach Greenwich. Because the RiverBus's primary clientele is commuters, you can buy a cheap "Explorer" ticket after 9:30 A.M. good for unlimited trips for the rest of the day, except for the 5:00 P.M. to 6:00 P.M. rush hour. But remember, the RiverBus does *not* run on weekends. For information, call 071-512-0555.

BY TRAIN. BritRail **"Network Southeast"** trains run from **Charing Cross Station** to Greenwich roughly every 30 minutes (more frequently at rush hour). The trip takes 15 to 20 minutes. If you plan to return by train as well and are starting after 10:00 A.M. (or anytime on weekends or holidays), buy a "Cheap Day Return" ticket. If you plan to return by Docklands Light Rail and the Underground (see below), buy a "One Day Travelcard," good for all three—again, after 10:00 A.M. and anytime weekends and holidays.

BY LIGHT RAIL. For a splendid bird's-eye view of the river and the entire Docklands complex, try the elevated **Docklands Light Rail**. Take the Tube to the **Tower Hill** station and then walk a few steps to the **Tower Gateway** terminus of the Docklands Light Rail green line, taking it to **Crossharbor**. There, walk across the platform and take the red line to **Island Gardens**. From here, take a 5-minute stroll *beneath* the river to Greenwich through the **Greenwich Foot Tunnel**. The foot tunnel was built in 1902 to make it easier for workers living on the south bank to reach the busy docks on the north. Docklands Light Rail operates from 5:30 A.M. to 9:30 P.M., Monday through Friday only; alternative bus service is offered on weekends. As above, the "One Day Travelcard" is the best fare bargain. Call 071-222-1234 for information.

🚶 A WALKING TOUR OF OLD GREENWICH

Distance: About 2 miles; allow 2 hours
Difficulty: An easy morning stroll
Total Elevation Gain: Negligible
Gear: Comfortable shoes or sneakers, rain gear, camera
Map: Free "Greenwich Places of Interest" map and *Historic Maritime Greenwich* brochure from the Tourist Information Centre

If, as the saying goes, "Every drop of the Thames is liquid history," then Greenwich has been history's witness, watching it ebb and flow like the tides for centuries. There is a Roman temple on the grounds of what today is Greenwich Park, but the village came into its own during the Middle Ages. Henry VIII was born here, as were his daughters, Elizabeth I and the ill-fated Mary I. The English fleet sailed from here to confront the Spanish Armada in 1588, and Francis Drake was knighted by Queen Elizabeth I here after sailing around the world. The *Gypsy Moth IV*, the tiny sailboat a latter-day knight, Sir Francis Chichester, sailed single-handed around the world, stands at Greenwich Pier, looking frail in the shadow of the great *Cutty Sark*, one of the last of the clipper ships to ply the China tea trade.

Greenwich's maritime history, and some of London's finest neo-classical architecture, are a few of the highlights of a pleasant 2-hour walking tour best begun at the pier. (Guided walking tours are offered by the Tourist Information Centre; check at its offices at 46 Greenwich Church Street for times.) From the *Cutty Sark*, walk up **Greenwich Church Street** and turn **left** into **College Approach**; in the middle of the block, turn **right** through a colonnaded archway to **Greenwich Market**. From the early 1800s, this was Greenwich's fish, meat, and

Past, present, and future London crowd the banks of Old Father Thames.

vegetable market. If you turn around, you can see the city's stern reminder to its shopkeepers: A FALSE BALANCE IS AN ABOMINATION TO THE LORD BUT A JUST WEIGHT IS HIS DELIGHT. (On weekends, the covered marketplace is packed with craftmakers' booths, and other open markets specializing in antiques, books, and prints are scattered around the center of town.) At the other end of the market, cross narrow **Turnpin Lane** and continue up an alley to **Nelson Road**, lined with antique stores and antiquarian booksellers. Turn **right**, walk to the corner, then turn **left** onto Church Street (which becomes **Stockwell Street**), but pause at the corner to admire a delightful art-deco brasserie, complete with curved corner, lots of black-and-white faux marbling, and a pair of elephants atop tall pilasters.

The "church" of Church Street is **St. Alfege's**, designed by Nicholas Hawksmoor and built upon the site where the Saxon bishop Alfege was murdered by invading Danes in 1012 for refusing to pay a ransom for the town. Continue up the street to the Ibis Hotel, turn **left**, and walk past a series of pretty bowfront Victorian shops. Then turn **left** again at

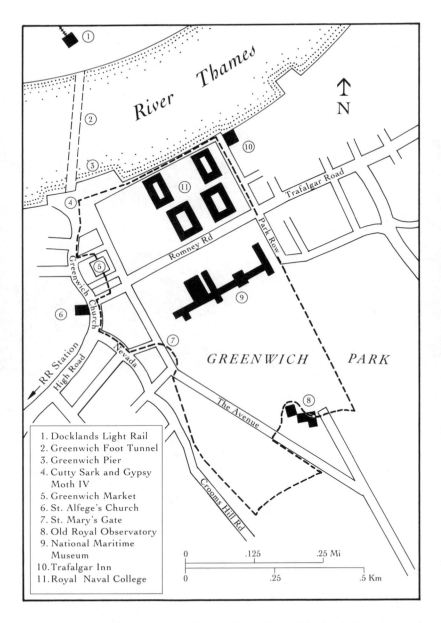

1. Docklands Light Rail
2. Greenwich Foot Tunnel
3. Greenwich Pier
4. Cutty Sark and Gypsy
   Moth IV
5. Greenwich Market
6. St. Alfege's Church
7. St. Mary's Gate
8. Old Royal Observatory
9. National Maritime
   Museum
10. Trafalgar Inn
11. Royal Naval College

the Old Rose and Crown pub, built originally in Elizabeth I's reign and rebuilt during Victoria's at the end of the last century. The route now passes the Greenwich Theater to end at the park. At **St. Mary's Gate**, turn **right**, past **St. Mary's Lodge**, and take the path uphill that follows the right-hand side of Greenwich Park. This path initially passes through a lovely herb and perennial border garden, with a series of handsome Georgian homes behind, lining the street. Watch for a distinctively massive Henry Moore sculpture on a knoll to the left. At **Croomshill Gate**, turn **left** and take the middle path across the hillside. At **The Avenue**, turn **left** again and walk downhill until you draw even with the **Old Royal Observatory**. Here, take the path to the **right** that sweeps around to the terrace in front of the building. The observatory, founded in 1675 and designed by Christopher Wren, is Britain's oldest scientific establishment. The observatory has since moved to the clearer air and lower ambient light conditions of Sussex; today the building houses the Museum of Astronomy (open Monday through Saturday, 10:00 A.M. to 6:00 P.M., Sunday 2:00 P.M. to 6:00 P.M.; closes at 5:00 P.M. in winter). Some of the most interesting aspects of the site are *outside*. The Greenwich meridian crosses the courtyard, providing the somehow deeply satisfying opportunity to place one foot in the western hemisphere and the other in the eastern. Nearby are the official measurement standards of the yard, foot, and inch—the last holdouts in an increasingly metric world. Here too is the twenty-four-hour clock that measures Greenwich mean time. And on the roof of the observatory is the world's first visual time signal, a red ball that is raised to the top of a mast at precisely 1:00 P.M. each day.

Better than any of these scientific benchmarks is the view from the terrace—perhaps the finest view of London there is. Directly below is another of Wren's masterpieces, the **Royal Naval College**. Across the river, architect Cesar Pelli's **Canary Wharf Tower**, the tallest in London, presides over the sprawling Isle of Dogs. Beyond that is London itself—the City, the West End, and, in the distance, the gentle swell of Hampstead Heath. Even without the rest of Greenwich's attractions, this view alone is worth the walk.

With the observatory's entrance at your back, walk past the statue of General James Wolfe and east on a narrow path. At the first path intersection, turn **left**, and walk downhill. At the bottom, the building on the left is the **National Maritime Museum**, with the world's largest collection of maritime artifacts. The museum is housed in a splendid neoclassical complex, the center of which is **The Queen's House**, designed by Inigo Jones for James I's consort, Anne of Denmark. Begun in 1616, it was the first Palladian building built in Britain. It is open the same hours as the observatory.

As it reaches the Maritime Museum, the downhill path passes through a wrought-iron gate and into **Park Row**. Follow Park Row toward the river, crossing **Trafalgar Road**. When you reach the river, with the Trafalgar pub on the right (a favorite of Dickens, Thackeray, Collins, and countless Members of Parliament), turn **left** along the river walk, with the **Royal Naval College** on your left and stop briefly at the

The ornate riverfront gates of Sir Christopher Wren's magnificent Royal Naval College

elaborate iron water gate. The purity and symmetry of Wren's design for the college (originally a hospital) is simply stunning: four buildings facing a central parade, each lined with long colonnades and supporting classical pediments, the whole composition topped with a pair of soaring cupolas. The college is not a museum, but its chapel and Painted Hall are open to visitors every day but Thursday from 2:30 P.M. to 5:00 P.M. A few more steps west along the riverbank return you to Greenwich Pier.

ALONG THE LONDON RIVER

This afternoon, leave Greenwich behind and explore more of "the London River." Begin by hopping the RiverBus at Greenwich Pier and taking it upriver to **London Bridge City Pier**. Along the way, the fast catamaran curves north around the Isle of Dogs—named, incidently, either for the hunting dogs Henry VIII kept there, or a corruption of the *dykes* that once riddled the marshy isle, or simply a corruption of *docks* (no one knows for sure). On the opposite shore is **Rotherhithe** and the **Surrey Docks** complex, once the heart of the wood products industry and now in the process of being redeveloped.

As the river curves left again, the boat passes two old riverside pubs, **The Grapes** and **The Barley Mow**. Soon thereafter, you pass the entrances to **Tobacco Docks** and **St. Katherine Docks**. Both banks

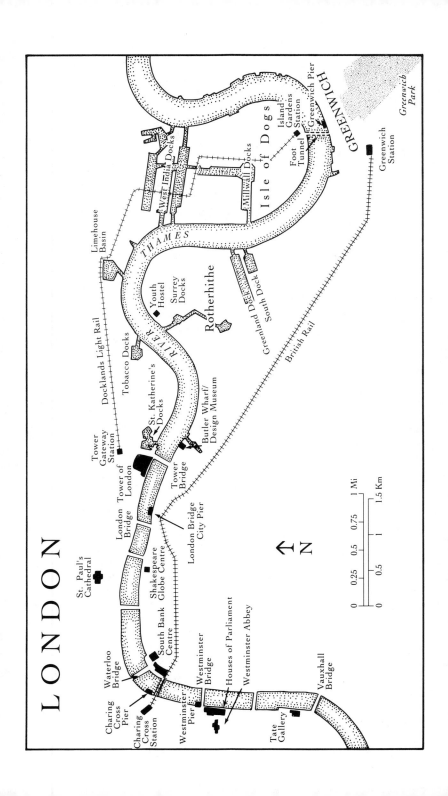

LONDON

St. Paul's Cathedral

Charing Cross Pier
Charing Cross Station

Waterloo Bridge

Westminster Pier

South Bank Centre

Westminster Bridge

Houses of Parliament

Westminster Abbey

Tate Gallery

Vauxhall Bridge

Shakespeare Globe Centre

London Bridge
Tower of London

London Bridge City Pier

Tower Bridge

St. Katherine's Docks

Tower Gateway Station

Butler Wharf/ Design Museum

Docklands Light Rail

Tobacco Docks

Limehouse Basin

West India Docks

Isle of Dogs

Millwall Docks

THAMES

RIVER

Youth Hostel

Surrey Docks

Rotherhithe

Greenland Dock

South Dock

British Rail

Island Gardens Station

Foot Tunnel

Greenwich Pier

GREENWICH

Greenwich Station

Greenwich Park

N

| 0 | 0.25 | 0.5 | 0.75 | 1 Mi |

| 0 | 0.5 | 1 | 1.5 Km |

are packed with imaginatively restored riverside warehouses and industrial buildings and, in a moment, the RiverBus draws up to London Bridge City Pier. Alight here and follow signs downriver to **Hays Galleria** and, 10 or 15 minutes farther on, the **Design Museum** at **Butler Wharf**, Terence Conran's monument to timeless commercial design (with both permanent and changing exhibitions).

From Butler Wharf, take the ferry across and upriver to **Tower Pier**, a few steps from the **Tower of London**. Here, you have a choice. You can visit the tower and later continue upriver to Charing Cross by RiverBus, perhaps walking along the **Embankment** to the **Houses of Parliament** and **Westminster Abbey**, and then take the sightseeing boat back downriver to Greenwich, or you can take the Tube from the Tower Hill station to the St. Paul's station and visit Wren's magnificent **St. Paul's Cathedral** or any of a number of other central London attractions (see Getting Around the Rest of London). Then (Monday through Friday only) return to Tower Hill, walk the short distance to the Tower Gateway terminus of the **Docklands Light Rail**, and spend the next half hour or so soaring above the architectural and historical spectacle of the Isle of Dogs: **West India Quay**, **Canary Wharf**, **Heron Quays**, and **South Quay**. At **Crossharbor** (where there's a Visitor Centre), switch to the red line (just across the platform) and continue on past **Mudchute** (with its incongruous farm) to **Island Gardens**. Then take the foot tunnel back to Greenwich.

GETTING AROUND THE REST OF LONDON

The trouble with London is that once you spend an hour you want to spend a lifetime. The museums, galleries, monuments, parks, shops, restaurants, pubs, neighborhoods, and passing scene offer almost limitless fascination. If you choose to spend the day doing the more usual London sights or plan to stay longer in the city, consider the walking tours described in the first two volumes of *The Best of Britain's Countryside*, or consult one of the London guidebooks listed in Further Reading. In the meantime, you'll need some tips on how to get around efficiently.

GET THE OFFICIAL MAP. Before you do anything else (unless you've already done so) buy the **British Tourist Authority's** inexpensive and invaluable *Official London Map*. Accept no substitutes. Send away for it in advance, buy a copy at the information desk when you arrive at the airport (see Day One), or head for either the Tourist Information Centre in Greenwich (if that's where you're staying) or the British Travel Centre at 12 Regent Street, a block south of Piccadilly Circus, open 9:00 A.M. to 6:30 P.M., Monday through Friday; 10:00

A.M. to 4:00 P.M., Saturday and Sunday, with longer Saturday hours in the summer. While you're there, you may want to pick up the Tourist Authority's *Quick Guide to London*, a slim brochure with descriptions, locations, times, and phone numbers for every major attraction in the city, plus other helpful information.

TAXI. If you're traveling with several people and it's the weekend (traffic during the week is horrible), consider taking cabs around the center of the city. They're roomy, the drivers are unfailingly friendly, helpful, and polite (saying "please" when you give directions warms them right up), and their knowledge of the city is astonishing. They spend from two to as long as four years traveling around London by bicycle or moped to learn what it takes to get a license (drivers call this "doing the Knowledge"). There are no better-prepared cabbies in the world. You can trust your driver to know precisely how to get where you want to go by the quickest route, no matter how circuitous it may seem. The fare, when split among three or four riders, will be competitive with the Tube, except over very long distances or in rush hour. (Tip roughly 15 percent.) A cab is available if its roof light is on. If you can't find one that's available, head for the taxi rank at the nearest hotel. Only use licensed, metered cabs; so-called "minicabs" are unlicensed and are free to charge whatever they like.

BUSES. The advantage of London's great bus system is that you get to see everything along the way. The disadvantage is that the system is impenetrably complex. If you're only in London for a day or two, skip the buses.

YOUR RENTAL CAR. Driving in London makes sense if you know the city well, have a gifted navigator, relish the strategic challenge of gridlock, and view driving as a blood sport. These details aside, there is this to say about driving in London: the signing is terrific. If you know what neighborhood your destination is in, and roughly what part of town that is, just follow the signs to that neighborhood, then use your London map to find the specific location. If you suddenly find yourself going in a direction apparently away from your target, don't panic, just keep following the signs. They're designed to steer you away from chronically congested areas and one-way traffic traps between you and your destination. As for parking, look for garages, or, if you won't be long, metered spaces. If you lead a particularly charmed life, you may be able to find unrestricted parking in some residential areas, but don't count on it. Under no circumstances park next to a double yellow line.

TUBE. There's almost nowhere in London that isn't a few blocks from a Tube station (look for the red circle bisected by a horizontal blue line that says UNDERGROUND). The route map is in your BTA London Map and on the wall in each station, and free maps are available from ticket agents in each station. Each line has its own name and color code. You can buy your ticket from the ticket agent's kiosk or, increasingly, vending machines. Then, you run the ticket through an automated gate and *keep it* to hand to another agent (or run through an exit machine) at your destination. In stations where two or more lines intersect, follow signs on the wall for the line you want. Many platforms have electronic signs that tell you how soon the next train will come and, if the line splits somewhere, which branch the next train will take. You can zoom across town quickly (in most cases faster than by cab) and the fares are relatively cheap. If you're planning on doing a lot of "Tubing," buy a one-day Travelcard, valid after 9:30 A.M. or anytime weekends and public holidays. Three-day passes are also available, if you're staying longer. The Tube is open Monday through Saturday from 5:30 A.M. to midnight, Sunday from 7:30 A.M. to 11:30 P.M. Safe, clean, reliable, and affordable, the Tube is your best bet.

◆DAY SIXTEEN

Home

*T*here are two rules for leaving Britain with your sanity intact: (1) Be patient; and (2) Give yourself plenty of time. Whether you're leaving from Greenwich or central London, you'll have to deal with several modes of transportation (any one of which could, and no doubt will, experience delays), and you'll be lugging bags (this is why they call it "luggage"). Pack the night before and start out early. Between seasonal fog, occasional strikes (usually at peak travel times), and other vagaries of air travel, it pays to check in with your airline the morning of your flight to determine its status. Your airline's number is either on your ticket envelope or in the phone book (or call Directory Enquiries 142).

The key thing to remember is that you must be at your airline's check-in counter at least two hours before departure—not in the terminal, or going through security, or even standing in line, but *at the check-in counter*. Get there late and the airline has every right to have given your seat away to someone else. If you've got a ticket that restricts changing flights (and virtually all discounted tickets have restrictions) you may find this situation not only inconvenient but also extremely costly.

Expect the airport check-in area to be chaotic. Gatwick and Heathrow are among the busiest airports in Europe, and all international flights tend to depart in roughly the same fashion in which they arrived: simultaneously. All flights to the States, for example, leave between mid-morning and early afternoon. Here are some tips for a smooth departure.

GETTING TO THE AIRPORT

FROM GREENWICH. If you still have your car, the first part of the drive to either airport will be a bit frantic, but be patient and watch the excellent road signs. For **Heathrow**, drive up to the top of Greenwich Park and take **Shooter's Hill Road** west. This is actually the A2. In about 2 miles (3.2 kilometers), the A2 forks right, but you switch to the **A202**, in the direction of Victoria Station, to cross the river via **Vaux-**

hall Bridge. Then, follow signs for **Kensington**, **Hammersmith**, the **A4**, and **The West**. Head out of town on the A4, which then becomes the **M4**, and you'll soon be at the Heathrow Exit. For **Gatwick**, take **Shooter's Hill Road** or **Trafalgar Road** east to the **A102**, the motorway that comes out of the Blackwall Tunnel, and follow it south, taking either the **A2** to Exit 2 of the **M25** or the **A20** to Exit 3 (either is fine). Then, take the M25 around to the southern fringe of the metropolitan area. Watch for the **M23** and take it south to Gatwick. To be safe, give yourself at least 2 hours to either airport.

If you're using public transport, take the BritRail train to **Charing Cross**, then follow signs to the **Embankment** Tube station. Take either the District (green) or Circle (yellow) line west. For **Gatwick**, get off at **Victoria Station** and take the **Gatwick Express** to the airport (leaves every 15 minutes; takes 30 minutes). For **Heathrow**, stay on the tube to the **South Kensington** station, change to a Piccadilly (blue) line train to the Heathrow **Terminals 1,2,3** station. To be safe, plan on the trip to either airport taking up to 2 hours. Baggage carts will available at the stations at both airports.

FROM CENTRAL LONDON. If **Heathrow** is your destination, you have three options. A **taxi** will cost more than £20 from the center of the city, but if you have a lot of baggage, door-to-door taxi service is hard to beat. If your budget is tight and you're traveling light, use the **Tube**. Take the Piccadilly (blue) line to Heathrow (*not* Rayners Lane or Uxbridge). The trip takes about an hour and costs about £2. If your hotel is near an **Airbus** stop (check with the front desk or call London Transport), the bus is an attractive alternative. It also takes about an hour and costs about £3. Getting to **Gatwick** is easier: take a cab or the Tube to Victoria Station and the BritRail **Gatwick Express** to the airport.

RETURNING YOUR RENTAL CAR

If you've kept your car until now, here's the most efficient way to return it: assuming you're traveling with someone else, drop them off at the departure terminal with the baggage, tickets, and passports. (They won't be able to go through security without you, but it will save you having to shift the bags an extra time.) Then take the car to the rental agency, stopping at a petrol station to top off the tank if you're expected to return it full. After completing the formalities, save your receipt; you'll need it if billing discrepancies arise (which they frequently do), and return to the terminal.

One of many colorful Londoners on Greenwich Pier

If you've spent last night some distance from the airport, leave plenty of extra time. Traffic around the airports is predictably heavy and delays are common, except on weekends. The signs to terminals, on the other hand, are clear, so you're unlikely to get lost.

OVERBOOKING

If you check in at least 2 hours before departure and find your seat's been given to someone else anyway, or that the airline simply overbooked, you may have a fight on your hands. Here's your armor. According to new European Commission rules, the airline must: (1) pay for your phone calls to your destination; (2) pay for your meals "in reasonable relation to the waiting time"; and (3) pay for a hotel room if they can't get you onto another flight until tomorrow. In addition, the airline must pay you a fine: 150 European Currency Units (or about $190) for flights under 3,500 kilometers (2,170 miles), and 300 ECUs (about $380) for longer flights. Indeed, if they book you on a later flight the same day, but the delay is longer than 2 hours for the shorter flight or 4 hours for the longer one, they must pay a fine of half this amount in each case. The airline won't volunteer this information; you have to know your rights.

VAT REFUNDS

Britain levies a value added tax (VAT) of 17.5 percent on all purchases. To encourage you to buy gifts nonetheless, Britain has a **Retail Export Scheme** by which the tax can be refunded for goods you take out of the country (thus, things you consumed in England—food, hotel, car rental—don't qualify). It's a great idea, but it's fiendishly complex in the execution. First, you have to be sure the shop you buy from participates (most, but not all, do). Second, some (but not all) stores require a minimum purchase (as high as £50 in some cases). Third, you have to remember to request a VAT Refund form from the sales clerk (they don't volunteer them), fill it out, have it signed on the premises, and get a self-addressed (but sometimes not stamped) envelope in which to return it after it's stamped by airport customs agents. Fourth, when you get to the airport you must find the customs agents' office and have them stamp the form. Unfortunately, they can require that you show them your purchases—which means you must do this before you check in (if the office is in the check-in hall), or retain your purchases as carry-on luggage. They may settle for receipts, but don't count on it. Finally, you simply slip the stamped form into the envelope and mail it from an airport postbox.

If you are lucky, the shop from which you made your purchase will be able to credit your credit card in dollars, once the refund has been processed. Otherwise, expect to wait several weeks (sometimes months), for your refund check. The check, however, will be in pounds and even major banks charge a hefty fee (as much as $50) to cash foreign checks. According to the British Tourist Authority, you can get around this problem by dealing with foreign currency-cashing firms such as the Deak International/Thomas Cook Foreign Currency Service (212-757-6915), Ruesch International (800-424-2923), or New York Foreign Exchange (800-346-3924). These firms charge small fees (typically $2 to $3.50). It's a lot of trouble, but if you've done some serious shopping, 17.5 percent is serious money.

GETTING TO THE DEPARTURE GATE

One last tip: don't linger in the Duty Free Shop at departure time. Gates at both Heathrow and Gatwick seem miles from the departure waiting lounge (you may have to take a shuttle train at Gatwick) and it takes time to get there. Don't rely on the announcements; watch the flight board in the departure lounge and make your way to the gate when the "Boarding" light comes on. The plane *will* leave without you if you're late.

Then settle in for the trip home . . . and begin planning your next two weeks in the best of Britain's countryside.

Further Reading

Backgrounders

Of the comprehensive guides to Britain or Wales, the *Insight Guides* series is the most imaginative and the most lushly illustrated. Separate books on *Great Britain* and *Wales* (published by APA Publications and distributed by Prentice-Hall Travel).

The finest regional guidebooks (with first-rate road maps) are the *AA/Ordnance Survey Leisure Guide Series*. Editions applicable to this itinerary include *East Anglia, Peak District, Snowdonia and North Wales, Brecon Beacons and Mid Wales, Forest of Dean and Wye Valley,* and *Cotswolds.* Published jointly by the Automobile Association and the Ordnance Survey.

Best book on natural history and wild areas: *Discovering Britain.* London: Drive Publications (for the Automobile Association) was published last in 1986. Check your local library.

Best books on London: *Insight Guides: London* (see above), and *London Access,* by Richard Wurman. New York: Access Press, 1991.

Accommodations Guides

FOR INNS AND SMALL HOTELS:

Brown, Karen. *English, Welsh, and Scottish Country Hotels and Itineraries.* Chester, Conn.: Globe Pequot Press, 1992.

Levitin, Jerry. *Country Inns and Back Roads: Britain and Ireland.* New York: Harper and Row, 1992.

Rubenstein, Hilary. *Europe's Wonderful Little Hotels and Inns: Great Britain and Ireland.* New York: St. Martins Press, 1992.

Stay at an Inn. London: British Tourist Authority, 1992.

FOR SELECT B&BS:

Stay on a Farm: The Official Guide of the Farm Holiday Bureau U.K. 1990. London: William Curtis Limited, 1990. **Far and away the best B&B guide for the countryside.**

Brown, Karen. *English Country Bed & Breakfasts.* Chester, Conn.: Globe Pequot Press, 1992. An excellent selection.

The Bed & Breakfast Guide to Great Britain. New York: Consumer Reports Books, 1992.

Welles, Sigourney. *The Best Bed and Breakfast in the World: England, Scotland, and Wales.* Chester, Conn.: Globe Pequot Press, 1992–93.

Good Room Guide. Excellent booklet listing first-rate B&Bs, published privately by Guestaccom, 190 Church Road, Hove, East Sussex, BN3 2DJ, or phone (0273) 722833.

YOUTH HOSTELS:

YHA 1992 Accommodation Guide. Available through Hostelling International/American Youth Hostels, P.O. Box 37613, Washington, D.C. 20013-7613, or phone (202) 783-6161.

FROM THE WALES TOURIST BOARD:
(contact nearest British Tourist Authority office—see Useful Addresses)

Wales: Bed and Breakfast. A detailed catalogue.

Wales: Hotels, Guest Houses, and Farmhouses. A detailed catalogue.

Wales: Somewhere Fresh. An illustrated brochure of hotels, guest houses, farmhouses, and other B&Bs.

Books on Food
FOR RESTAURANTS:

Jaine, Tom. *The Good Food Guide 1990.* London: Hodder and Stoughton (for the Consumers' Association), 1990.

FOR PUBS:

Aird, Alisdair. *The 1992 Good Pub Guide*. London: Ebury Press, 1992.

Hanson, Neil. *The Best Pubs of Great Britain*. Chester, Conn.: Globe Pequot Press (compiled by the Campaign for Real Ale), 1989.

Books on Wales

Bailey, Anthony. *A Walk Through Wales*. New York: HarperCollins, 1992. An excellent update on Borrow and Morton.

Borrow, George. *Wild Wales*. London: Century, 1989. A classic, originally published in 1862.

Morton, H.V. *In Search of Wales*. London: Methuen, 1986. Charming account of a 1932 tour. Check your local library.

Useful Addresses

British Tourist Authority Overseas Offices

UNITED STATES:

551 5th Avenue
Suite 701
New York, NY 10176
(212) 986-2200

625 N. Michigan Avenue
Chicago, IL 60611
(312) 787-0490

2850 Cumberland Parkway
Atlanta, GA 30339
(404) 432-9635

World Trade Center
Suite 450
350 S. Figueroa Street
Los Angeles, CA 90071
(213) 628-3525

CANADA:

111 Avenue Road
Suite 450
Toronto, Ontario M5R 3T8
(416) 925-6326

AUSTRALIA:

210 Clarence Street
Sydney, NSW 2000
(02) 267-4555

NEW ZEALAND:

Dilworth Building
Third Floor
Cnr. Queen and Customs Street
Auckland 1
(09) 3031 446

National Tourist Boards

English Tourist Board
Thames Tower
Black's Road
Hammersmith, London W6 9EL
(071) 846 9000

Wales Tourist Board
Brunel House
2 Fitzalen Road
Cardiff CF2 1UY
(0222) 499909

National Parks Covered in This Book

Brecon Beacons National Park
7 Glamorgan Street
Brecon
Powys LD3 7DP
(0874) 4437

Peak National Park
Aldern House
Baslow Road
Bakewell
Derbyshire DE4 1AE
(062981) 4321

Pembrokeshire Coast National
  Park
County Offices
Haverfordwest
Dyfed SA61 1QZ
(0437) 764591

Snowdonia National Park
Penrhyndeudraeth
Gwynedd LL48 6LF
(0766) 770274

Other Helpful Organizations

Automobile Association
Fanum House
Basingstoke, Hants. RG21 2EA
(0256) 20123

Countryside Commission
John Dower House
Crescent Place, Cheltenham
Gloucestershire GL50 3RA
(0242) 521381

The National Trust
36 Queen Anne's Gate
London SW1H 7AS
(01) 222 9251

Ordnance Survey
Romsey Road, Maybush
Southampton SO9 4DH
(0703) 792763

Ramblers' Association
1/5 Wandsworth Road
London SW8 2XX
(01) 582 6878

Index

About the authors

Bill North is a writer and independent public policy consultant. **Gwen North** is a consultant in fashion merchandising. Avid travelers, the Norths created The Two-Week Traveler Series for independent, sophisticated travelers with wide interests but limited vacation time.